The FinTech Nation

Excellence Unlocked in Singapore

The FinTech Nation

Excellence Unlocked in Singapore

VARUN MITTAL
Singlife, Singapore

LILLIAN KOH
Fintech Academy, Singapore

World Scientific

NEW JERSEY • LONDON • SINGAPORE • BEIJING • SHANGHAI • HONG KONG • TAIPEI • CHENNAI • TOKYO

Published by

World Scientific Publishing Co. Pte. Ltd.
5 Toh Tuck Link, Singapore 596224
USA office: 27 Warren Street, Suite 401-402, Hackensack, NJ 07601
UK office: 57 Shelton Street, Covent Garden, London WC2H 9HE

British Library Cataloguing-in-Publication Data
A catalogue record for this book is available from the British Library.

THE FINTECH NATION
Excellence Unlocked in Singapore

ISBN 978-981-12-4915-0 (hardcover)
ISBN 978-981-12-5028-6 (paperback)
ISBN 978-981-12-4916-7 (ebook for institutions)
ISBN 978-981-12-4917-4 (ebook for individuals)

For any available supplementary material, please visit
https://www.worldscientific.com/worldscibooks/10.1142/12640#t=suppl

Typeset by Diacritech Technologies Pvt. Ltd.
Chennai - 600106, India

CONTENTS

ACKNOWLEDGEMENTS

As we embark on this exciting journey with the second book from Fintech Nation, a not-for-profit platform Fintech Nation to nurture and scale the FinTech ecosystem in Singapore, we would like to express our heartfelt gratitude to the individuals and organisations who have played a pivotal role in making this endeavour possible. Their unwavering support and dedication have been instrumental in shaping the vision and mission of Fintech Nation.

First and foremost, we extend our deepest thanks to the founders, investors, and industry leaders who have generously shared their invaluable insights and expertise with us. Your contributions have been instrumental in shaping the direction of Fintech Nation and have enriched the collective knowledge of the FinTech community.

We also sincerely thank Elevandi and its dedicated staff, particularly Pat Patel and Rebecca Martin. Their steadfast support and commitment to Fintech Nation and all its initiatives have inspired and encouraged us throughout our journey.

Furthermore, we are grateful to Thunes and its founding partners, Irina Chuchkina and Mansi Chopra, for their pivotal role as partners in Fintech 65, the talent pillar of Fintech Nation. Your partnership has enabled us to nurture and develop the next generation of FinTech talent, paving the way for a brighter future in our industry.

The support of the Singapore FinTech Association and its leadership team, Shadab Tayabi, Reuben Lim, and Shakeel Rashid, has been invaluable in driving Fintech Nation's events and community engagement initiatives. We sincerely thank you for your collaborative efforts and commitment to the FinTech ecosystem.

We also would like to acknowledge the researchers, interns and friends of Fintech Academy like Emily, Chiew Hong and David who provided unstinting support.

Last, but not least, we want to express our gratitude to the dedicated volunteers who make up the Fintech Nation team. Chris Lim, Vanessa Ho, and Kai Zen Theng have been instrumental in various facets of our platform, from managing platforms to fostering community engagement and marketing. Your selfless contributions have not gone unnoticed, and we deeply appreciate your tireless efforts.

Through the collective efforts and unwavering support of these individuals and organisations, Fintech Nation continues to thrive and make a meaningful impact in the world of FinTech. We look forward to our community's continued growth and success and the positive changes we can bring to the FinTech landscape.

Thank you all for being part of this incredible journey.

FOREWORD

In the fast-paced realm of FinTech, where innovation and adaptability reign supreme, Singapore has emerged as the pre-eminent FinTech hub in the Asia-Pacific region. With over 1,500 FinTech companies headquartered in Singapore, large investments continue to drive rapid growth in the sector.

The nation has very efficiently harnessed its financial and technological prowess while developing a comprehensive regulatory and support infrastructure that prioritises Environmental, Social and Governance (ESG) and sustainability issues for financial institutions. Having been part of this journey since the early days, I am honoured to introduce you to the remarkable story of Singapore's FinTech evolution.

In just five years, FinTech investments in Singapore have grown 18-fold, from USD230M in 2017 to more than USD4B in 2022, attracted by Singapore's open economy and strong infrastructure. This is also a testament to Singapore's unwavering commitment to fostering innovation and the result of solid infrastructure and a robust regulatory framework that has made the country a prominent international financial centre.

Central to this ascent is the Monetary Authority of Singapore's forward-looking and balanced posture of encouraging FinTech innovation while guarding against risks through sandboxes and industry-led pilots. These initiatives balance encouraging or fostering innovation and safeguarding against potential risks, ensuring that Singapore remains at the forefront of global FinTech innovation.

The nation's push to empower consumers with increased accessibility to their financial information has enabled FinTech to be a key vector of growth for the Singapore economy. This transformation has been made possible through legitimate consent mechanisms and the establishment of an open financial platform, SGFindex-SG Financial Data Exchange.

Within the FinTech spectrum, digital payments have emerged as the undisputed powerhouse. The issuance of four new digital bank licences clearly indicates Singapore's commitment to fostering competition and financial inclusion. The focus on financial inclusion is forcing a distribution architecture that will eliminate obstacles to transferring funds and providing credit.

However, Singapore's small market size necessitates a global outlook for FinTech companies. Fortunately, Singapore's robust legal and financial infrastructure provides a launchpad for these enterprises to venture beyond its shores confidently.

This book delves into the heart of Singapore's FinTech landscape, revealing the inspiring stories, the visionary leaders, and the transformative technologies that have propelled this nation to global prominence. As you turn the pages, you will gain valuable insights into the collaborations, regulatory wisdom, and entrepreneurial spirit that define Singapore's FinTech prowess. "FinTech Nation" is not just a testament to the past and present of FinTech in this remarkable city; it is also a roadmap for the future — a future where innovation, technology, and finance converge to create a more inclusive, efficient, and prosperous world.

With a conducive regulatory environment, a highly skilled workforce, and an unyielding dedication to embracing technological advancements, Singapore will continue to grow rapidly as a global FinTech centre.

Neil Parekh
Nominated Member of Parliament
Singapore

PREFACE

Singapore has become a flourishing financial centre of international repute and a flag bearer for FinTech innovation in eight years, from the setting of the FinTech department in the Monetary Authority of Singapore (MAS) in 2015 to 2023. Despite being a small island of 5.7 million inhabitants, our city-state tops the ASEAN region in terms of literacy, life expectancy, mobile phone usage, internet penetration rate, and cosmopolitan population. Singapore has one of the lowest unemployment rates at 2.8%. It is regarded as one of the easiest countries to do business in, ranked second worldwide, with regulations that allow for followership of companies. Singapore has a literacy rate of 96.8% and near-complete internet coverage across the island. Born as a humble trading port, Singapore has developed this far due to its strategic advantages. Consequently, it acts as the bridge between the Asia-Pacific region and the rest of the world, enabling its financial services sector to flourish. Financial services and the fractional banking system are vital social and public order components. Regulated industry segments like financial services thrive in a society with a deep respect for law and authority.

In addition, factors such as a sound economic and political environment, favourable legal and tax policies, a reputation for integrity, strict enforcement against crime and money laundering, and reliable support for financial innovations have contributed to Singapore's status as The FinTech Nation. As a result, the financial industry is a critical player in the country's financial market segment and has become one of the strongest in the world.

One of the critical attributes of Singapore is a national character built on survival instinct and an obsession with success. Singaporeans, by nature, are *Kiasu* (fear of missing out) and wear it as a badge of honour. Similar to Israeli *Chutzpah*, it has both positive and negative connotations. Being *Kiasu* drives Singaporeans to be constantly paranoid, doing what it takes to succeed. It creates a certain fanaticism about meritocracy and instils a belief that one can never be complacent. In a regulated industry, our desire to excel pushes us to comply with constantly changing regulations to meet market demands. Our durable social fabric supports adherence to order and authority. It is a significant asset in developing and supporting a heavily regulated industry like financial services.

The FinTech journey of Singapore has been a story of relentless pursuit of excellence to build a global financial service hub with limited means and many aspirations. The slogan "Dream big. Start small. Move fast." brought together regulators, startups, investors, corporates and everyone else to achieve a common goal. As the ecosystem evolved, the mission of the ecosystem became to nurture and scale a FinTech hub which is "Responsible, Viable, Inclusive".

The key principles which established Singapore as a FinTech Nation have been an obsession with excellence referred to as **RFFL (Right First, Fast Later)**, a unique model of economic and legal policies known as **Singanomics** and lastly, an organised and controlled model of a new idea development termed **Garden Innovation.**

Singapore DNA is to focus on being **Right First and Fast Later**. It reflects the roots of the country's "*Kiasu*" nature. In the long run, it does not matter who came first but who did things the right way. Singapore's economic policies are a unique example of balancing social welfare with economic development. Singapore develops regulations and policies incorporating community stakeholders' voices in the process.

Singapore has limited natural resources, creating a need for efficiency in every aspect of life. Unlike the international model of Innovation Jungles, which focuses on advocating disruption, Singapore practises a more conciliatory approach to **Garden Innovation**. Prime Minister Lee Kuan Yew introduced the "garden city" vision on 11 May 1967 to transform Singapore. The approach has since been adopted across all walks of life. In the journey to becoming a FinTech Nation, Singapore picked vital focus areas of innovation like payments, blockchain, artificial intelligence, retirement solutions and green finance. It then provided all possible resources to nurture them like a compassionate gardener.

As a small country built on the foundations of trade and commerce, Singapore has long practised **Singanomics** — a system of economics which orchestrates a balance between state-driven development, staged liberalisation, and efficient private enterprise.

An iron fist in a velvet glove provides global competitiveness and excellence by leveraging policy and other governance instruments of influence. Singapore's approach lets market forces define most outcomes, while a progressive government develops the broader structure and guidelines.

In short, as laid out above, these principles form the pillars of this nation's relentless pursuit of success. This spirit of excellence likely attracts people across the region to build their ventures in finance and technology here. So whilst policies and systems structure and direct change create the backdrop for the FinTech development, the **PEOPLE** behind the scenes, the ones with the dynamic vision and creative drive, breathe life into paper-bound dreams.

> *"Everything MAS does is work-in-progress. There is no finite point at which to declare this is our legacy, and everything will be great from now on. This is a process of continuous improvement. It's like innovation that you always do something better. So many*

> *exciting things are happening in the technology area. It's not a question of legacy but an ongoing process of innovation. You need to have that mindset and culture across the financial industry. But because this industry is inherently riskier than other industries, we need to do this innovation prudently."*
>
> *Ravi Menon, Managing Director of MAS*

The first book on "Singapore, The Fintech Nation", traced Singapore's journey from 2015 to 2020, starting with establishing regional hubs and internationalising FinTech innovation. It became a bestseller on Amazon, Kinokuniya, and Lazada, with a foreword by MAS Managing Director, Ravi Menon, and an opening chapter by Chief FinTech Officer of MAS, Sopnendu Mohanty. Moreover, the book played an integral role in codifying the key principles that established Singapore as a FinTech Nation. The second book in the series which you are reading now, continues the legacy and foundation set up by the first book, bringing together the community to share stories of the past and vision for the future.

The book aims to offer provocative insights into current FinTech transformations and developments in Singapore since 2015. It provides unprecedented insights into industry leaders' and founders' journeys. It serves as a highly informative and exhaustive guide to what goes on in the real FinTech industry, complete with stories of founders and enablers of the FinTech ecosystem, including access to capital, customers, talent, and policy initiatives which have made them and Singapore successful. It shared some untold stories and exciting journeys of the founders of the various FinTech enterprises and prominent players. It traces Singapore's FinTech journey since its inception (2015), the establishment of regional hubs and the internalisation of FinTech innovation. It captures the remarkable transformations and developments that have unfolded in Singapore since 2015, shaping the FinTech landscape over the years.

This book is not just another mundane account; it delves deep into the very heart of the industry, unraveling the awe-inspiring stories and extraordinary journeys of visionary leaders and trailblazing founders. With unprecedented access to their experiences, it offers a highly informative and comprehensive guide, shedding light on the inner workings of the real FinTech industry.

Through this book, one learns about a world where access to capital, customers, talent, and policy initiatives are cleverly conceived to be the stepping stones to success. The book also shares the secrets behind Singapore's triumph as a FinTech hub and reveals unparalleled insights into the forces that propelled it to the forefront of innovation. From untold stories of resilience and determination to exhilarating tales of triumph, this book unravels the captivating narratives of the brave entrepreneurs who have carved their paths in the FinTech ecosystem.

We would like to express our appreciation to the 80 founders, trailblazers, and enablers we interviewed. This book provides valuable insights into the stratifications of the ecosystem though it is not exhaustive. It unlocks the stratifications that lie within, revealing the multifaceted layers of the FinTech revolution. We have limited the discussion of FinTech to only financial services. But, of course, FinTech has evolved so much that it is pervasive in most industries today, from agriculture to healthcare and even the military. Since FinTech began as a disruption to financial services, we will focus on its genesis, evolution and impact on this industry.

ABOUT THE AUTHORS

Varun Mittal is a seasoned professional adept at the cross-section of digital business building and financial services in Southeast Asia and global emerging markets. He has developed and implemented strategy, technology rollout, ecosystem management, and regulatory engagement for financial institutions and digital and internet technology companies.

He serves as the Chief Digital Officer and Chief Innovation Officer at Singlife, managing digital products, platforms and ecosystems for insurance, payments and financial advisory business verticals. Earlier in his career, he served as a Partner at EY, leading global emerging markets fintech and ASEAN digital banking practice supporting fintech startups, financial institutions and regulators. Previously, he was part of the founding team at helloPay (acquired by ANT Financial, Alibaba Group), led payments for Samsung in ASEAN and developed regional mobile payment solutions at Singtel Group. Varun undertook his MBA at the National University of Singapore and graduated as a computer science engineer.

As an avid investor in startups in Southeast Asia, he has invested in over 50 startups with five exits through his investment vehicle, Boleh Capital. He is the founder of the Fintech Nation, a not-for-profit platform comprising a book, mentorship platform and investment fund (Fintech Nation Fund) to support the fintech ecosystem in Singapore. As an accomplished author, he has written multiple books covering the journey and evolution of Singapore as a global fintech hub. He has been awarded as one of the top ten people in Singapore Fintech by the Monetary Authority of Singapore in 2019 and 2021.

Dr Lillian Koh, Ph.D has dedicated her life to education and impact work. She began her career at the Ministry of Education and taught post-graduate courses at the Nanyang Technological University (NTU) Singapore. She was Advisor to the NTU Investment Interactive Club and Chair of the Center for Financial Literacy at National Institute of Education, leading successful financial education programmes for schools and institutes of higher learning in Singapore. She was Faculty Associate at A*STAR and Principal Investigator of research grants at NTU. After these 34 years, she served as the Director of Research at Curtin University, Singapore. She founded Fintech Academy, which spearheads talent development programmes and certifications for fintech, in collaboration with universities and Institute of Banking and Finance (IBF). Her contribution to national service includes serving as Advisor to Talent Programme at the Singapore FinTech Association in the early days as well as Advisor to the Institute of Blockchain Singapore. Appointed International Consultant by the World Bank, she was also consultant to National Healthcare Group, Pearson, Citigroup and UNESCO.

She is also the Director of the Center for Research and Innovation @ NTUitive, a spin-off of NTU and is Advisor to Global Entrepreneurship Network (GEN) Singapore. Dr Koh co-authored *Singapore: The Fintech Nation*, one of the first books about Singapore's financial technology journey and also the first International Handbook of Financial Literacy by Springer.

Chapter 1

AN ECOSYSTEM PLAYBOOK: ENGAGE, EXPERIMENT AND EXECUTE[1]

> *"You can't connect the dots looking forward; you can only connect them looking backward. So you have to trust that the dots will somehow connect in your future. You have to trust in something — your gut, destiny, life, karma, whatever. This approach has never let me down, and it has made all the difference in my life."*
>
> *Steve Jobs*[2]

It is hard to predict future outcomes when you start a greenfield work in nascent space, and I was in a greenfield situation five years ago in a developing area called FinTech. On 3 August 2015, I took up a new job as the Chief FinTech Officer of the Monetary Authority of Singapore (MAS) after a long stint at Citibank. I was apprehensive, excited and also

[1] This Chapter is contributed by Sopnendu Mohanty, Chief FinTech Officer, Monetary Authority of Singapore.

[2] Prepared text of the Stanford Commencement Address delivered by Steve Jobs, CEO of Apple Computer and of Pixar Animation Studios, 12 June 2005, https://news.stanford.edu/2005/06/14/jobs-061505/

optimistic about the possibilities of developing a body of work which is both transformative and foundational. Early expectations were set on how the success would look like after Managing Director, Ravi Menon's speech, "A Smart Financial Centre" at Global Technology Law Conference 2015 on 29 June 2015,[3] where he laid out a framework to establish ourselves as a smart financial centre by 2020. Fast-forward and now at the end of the five-year journey, when I look back, it feels like we had an excellent plan to execute and deliver. The reality is we didn't plan for this outcome nor had a pre-defined five-year strategy. Instead, we agreed on two things — first, build a competent team within MAS, and to outsiders, we will act as enablers with an entrepreneurial spirit; secondly, a guiding rail to take the journey which was, "we will **engage deep**, we will **experiment a lot**, we will **execute our promises**, and we will be **empathy driven**".

This book goes in-depth to extract insights on elements which explain the DNA of Singapore as a FinTech hub. For this chapter, with the risk of oversimplifying the remarkable growth story, I have presented an overview of various drivers and its effects in facilitating sustainable and inclusive growth of an ecosystem in a nutshell. I have also articulated how these drivers became critical components of the playbook to create a world-class inclusive ecosystem. The construct of these drivers came from precious and extensive insights gained by working with talented and compassionate colleagues, professionals and innovators who have shaped and refined every step in our mission to establish a global FinTech platform. It is essential to point out that throughout the five-year journey, another critical aspect which is very much visible in spirit and action was the concept of platform thinking. As with any platform thinking, there are two parts: (a) an open platform to create; and (b) a trusted, well-governed and interoperable platform to distribute safely. Today, the platform has evolved, and is

[3] "A Smart Financial Centre" — Keynote Address by Mr Ravi Menon, Managing Director, Monetary Authority of Singapore, at Global Technology Law Conference 2015 on 29 June 2015, https://www.mas.gov.sg/news/speeches/2015/a-smart-financial-centre

continuously progressing for the brightest and most courageous to develop solutions to solve societal needs for inclusive and safe financial systems, and at the same time, to use Singapore as a springboard to expand globally.

The history of technology-driven innovation is fraught with periods of irrational exuberance, boom cycles and a sudden burst of the boom cycle. The innovation narrative gets fast laced with echo chamber conversations, big bets, big promises, and a massive rush of talent, founders and investors looking to make the best out of the boom. FinTech is no different. Almost close to a decade after the dotcom bubble (2001–2002), followed by the global financial crisis (2008–2009), led to the birth of FinTech Innovation. Since then globally, by 2015, investment in FinTech reached close to USD20B with a jump of more than 100% from the previous year. Going by the history of boom and bust cycles, we started our FinTech journey almost at the midpoint of technological exuberance, and jurisdictions like the UK, US, and China have already built thriving FinTech centres. Although, starting mid-way had its advantages and disadvantages; the edge was in leveraging on all the progress and advancements made by other jurisdictions, but starting late in our small domestic market size was a stiff initial hurdle.

Constraints Force a New Approach

When we started, the common perception was that FinTechs were threatening to eat the banks' lunch. The growing success of FinTechs was due to their ability to deliver superior payment services, smarter lending facilities and customer-centric digitised banking services. In contrast, incumbent financial institutions (FIs) were still operating with complex legacy models compounded with legacy technology; hence, the customer's experience was far from being delightful. However, FIs, despite being woefully short in delivering customer-centric product and services, the trust factor was still their vantage point. Hence, we saw merit in taking a comprehensive and inclusive approach to champion collaboration between

FIs and FinTechs, where FinTechs will bring best-in-class technology and user experience, and FIs can provide the necessary trust and institutional stability. As we moved along, we introduced a series of regulatory responses by fine-tuning existing regulatory policies.

Furthermore, we introduced comprehensive regulatory reforms in payment service areas. This brought many FinTechs under the regulatory ambit to improve trust and confidence in the changing financial systems. Thus, the constraint of small market size was overcome by making Singapore predominately a hub for business-to-business (B2B) FinTechs, which focused on digitising firms engaged in financial services. At a broader level which includes all kind of FinTechs (i.e., B2C, B2B, B2B2C), Singapore became a launchpad for startups to pilot new ideas, raise funds and access the growing market within few hours of a plane ride.

Looking back, I have framed the hub development with four anchor drivers that helped us to grow Singapore as a vibrant FinTech hub. These anchor drivers were Continuous **Innovation**, Collaborative **Network**, Comprehensive **Ecosystem**, and Conducive **Regulation (INER)**. The INER approach has made the Singapore FinTech hub conducive, comprehensive and collaborative, and the hub has grown to great heights since then, and the success is not an accident. It is a carefully orchestrated process where the capital, talent, market access and progressive regulations, operates optimally.

Innovation Effect — Lead the Change You Want to Be

For a nation to be a leading global centre for a tech-driven sector, the first building block which we developed was a strong innovation character for the financial sector. Hence, there was this necessity to invigorate a culture of innovation at various levels and among diverse stakeholders. The change started with a movement to adopt an experimentation culture among FIs,

FinTech companies and public sectors to do pervasive trials on new ideas. Therefore, we started popularising "**Dream Big, Start Small and Move Fast**" among the community.

To boost innovation adoption, we had announced on 20 June 2015, a substantial SGD225M financial incentive scheme to help financial firms set up innovation labs and to fund infrastructure to deliver FinTech services:

> *"The Financial Sector Technology & Innovation (FSTI) scheme is one of several programmes aimed at establishing Singapore as a smart financial centre, which in turn is part of the Government's 'smart nation' initiative."*
>
> *Ravi Menon*[4]

The scheme had a productive impact on Singapore's financial sector's innovation landscape. Over the next five years, Singapore saw over 40 global financial service institutions setting up their innovation labs and launched more than 500 innovation projects.

We also created a regulatory environment to foster engagement of regulators in the innovation process. There was a perception then that regulation is a barrier to innovation and FinTech development. To address this negative perception, few regulators like the Financial Conduct Authority (FCA) of UK and ourselves started thinking of providing a regulatory Sandbox to engage with startups and FIs on innovative ideas and programmes. Therefore, we initiated a consultation paper on 6 June 2016, to launch a regulatory Sandbox by the end of 2016. Expansive in our approach, we are the first to offer it to both FIs and FinTechs, only for production systems with real customers, and the window to apply for the Sandbox was kept open throughout the year. Further, we regularly communicated the concept of experimentation with

[4] Ravi Menon, Managing Director of the Monetary Authority of Singapore (MAS), https://www.straitstimes.com/business/banking/225m-boost-for-financial-technology

"appropriate safeguards to contain the consequences of failure for customers rather than to prevent failure altogether",[5] through our speeches, public messages and other communication platforms.

> *"MAS aims to provide a responsive and forward-looking regulatory approach that will enable promising FinTech innovations to develop and flourish. The Sandbox will help reduce regulatory friction and provide a safer environment for FinTech experiments. We believe this will give innovations a better chance to take root."*
>
> *Jacqueline Loh*[6]

Network Effect — Build a Perceptual Scale

We saw early in our journey that to build a vibrant hub, we needed to create a mutually beneficial network of partners, collaborators and shared interest for a transformative programme, and also have the scale to make the impact. We established a global network spanning from Asia to Latin America, which gave the much-required perceptual scale character to the hub. We worked at a furious pace to build a partnership with our counterparts, almost one agreement in every two months was the rate at which we will have a formal agreement with a country. Now over five years, we have made more than 30 FinTech Co-operation Agreements (CAs) with our international partners to foster closer cooperation on FinTech and to promote innovation in financial services with respective markets.

---

[5] MAS Media Release, "MAS Proposes a "Regulatory Sandbox" for FinTech Experiments", 6 June 2016, https://www.mas.gov.sg/news/media-releases/2016/mas-proposes-a-regulatory-sandbox-for-fintech-experiments

[6] Jacqueline Loh, Deputy Managing Director of MAS, https://www.mas.gov.sg/news/media-releases/2016/mas-proposes-a-regulatory-sandbox-for-fintech-experiments

Building such networks helped the Hub in accessing and stitching mutually beneficial relationship among a wide range of diverse FinTechs, global talents, investors and policymakers. This led to making the Singapore hub as the gateway to Asian growth. It attracted over 1,000 FinTech companies to make Singapore as their global base or the regional base for their operations. Cumulatively, the Hub attracted over USD4B worth of investment needed for these companies to establish and kick-start their growth. Many international programmes benefited from such agreements; the plan to build payment rails connectivity with India and Thailand, collaboration with Kenya on jointly hosting AFRO-ASIAN FinTech festival, and the multiple countries engaged with Project Ubin to work on distributed ledger technology (DLT) and central bank digital currencies (CBDC) are few such examples. Further, it cemented the role of Singapore in global FinTech development mindshare, and the foundation to build a long-lasting international relationship was securely anchored.

> *"We have gathered in Nairobi to celebrate the newest bridge for financial innovation, bringing together more than three-quarters of the world's population. The motivation is the conviction that FinTech offers a great opportunity for transforming many lives, in Africa and Asia, and the rest of the world. We can only imagine what the consequence of this Afro-Asia FinTech Festival will be over the next 50 years. Through this Festival, and in the amount of talent that has been brought together, collaboration offers the best chance for creating an effective ecosystem for financial innovation."*
>
> *Dr Patrick Njoroge*[7]

[7] Dr Patrick Njoroge, Governor, Central Bank of Kenya, https://www.mas.gov.sg/news/media-releases/2019/singapore-and-kenya-establish-fintech-cooperation-at-inaugural-afro-asia-fintech-festival

Ecosystem Effect — Inclusive Engagement Approach

A deep and resilient ecosystem is the backbone of a thriving technology hub. Singapore's approach was not to choose between FIs and new FinTech players but to provide a conducive environment for both to innovate, compete and collaborate, which will then create a thriving innovation environment. So right at the onset of the FinTech journey, we had a focused task to build a comprehensive ecosystem which includes all stakeholders like the academia, investors, developers, FIs, regulators and others. Vibrant ecosystems bring together diverse and collective insights to sharpen the value and effectiveness of the sector. We worked with each stakeholder community and initiated various ecosystem building programmes to inject FinTech development via an ecosystem approach.

We worked with the industry to facilitate greater collaboration not only at a coordination level but also at a policy level. We encouraged the development of open application programming interface (APIs) among FIs to enable efficient data sharing, we promoted the responsible use of the cloud. Our research institutes started partnering with FinTechs and FIs on data analytics and digital transformation projects. Our universities and polytechnics updated their curriculum and internship programmes to help their students on FinTech skills. In 2016, with the five local polytechnics, we agreed on a "*framework to review and enhance the polytechnics' curricula in the next three years to prepare and equip their graduates with the skill sets necessary to take on the new FinTech-related jobs emerging in the financial sector*".[8] In the same year (2016), Singapore FinTech Association (SFA) was created, which is "*a*

[8] Joint Media Release, "MAS and Local Polytechnics Sign Memorandum of Understanding to Promote Skills Development in Financial Technology", 3 October 2016, https://www.mas.gov.sg/news/media-releases/2016/mas-and-local-polytechnics-sign-memorandum-of-understanding-to-promote-skills-development-in-fintech

cross-industry non-profit initiative, intended to be a platform designed to facilitate collaboration between all market participants and stakeholders in the FinTech ecosystem".[9] The SFA has grown rapidly and has now more than 800 members, organised hundreds of community-building exercises, and more than 50 FinTech association Memoranda of Understanding (MoU) around the world.

> *"We are promoting innovation in finance in a comprehensive way in Singapore. It requires a whole ecosystem. It requires bringing a whole range of players together — the technology players, finance players, startups, and both global and local Singapore players."*
>
> *Tharman Shanmugaratnam*[10]

▸ A Digital Avatar of the Ecosystem: API Exchange (APIX)

While we encouraged FIs to test and introduce these innovations where they are relevant, they were expected to perform their own due diligence when collaborating with innovative startups. However, there was this long bridge to nowhere between startups and FIs. Most of the startups walking on that bridge to reach FIs internal tech environment had a remarkable failure rate, and only a handful could make it. Various legacy and perception challenges were stumbling blocks in that journey.

Therefore, with support from the International Finance Corporation (IFC) and the ASEAN Bankers Association (ABA) to establish the ASEAN

[9] About Singapore FinTech Association, https://singaporefintech.org/

[10] Speech by Tharman Shanmugaratnam, Deputy Prime Minister and Coordinating Minister for Economic & Social Policies, also Chairman of the Monetary Authority of Singapore, at the launch of Singapore FinTech Festival (SFF) at Asia Society, New York City, on 12 April 2016, https://www.bis.org/review/r160425f.htm

Financial Innovation Network (AFIN) industry Sandbox. The AFIN platform's flagship product API Exchange (APIX), enables experimentation between FIs and FinTech companies in ASEAN to collaborate, broaden and deepen access to digital financial services across ASEAN.

The APIX genesis is from a casual conversation between myself and a senior official from IFC. During that conversation, I drew an approach on a tissue paper to improve the financial inclusion capacity of FIs by focusing on helping the FIs to digitise faster rather than only introducing neo-FinTechs/TechFins. Many exciting interactions followed the initial conversation, and finally, we crafted a solution prototype which was launched by India's Prime Minister Narendra Modi and Singapore's Deputy Prime Minister Tharman Shanmugaratnam at the Singapore FinTech Festival on 14 November 2018. The initial idea of APIX had the privilege of accessing the brilliant engineering mind of Pieter Franken, a Tokyo based Deep-Tech innovator; passionate inclusion champions — Vivek Pathak, Rachel Freeman and Ivan Mortimer-Schutts from IFC; super product specialists — Navin Suri, CEO Percipient, and Matthias Kröener, founder of digital challenger bank Fidor; market expertise inputs from Michael Tang and Mohit Mehrotra of Deloitte, and my competent deputy, Damien Pang.

The AFIN platform also allows ecosystem participants to observe the experiments and benefit from the insights gleaned, and to spur discussions on cross-border collaboration throughout the region. APIX is now close to three years in its journey and has evolved to be a fast-growing digital hub for three key areas: (a) market place of FinTech solutions; (b) a public Sandbox for developing pilots and learning how to partner with FinTechs; and (c) facilitate integration of FinTech solution with FIs to facilitate transformation. The APIX platform continues to evolve in its approach to support the ecosystem and has progressively sharpened its value proposition. During the COVID-19 pandemic, when we went through the massive lockdown, APIX became the core ecosystem platform which kept the ecosystem engaged. It became a platform to raise capital, to host global hackathons, do deep-dive digital transformation gap analysis by FIs. It also became a platform to operate various COVID-19 related incentive schemes and provided the digital backbone to many global ecosystem events.

Building a Global Knowledge Platform for the Worldwide Community — Singapore FinTech Festival (SFF)

Over last four years, we have built the world's largest engagement platform for the global FinTech community, popularly known as Singapore FinTech Festival (SFF) which provides a platform for the FinTech community to connect, collaborate and initiate partnerships. Whether you are a startup, technology company, investor, FIs, research institute, policymaker or innovation professional, the SFF provides five days of intense interactions and discussions to further global FinTech development. The festival was born out of a series of humorous stories involving my colleague and brilliant execution specialist Roy Teo, a spirited Ong-Ang Ai Boon, Director of The Association of Banks in Singapore and myself. Each of us had a deep passion for building something special with no barrier to our ambitions, and we had a healthy diversity in our thinking, but came together on many crucial choices to make it happen.

SFF has catalysed Singapore's global brand as a FinTech hub, and our outreach to make the platform accessible and affordable to the international community from more than 100 countries has made the festival the most impactful global annual gathering of the brightest minds. The SFF has amplified our inclusivity and sustainability focus in promoting innovation and significantly upgraded the role of our hub as a global knowledge centre. The SFF is hailed as one of the marquee successes of the Singapore ecosystem, which today has an impressive list of global leaders gracing the event over the last four years. In 2019, it attracted over 60,000 delegates, 1,000 exhibitors and 500 international speakers.

"In Singapore, it is often windy. Winds here bring change, and opportunity. Historically, they blew ships to its port. These resupplied while waiting for the Monsoon to pass, for the seasons to change. 'Change is the only constant', wrote the ancient Greek philosopher, Heraclitus of Ephesus. Singapore knows this. You know this. It is the true spirit of the Fintech Festival — opening doors to new digital futures; hoisting sails to the winds of change."

Christine Lagarde[11]

Regulation Effect — Enabling Regulatory Environment

Having a conducive regulatory environment is key to the success of the ecosystem. It is not uncommon for FIs to innovate. It has been part of the competitive landscape, and innovation is a key differentiator. We have been encouraging and welcoming FIs to "*develop and apply new technologies into the financial ecosystem to enhance value for customers, increase efficiency, manage risks better, create new opportunities and improve people's lives*".[12]

Our existing regulatory regime had a solid framework for defining regulatory expectations by adopting new technology approaches. The fast-emerging FinTech startups introducing disruptive innovation with the use of modern technology necessitated specific new regulatory requirements fit for disruptive innovation. Instead of a "one-size-fits-all" regulatory approach, a risk-based approach to FinTech innovation was taken.

[11] Christine Lagarde, IMF Managing Director, at Singapore FinTech Festival (SFF) in 2018, https://www.imf.org/en/News/Articles/2018/11/13/sp111418-winds-of-change-the-case-for-new-digital-currency

[12] Consultation Paper on FinTech Regulatory Sandbox Guidelines, 6 June 2016, https://www.mas.gov.sg/-/media/MAS/News-and-Publications/Consultation-Papers/Consultation-Paper-on-FinTech-Regulatory-Sandbox-Guidelines.pdf

Over five years, many such regulatory changes were introduced to strengthen the conductivity of the hub.

▸ *Facilitating Business Models, Streamlining Existing Regulations and Supporting Investment Innovation*

To encourage and enable experimentation of solutions that utilise technology innovatively to deliver financial products or services, we introduced **Regulatory Sandbox** in November 2016, and further refinement to it with the **Sandbox Express** in September 2019. The agile approach in adopting a useful regulatory sandbox was demonstrated in the innovative process of introducing the express variant. This pre-defined Sandbox with pre-determined boundaries, expectations and regulatory reliefs provided a templatised version for the experimentation approach, and we promised FastTrack applications, with an approval decision granted within 21 days. Today, we have more than 10 successful FinTech companies who had "graduated" from the Sandbox, and they are shaping the new frontier innovation in their respective focus areas.

The FinTech market was going abuzz with new emerging business models, and we responded promptly with guidance on crowdfunding in June 2016, clarification on Initial Coin Offering (ICOs) and new guidelines on Robo-Advisory in October 2018 to make it easier for digital advisers to set up in Singapore. We introduced the streamlining of existing regulations by revisiting the rules governing the booming payment sector and the Payment Services Act 2019 commenced in January 2020. The new licensing framework was based on the concept of activity-based licensing, where the payment regulation was broken down to seven different licensing modules based on their activities and a proportional regulation expectation being applied. We also included the new types of payment services such as digital payment token services. Further, guidelines on online distribution of Life Policies with no advice was issued in June 2018 to promote digital insurance industry. Finally, a new Digital Banking Licence was introduced in June

2018, to allow entities, including non-bank players, to conduct digital banking businesses in Singapore.

To support FinTech investments, we made adjustments to anti-commingling Framework in June 2017 to make it "*easier for banks to conduct or invest in non-financial businesses*"[13] and banks can engage in the operation of digital platforms for online purchases. A simplified licensing regime for venture capitals (VCs) was introduced in October 2017 to shorten authorisation process for VC managers by focusing on existing fit-and-proper and anti-money laundering (AML) standards rather than track record and capital requirements. Further, a New Variable Capital Companies (VCC) Framework was implemented in January 2020 to allow a "*new corporate structure that can be used for a wide range of investment funds*"[14] and provide fund managers greater operational flexibility and cost savings.

To strengthen the resilience of the sector while encouraging the use of innovative technologies, changes were made to regulatory stance on cybersecurity, cloud computing and use of public data infrastructure. We issued Cyber Hygiene Notice in August 2019, new guidance on Cloud Services in July 2016 and a circular on Use of MyInfo and Non-Face-to-Face (NFTF) verification in January 2018. MyInfo is a verified source of identification information, which FIs can leverage to carry out proof of customer identity, and provided adequate measures to guard against impersonation.

[13] MAS Media Release, "MAS Streamlines Framework for Banks Carrying on Permissible Non-financial Businesses", 28 June 2017, https://www.mas.gov.sg/news/media-releases/2017/mas-streamlines-framework-for-banks-carrying-on-permissible-non-financial-businesses

[14] MAS Media Release, "MAS and ACRA Launch Variable Capital Companies Framework", https://www.mas.gov.sg/news/media-releases/2020/mas-and-acra-launch-variable-capital-companies-framework

The Managing Director of MAS, Ravi Menon, has been named the best central bank governor in Asia-Pacific for 2018 by UK-based magazine, *The Banker*. *The Banker* said in an article pertaining to the award to Ravi: "*The Monetary Authority of Singapore (MAS), the country's central bank, stands out for its cutting-edge regulatory approach to FinTech while maintaining macroeconomic stability. These are the key reasons for selecting Ravi Menon, Managing Director of MAS, as the Central Bank Governor of the Year for Asia-Pacific*".[15]

Sustainable FinTech: Pioneering a Global Network

FinTech is instrumental in democratising financial services and fostering inclusive growth. In sustainable FinTech, innovations can bridge the financial divide, ensuring that underserved and marginalised populations have equal access to opportunities within the global financial network. Blockchain technology, for example, has the potential of enhancing supply chain sustainability, reducing carbon footprints, and promoting responsible consumption within a globalised market.

FinTech has the power to drive positive environmental and social change. In the rapidly evolving world of FinTech, sustainability is not only an aspiration but an essential foundation for growth and impact. Through a collaborative global network, FinTech can spearhead sustainable financial practices, ensuring a flourishing tomorrow for individuals, businesses, and the planet. Let us embrace this convergence of finance and sustainability, uniting in purpose and innovation for a brighter, more sustainable future.

The urgency of sustainability within FinTech cannot be overstated. Climate change, economic disparities, and social inclusion demand that FinTech

[15] The Business Times, "MAS chief Ravi Menon named best central bank governor in Asia-Pacific", 4 January 2018, https://www.businesstimes.com.sg/banking-finance/mas-chief-ravi-menon-named-best-central-bank-governor-in-asia-pacific

becomes a catalyst for sustainable development. Therefore, there is a compelling case for aligning FinTech initiatives with sustainability goals to drive positive global impact. Sustainable finance forms the bedrock of a future-ready financial industry. This will include sustainable investment practices, ethical funding models, and the role of FinTech in advancing sustainability-focused financial solutions, illustrating the potential for a greener and more equitable global economy.

In conclusion, working together as an ecosystem will ultimately help us all to create the foundation for a sustainable and resilient financial services ecosystem, one that provides greater access to necessary financial resources and drives financial inclusion for all excluded sections. I am eternally thankful for the opportunity to be part of this remarkable journey by restating my idol, Steve Jobs, quote: "*You have to trust in something — your gut, destiny, life, karma, whatever*".

Chapter 2

BUILDING IT RIGHT, FOR GOOD

To those unfamiliar with Singapore's legal culture, the concept of "fines" for specific public transgressions is almost unbelievable. People cannot comprehend how Singapore regulates its high fines, from USD1,000 for feeding birds in public places to the severe penalty for chewing gum in the entire island nation. However, Singapore's detail-oriented nature extends beyond controlling these minuscule acts and has played a vital role in shaping the country's business ecosystem. A positive attitude towards foreign and local businesses drives Singapore's renowned ease of business. With an optimum level of regulation, Singapore has developed a near-utopic ecosystem where businesses work in tandem with the regulators, leading to maximum compliance.

As a small country with limited natural resources, Singapore has been built on a sound international legal and business-friendly system. Two qualities that enable businesses to thrive are predictability and enforceability, and Singapore works incredibly hard to bring both to life.

Financial Services

One phenomenal advantage that the financial services industry in Singapore enjoys is having all its different segments — banking, insurance, capital markets and most importantly, the central bank — housed in a single entity under the Monetary Authority of Singapore (MAS). It drastically simplifies business dealings, as any challenges to regulatory jurisdiction or the need to manage multiple agencies are eliminated. Singapore is likely the only country that unifies all these institutions under one roof. As a result, policy alignment, efficient resource deployment and ease of doing business are consistently delivered.

As technology and business models evolve, regulations must keep up or risk becoming redundant. Such changes would impact financial technology startups and financial institutions (FIs) that want to experiment with new ideas while remaining compliant. In true *kiasu* spirit, the government takes action that pushes the envelope to its breaking limit. This can be seen in the regulatory openness practised by MAS. As one of the five key pillars in Singapore's FinTech ecosystem, regulatory openness manifests in policymaking, optimising the overall regulatory environment and encouraging competition.

> *"While we are a no-nonsense regulator, we are also highly facilitative of innovation because we believe that innovation will increasingly be important for the progress of the financial sector. So we want to create an environment that promotes innovation without compromising soundness."*
>
> *"It has to be both. If we had a reputation for being a light regulator, we would attract the wrong players. We want to attract good players. And good players often want to be regulated. Take some cryptocurrency intermediaries, for instance: the sound,*

well-managed entities want to be regulated because being licensed by someone like MAS gives them more credibility in the market."

"I've always felt [that] our strong regulatory regime has been a significant positive for our efforts to grow and develop the financial sector. Most of the time, it's not a trade-off. It is how the two — regulation and promotion — work together to create an environment that promotes innovation while ensuring safety and public confidence."

Ravi Menon[1]

In the FinTech ecosystem, partnership and collaboration are essential. Unfortunately, many startups sometimes struggle to get their voices heard by more prominent players and get passed over for collaborative opportunities with incumbents. Despite this, the ecosystem remains a pillar of support for entrepreneurs, thanks to the commitment of ambassadors of FinTech who worked doubly hard to connect startups and incumbents. MAS plays an important part by promoting FinTech connectivity, launching open application programming interfaces (APIs), and encouraging big banks and insurance companies to provide fair and reasonable access to data. FinTech companies can access this and serve the customers as well. The industry's primary focus is to bring the best value to the consumers, with the government pushing for Singapore to become a brilliant nation.

Disruptive technology, increased big data availability, new business models and value chains are transforming how banks serve customers, interact with third parties and operate internally. Management of risks must keep

[1] Ravi Menon, Managing Director at MAS, in an interview with *Bloomberg Quint* in November 2018, https://www.bloombergquint.com/technology/fintech-and-the-monetary-authority-of-singapore-interview

up with this dynamic environment, including the evolving risk landscape. In financial services, exposure to risks may have significant repercussions.

MAS encourages experimentation in FinTech so that promising innovations can be tested in the market and have a better chance for broader adoption in Singapore and abroad. It aligns with a general aim to transform Singapore into a smart financial centre by increasing efficiency, improving the ability to manage risks, creating new opportunities and improving people's lives. This has manifested in the MAS FinTech Regulatory Sandbox, a testing environment that isolates untested code changes and outright experimentation from the production environment or repository.

The MAS FinTech Regulatory Sandbox was launched in 2016 to facilitate live experiments of innovative financial services and business models within specified boundaries. It establishes a conduit and strengthens the engagement channels between firms (both regulated and unregulated) and MAS on innovative ideas and regulatory clarifications relating to them.

A vital aspect of this approach is that Singapore uses the Sandbox as an exception rather than the norm. For example, if existing regulations cannot support an idea or technology, it enters the regulatory Sandbox for evaluation. However, only six companies graduated from the Sandbox after the second year. Hence, the ecosystem saw the need for a faster solution.

It led to the launch of a first-of-its-kind experiment known as the "Sandbox Express" to complement the initial Sandbox approach. Under the Sandbox Express, applicants can begin market testing in the predefined environment within 21 days of applying to MAS. In typical Singaporean fashion, everything is considered a perpetual work in progress and continues to evolve according to experience and feedback. In 2022, Sandbox Plus was introduced as a one-stop assistance in regulatory support and financial grants.

Globally, most regulators measure the success of their Sandbox process and approach by looking at the number of companies that enter and graduate from it — the more, the merrier. MAS took a diametrically opposite approach. First, it sought to understand why companies were seeking access to the Sandbox and found the following main motivations:

- Aspiration to extend existing products due to the evolution of technology to include digital know your customer (KYC), digital advice and sale of products under categories such as insurance and wealth.
- New products envisioned by FinTech companies not covered under existing regulations, such as peer-to-peer (P2P) lending, crowdfunding and digital assets.
- Aspirations and requirements to prove new technologies like smart contracts and blockchain can be used in regulated financial service companies.

Instead of defining the success of its Sandbox by the number of graduates, the number of companies that applied and selected was kept small by clarifying or expanding existing regulations to encapsulate various innovations. As a result, this country which has 1,000 startups and more than 150 banks, has only 14 projects which have graduated from the sandbox as of September 2023 and continue to operate as a business. There have been more projects which have entered the sandbox but are either unsuitable on regulatory levels by MAS or are deemed to be commercially unviable by the applicants.

In a personal interview, Samuel Hall, CEO of Rainmaking from 2016, points out, "There are two approaches that a regulator can take: to let a thousand flowers bloom and see which ones survive, or to follow them closely via the Sandbox". While the Sandbox approach is more labour-intensive, this methodology has a higher success rate. The Sandbox allows MAS to filter out projects by setting high barriers to entry. It also allows MAS to control who enters the industry by setting even higher exit standards from the Sandbox.

Ultimately, the world drew parallels between regulatory sandboxes and social media platforms, urging more users to spend more time in them. However,

Singapore's unique perspective led them to look at the Sandbox as a customer service centre where success is measured by how few people need it. If necessary, they should leave as soon as possible. Over eight years, from 2016 to 2023, only 14 players graduated, making it just one to two graduates yearly.

Interestingly each of the graduates from the sandbox was a local FinTech startup aspiring to test a new concept in Singapore instead of incumbents trying to test new concepts. The approachability and flexibility of regulators to create a safe space for testing new ideas set the Singaporean approach to innovation and experimentation apart. Overall, there were three players in insurance, one in remittance and 10 in capital markets in the first eight years of operations.

Thin Margin focused on creating convenience for customers seeking money-changing and remittance solutions by bringing them to the doorstep beyond the traditional realm of services being rendered only from the physical shops of the advisors.

Policypal, Pand.ai and Trade Risk Solutions are focused on insurance, with the first two focused primarily on offering insurance digitally to simplify customer onboarding and reduce the overall cost of operations. On the other hand, Trade Risk Solutions looked at bringing risk-sharing principles with reinsurers to the insurance advisory space. All three graduates in the insurance space ultimately acquired a direct insurance broker licence.

Capital markets majority that witnessed most of the action in the regulatory sandbox saw activities focused into two main areas with an even split. Five of the 10 capital markets-focused graduates out progressed to acquire a Capital Markets Service (CMS) Licence, and the other five received a Registered Market Operator (RMO) Licence. CMS Licence players focused on primary market activities like facilitating the primary issuance of different types of securities, e.g., equity, debt, real estate, and syndicated loans on primary markets (including tokenised assets). The graduates from this category are Kristal Advisors, ADDX, Propine Technologies, Hg

Exchange (now known as Alta Exchange) and HydraX Digital Assets. RMO Licence players focused on trading and investment activities, digitising and disintermediating pre-trade, trade execution and post-trade activities. The graduates from this category are Bondevalue, Synoption, ECXX Global, LabyrinthX Technologies and DigiFT Tech.

Source: https://www.edb.gov.sg/en/business-insights/insights/how-singapore-s-fintech-regulatory-sandbox-is-helping-fintech-innovators-accelerate-time-to-market.html

FinTechs in Insurance Market

When Singapore embarked on its journey to embrace the regulatory Sandbox, a key question in the community was how the process would work. Valenzia Yap is the founder of PolicyPal and was its CEO from 2016 to 2022. For the first time, she built a startup in financial services, a domain often considered one of the toughest to break into. She realised that every consumer has some insurance, which would solve many problems if there were a platform that people could use as a centralised depository of insurance policies. PolicyPal was the first startup to graduate from the MAS FinTech Regulatory Sandbox, having entered the Sandbox in March 2017. The six-month Sandbox trial allowed PolicyPal to test the technology and validate its distribution model in Singapore.

InsurTech was not a standalone vertical in 2016; it has gained recognition over time, as the growth figures prove. Previously, it used to focus on providing a comparison between different policies. Next, insurance companies tried building chatbots to replace insurance agents, but it needed to gain traction. Insurance products are notoriously complex. Insurance is a unique, intangible product because a customer buys peace of mind. PolicyPal tried out chatbots as well but lost customers because they felt there needed to be more support. Today, it utilises a hybrid approach where a chatbot answers FAQs, but customers can also reach out to customer service for complex queries. InsurTech companies are even testing out blockchain technology for claims automation. However, the data is private for this initiative to gain traction.

> *"Imagine a day where you don't need to dig through your insurance policies, a day when you can just pick up your phone to find out what coverage you have."*
>
> *Valenzia Yap, 2020, in a personal interview on her vision in setting up PolicyPal*

Val built a founding team surrounding this vision. They aimed to keep it an open platform, with customers being able to upload all their policies. To achieve this, PolicyPal had to get its insurance broker licence. However, that required SGD300,000 in paid-up capital which was a challenge then.

As such, it decided to apply for the MAS FinTech Regulatory Sandbox, as MAS had just rolled out the full whitepaper for the Regulatory Sandbox. As a result, PolicyPal was accepted into the Sandbox and was supported and connected with MAS from the beginning.

Val explored how an insurance broker could roll out products in the Sandbox and tested selling life and bicycle insurance via the platform. Val shares that the Sandbox was a great experience as she also learnt how to work with the regulators.

The challenges that PolicyPal faced stemmed from the fact that it needed an existing customer base. As a result, the insurance broker had to build it from scratch, identify what customers were looking for, and ensure that its product addressed that need. One example was the launch of employee benefits for small and medium-sized enterprises (SMEs). The SMEs needed a more complex platform to manage employee movement and obtain coverage instantly. They previously had to deal with voluminous paperwork. PolicyPal recognised this pain point and solved this in a very pointed manner.

PolicyPal also faced challenges in fighting against experienced personnel in banks and insurance companies. However, as a new company, it had a fresh perspective on building products and focused on doing it from a consumer's perspective. In the long run, it aims to connect and join forces with FinTech players to become stronger.

AMTD Group acquired PolicyPal in June 2020. Since the acquisition, PolicyPal's user base and product offerings have grown significantly. PolicyPal's next step is to work with AMTD to support digital bancassurance. As an insurance partner for AMTD Digital, PolicyPal has an edge in its ability to integrate and provide core support to the entire FinTech ecosystem.

The company has launched claims automation for travel insurance and flight delays. However, Val shares that she and her team still need to be able to do it for all types of policies. With increasing digitisation and the growth of open APIs, PolicyPal can start connecting the dots and progress towards more automation for claims processing. They are also exploring the Internet of Things (IoT)-based insurance down the road and tracking data using IoT devices. Val shares an example of motion detection for older people, which monitors them and sends signals to their children's mobile phones as a new form of insurance protection. She believes they will be able to do this and more with partners.

In June 2021, Pand.ai, an AI startup, was accepted into the MAS FinTech Sandbox. This began a thrilling journey, allowing Pand.ai to safely explore and develop its innovative GINA platform, an AI-driven insurance aggregator.

During the application process, Pand.ai representatives met with officers from MAS several times, physically and virtually. Tough questions and genuine interest characterised these meetings, as the MAS officers sought to understand the value GINA could bring to consumers in Singapore. However, despite the rigorous questioning, the officers were very supportive and offered guidance throughout the process.

Once accepted into the sandbox, Pand.ai spent a few months integrating with insurance partners before releasing GINA to the public on 30 November 2021. The initial version of GINA was a WhatsApp-based aggregator featuring partnerships with three insurance companies. While the platform was slow, it eventually gained traction and sold over 30 car insurance policies within the first three months, starting from a zero base.

Interestingly, GINA's growth rate accelerated during the second and third months of operation. This can be attributed to 33% of customers coming through referrals, showcasing the platform's growing popularity and user satisfaction. In addition, by the end of the sandbox period, Pand.ai had successfully applied for and obtained a direct insurance broker licence.

This licence enabled the AI startup to realise its long-term vision of using a WhatsApp chatbot to sell insurance products directly. As a result, GINA

2.0 was released on 30 November 2022, featuring real-time transaction capabilities. Today, GINA is fully integrated with six insurance partners, offering users a seamless and efficient experience.

> *"The FinTech Sandbox provided a safe environment to experiment with novel concepts without incurring high compliance costs upfront. I also want to thank the folks at MAS for their support and guidance throughout the Sandbox programme. They genuinely want to help to build up the FinTech ecosystem here. They are not only great regulators; they are great human beings."*
>
> *Chuang Shin Wee, CEO, Pand.ai*

It is often assumed that regulatory sandboxes are catered for startups rather than for traditional corporates. However, it was not the case for MetLife, Inc. MetLife, the holding corporation for the Metropolitan Life Insurance Company, is among the largest global providers of insurance, annuities, and employee benefit programmes, with 90 million customers in over 60 countries. Inspired by the ecosystem, one of the largest insurers worldwide decided to use Singapore as a testbed for its global FinTech experiments. MetLife does not have a retail insurance business in Singapore. As such, it was a big step for the corporation to undertake a live test to prove the capabilities of blockchain technology in insurance. Since Metlife does not have a Singapore business, they did not graduate from the sandbox to obtain a full licence.

Vitana was the first in many regards to enter Singapore's FinTech Regulatory Sandbox. It was the first blockchain application and corporation to embark on a long journey, a lending testament to the applicability and flexibility of Singapore's regulations. It is at the Sandbox where real data is available for testing the robustness of the blockchain solution.

Vitana was the first to enter Singapore's FinTech Regulatory Sandbox. It was launched under LumenLab, the Singapore-based innovation centre of MetLife Asia, by **Subhajit Mandal**. Subhajit, affectionately known as

"Mondy" amongst the FinTech crowd in Singapore, began his career as a trader. After completing his undergraduate studies in India, Mondy came to Singapore to complete his Master's in Finance at the National University of Singapore (NUS). His first venture was Sentinance — a sentiment analyser that quantifies market sentiment and incorporates it into existing trading and investment strategies — launched in 2012. A few years later, Mondy helped launch Vitana in 2018 as the director of LumenLab, leading its FinTech initiatives. It is the first health insurance product that utilises blockchain technology to make automatic payouts possible. It offers pregnant women in Singapore financial protection for gestational diabetes. With one in five expectant mothers falling victim to gestational diabetes, Vitana provides a solution by connecting electronic records via mobile devices to issue policies within minutes. Payouts happen automatically upon diagnosis. The Sandbox allowed Mondy to test how blockchain can make insurance more seamless.

The journey through the Sandbox had its share of ups and downs, during which Mondy developed a unique relationship with the team in MAS, discovering new areas and unanticipated challenges.

> *"At no point did I feel like I was denied anything for the sake of denial — it was always for legitimate reasons and new learnings for the whole ecosystem."*
>
> *Subhajit Mandal, 2020, in a personal interview, on the challenges in setting up Vitana*

Data security remains to be of paramount importance when it comes to HealthTech, which was one of the reasons Mondy was unable to go ahead with his original plan of life insurance. Vitana uses parametric underwriting on the customer's mobile device. It ensures improved data security as the insurance company would not require access to underlying medical data to confirm insurability. Vitana's success is a blueprint for parametric insurance products in the future.

FinTechs in Capital Market

Capital markets are the foundation of a thriving financial services hub as they ensure that the lifeblood of private enterprise is available and accessible to all. Both Temasek Holdings and GIC are owned by the Singapore government, with combined assets under management of over USD800B, making Singapore one of the most substantial government-linked investments in the world. To ensure significant asset diversification, GIC must invest mostly outside of Singapore. At the same time, Temasek is an investor in some of the largest local Singapore companies like Singapore Airlines, SingTel, DBS Bank and SP Group.

Singapore is a small domestic market with a population of roughly 5 million; hence, there needs to be more volume and potential to scale for public markets like stocks. Additionally, there are limitations around the presence of anchor investors to support significant capital raises. These challenges are addressed by nurturing a diverse and scalable private markets ecosystem comprising private equity, venture capital, fixed income and security token providers. Private markets, by design, operate across the border and sit well with the country's broader trade and economic priorities. In addition, Singapore's adherence to common law and reputation for ease of doing business has attracted asset and wealth managers worldwide.

Raghav Kapoor, the founder of Smartkarma, says, "If Singapore does everything like the rest of the world, it will become 'SingaBore', which won't be fun". Singapore needs to chart its path to be aligned with its unique needs and capabilities. Raghav drives product strategy, oversees technology development and maintains a hands-on approach to the company's day-to-day operations. With Smartkarma, Raghav sets out to reinvent how investment research is sourced, priced and distributed, and he states in his interview with us, that "SmartKarma aims to be a global business platform". When asked whether Singapore is ready to be labelled as the FinTech capital of the world, Raghav cites the concept of herd mentality in his response,

"The FinTech industry in Singapore has thrived, and we should carve our identity; we should be proud of what we have achieved as a nation and lay claim to this title". Despite Singapore's favourable business ecosystem, some structural inconsistencies present resulted in local companies having to list overseas. An example would be the Singaporean startup Razer listed in Hong Kong. In Raghav's opinion, there is a wide gap between investment opportunities in privately held companies and publicly listed ones, with too many regulations surrounding the public side, resulting in companies staying private for a longer period.

As an international trade centre, both private and public capital markets are crucial to ensuring Singapore's continued growth, and they are reflective of broader ecosystem trends. In the last few years, technology has helped address some of the challenges typically associated with private markets, like high minimum investment amount, limited price transparency and long holding periods. In addition, enabling experiments in the MAS FinTech Regulatory Sandbox and encouraging the use of blockchain have brought about democratisation for most facets of the private market. Currently, at least five platforms are either present inside or graduated from the Sandbox, representing half of their total intake to date, serving private market participants.

Another driver for developing private markets was the presence of industry veterans who worked with global players before launching their platforms in Singapore. The private markets trend got a boost from a generation of industry veterans who wanted to bring democratisation to this untapped market opportunity. These people with high-paying jobs were driven by hunger to create impact and achieve long-term structural changes in private market operations. Some of the examples of capital market innovation have been the first regional bond exchange set up by BondEvalue, the largest startup fundraising platform in the region offered by Fundnel, private market exchanges from ADDX and Capbridge, Propine as digital asset custodian and Synoption for structured foreign exchange (FX) note products.

Private and public capital markets ensure Singapore's continued growth as a trade hub. However, private markets are governed by different dynamics than public markets. For example, regionally, Hong Kong acts as a gateway to the Chinese market and is able to tap on larger public market flows. In comparison, there is competition in Southeast Asia between different public market exchanges, including the local ones in Indonesia and Thailand.

However, Singapore believes private markets are a space where the country could play a much larger role as larger corporations and companies treat the city-state as a gateway into ASEAN. Thus, Singapore has focused on private markets and what can be done regarding innovation in this space.

The key issues with private markets are high barriers to entry, limited information and a need for more transparency.

When blockchain came to the forefront, it brought the opportunity to solve many of these gaps in the private market. Singapore recognised this and encouraged blockchain innovation through regulatory-driven initiatives. An example of a well-thought-out regulatory initiative is Project Ubin.

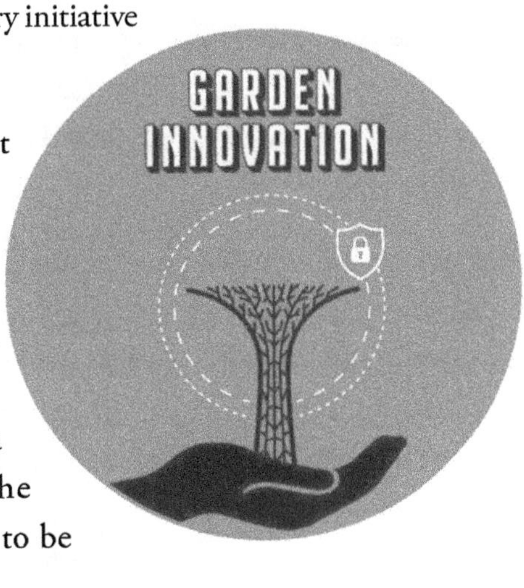

Many industry veterans felt that something could be done to enable the private markets, given the proliferation of innovations across the private sphere. But, of course, not all capital market innovations utilise blockchain. Still, there was a definite move towards this as the industry realised that more needed to be done to support private markets. This was done in a curated way defined earlier as **Garden Innovation**.

BondEvalue operates the world's first blockchain-based bond exchange, which focuses on allowing individuals to trade fractionalised bonds. Unlike equities and FX markets that have already been digitally disrupted, bonds have remained largely unchanged for decades. To this day, trading occurs over-the-counter (OTC), a euphemism for phone-based trading.

The company's founders are Rahul Banerjee and Rajaram Kannan, who were classmates during their MBA and quit their banking jobs to start BondEvalue. Before setting up BondEvalue, Rahul was at Standard Chartered as its Global Head of International Corporates in Financial Markets Sales. Likewise, Rajaram quit DBS Bank, where he was Senior Vice President and Head of Treasury and Markets Technology. Together they embarked on a journey to make bonds accessible to a broader audience.

Looking back, Rahul believes a confluence of factors led to the birth of the Bond Exchange. In 2016, Singapore witnessed the beginning of the FinTech boom. Creative juices flowed in every bank, board room and bar across the island nation. However, there needed to be more innovation in the debt capital markets. Even bond prices were not easily available to individual investors. Hence, BondEvalue was born to "bring transparency to bonds".

The team at BondEvalue use their deep domain expertise to level the playing field for consumers by moving the bond market towards exchanges. Bonds are more mathematically intricate than most other aspects of finance. While calculating yields of the 8 million plus bonds today is hard, doing so in real-time is even more complex. As a result, innovation in the bond market needs to catch up with developments in the equity space. Raj and Rahul were inspired to fractional seconds for investors who cannot meet the typical minimum investment amount of about SGD250,000. This high minimum denomination prevents people with less than SGD5M in investible assets from owning a diversified bond portfolio.

As a specialised exchange for bonds, BondEvalue improves the vital infrastructure of the capital markets. For example, while bonds traditionally traded over the counter settle after two days, BondEvalue allows bonds to settle instantly, similar to stocks. Another advantage is that trading happens in a fully electronic mode.

The fractional bonds called Bondblox are backed by the full bonds lock-boxed with one of the world's largest custodians. Like most large exchanges globally, BondEvalue also operates on a B2B2C model. Its members are banks, brokers and consumer-facing FinTech from across the world.

Rahul believes that in addition to Singapore being the FinTech capital of the world, it is also the centre of the new-age bond market. BondEvalue was the first entrant to the MAS's Sandbox Express and the first to exit the programme successfully after completing its experiments. BondEvalue's journey has been massively accelerated due to this Sandbox framework leading it to expand its offerings to onboard customers directly without dependence on banks and brokers as intermediaries. Bondevalue is now operating both B2B2C and B2C business models in parallel, thus covering all the bases in the fixed income space.

SynOPTION holds the RMO licence granted by MAS for trading OTC derivatives. The company's innovative approach led to its status as the first firm in the MAS Regulatory Sandbox for RMO in 2020. Furthermore, SynOPTION has received the Commodity Futures Trading Commission's Swap Execution Facilities exemption, enabling it to operate and onboard US entities.

Financial institutions constantly looking to trade options require tools to manage the option's lifecycle. Such tools and operations include the ability to analyse markets, execute trades, distribute pricing to clients and manage risk through the option lifecycle.

SynOPTION offers a diverse range of products tailored to meet the unique requirements of its clients. The company provides Optimus, a regulated institutional platform that empowers clients to analyse and trade on FX Options instruments and strategies. With Titan, SynOPTION offers FX options white label solutions, enabling firms to efficiently manage FX options trading and workflow through fully-branded user interfaces or APIs. It serves the Crypto Options analytics and trading platform, allowing for trading on structures across exchanges, altcoins, and exotics via OTC. Additionally, SynOPTION provides Omega, a risk management platform that allows portfolio managers and CIOs to assess multi-venue, multi-asset, and multi-product risks in a modular and efficient manner.

The product scope of SynOPTION encompasses various use cases. The company supports trades in FX, Digital Assets, and Precious Metals, providing a multi-asset trading experience. Its products are compatible with Over-the-Counter (OTC), Exchange-based, and Decentralised (DeFi) trading, ensuring versatility across multiple venues. From Cash to Linear products, from vanilla to exotic options, SynOPTION technology supports a wide range of products, offering extensive multi-product support.

Looking towards the future, SynOPTION is focused on expanding its engineering team capabilities and extending its client coverage to Europe and the US. The company remains committed to meeting its clients' evolving requirements and continuously enhancing its product offerings.

ECXX is a security token exchange based in Singapore. It enables companies, real estate companies and funds to unlock value from illiquid assets by tokenising them and providing a marketplace where they can be traded back and forth while being compliant and regulated. When they first started in 2018, they realised that the space is dominated by tokens and coins, which are often securities but issued without proper guidelines and consumer protection is often neglected. While securities laws under the Securities and Futures Act were not new, the infrastructure and legal framework of 2018 mainly dealt with traditional assets and structures. They engaged MAS on day one to offer security tokens to the masses.

In the global asset classes, the combined market cap runs into trillions. Real estate is the largest at USD326.5T. This is not surprising, considering real estate is popular amongst many investors globally. However, it is plagued with inefficiencies like the transfer of land titles, physical paperwork, and multiple intermediaries having to get involved in each transaction. A typical real estate transaction takes approximately six months for the sales process to complete. We believe tokenisation will remove the inefficiencies and enable more value to be unlocked. This extends to other asset classes like art and private equity. Fractionalisation and tokenisation drive new participants' adoption and entry, allowing more to partake in the Web 3.0 industry. Users can now own their digital assets online (with a proper legal anchor), thus enabling them to be a stakeholder instead of a user. This story extends to purely digital native tokens in which users can hold and invest.

ECXX entered the FinTech Sandbox express in August 2020 and obtained its RMO licence in January 2022. It enabled ECXX to carry out tokenisation experiments for different assets. The regulatory nod allowed ECXX to carry out regulated activity and drive the tokenisation of real-world assets (RWA). Their sandbox journey enabled us to map the entire process of wrapping the different assets with legal construct, thus enabling institutional and accredited investors to invest with a peace of mind. Digital assets will become a mainstream asset class, and ECXX is well-placed to help companies unlock the value of physical assets.

While FinTech solutions look at creating more direct-to-customer offerings to bring new asset classes and opportunities to end customers, it is important for regulators to vet such use cases.

Private Markets, Digital Advisory and Digital Assets were the key areas seeing innovation and new business models. While Kristal focused on recreating a virtual private bank comprising digital advisory, public market, private market and structured products, players like ADDX and Alta focused on private markets. Alta, which counts Binance as an investor, also ventured into the digital asset vertical, while players like HyraX and Propine focused deeply on the domain.

ADDX was the first regulated platform in a major global financial centre to offer issuance, settlement, custody and secondary trading of digitised securities. MAS awarded it a CMS licence. Through the platform, it provides investors access to investment opportunities which are outside reach. Issuers on the platform can similarly gain access to otherwise inaccessible segments of the capital markets in a secure, compliant and cost-effective manner. Principal shareholders include SGX and Heliconia; key partners include PwC, CIMB Bank and SAC Capital. ADDX saw an inequality in the accessibility of capital. Those who cannot get capital continue to be restricted, and inequality widens. Therefore, blockchain and DLT are central to the company's business model. Darius Liu, COO at ADDX, shares that from the perspective of finance professionals, he has observed this inequality gap in the private markets and has utilised DLT to narrow this gap together with his team at ADDX.

Ultimately, ADDX is a platform that aims to better facilitate the flow of capital in the private sphere. It is the first entity of its kind to graduate from the MAS FinTech Regulatory Sandbox successfully. It graduated with two Capital Markets Services and one Recognised Market Operator licence and is also a licensed custodian. The platform, or the marketplace, is seamlessly integrated with the custodian function, allowing smooth trading. As a result of technology, it can also charge a low fee as a trading commission. In addition, smart contracts have allowed for automating many workflows at ADDX.

Darius shares that the most recent and impactful innovative development in capital markets infrastructure is the electronification of trading and markets. He added that adherence to these rigorous standards and regulatory clarity is crucial to minimise the risks of new entrants in the financial services industry. The MAS FinTech Regulatory Sandbox enables financial institutions and FinTech players to experiment with innovative financial products or services in a live environment but within a well-defined space and duration.

The evolution of capital markets is being witnessed, wherein digitalisation is transforming the financial markets and bringing the numerous benefits of blockchain to various parts of the capital markets lifecycle. However, legacy technology systems only support digital or tokenised assets with a relatively inexpensive modernisation process. At the same time, there is an increasing demand for regulatory-compliant infrastructure with the entry of financial institutions and mounting pressure from regulators. Partnerships with appropriately licensed and technologically capable fiduciary partners have become necessary for companies wishing to participate in the Web 3.0 financial markets.

Hydra X is a Singapore-headquartered financial technology company that provides financial markets infrastructure for financial institutions, including regulated entities looking to transition into the Web 3.0 financial markets. It has a regulatory-compliant ecosystem of technology infrastructure and licensed entities that cover the end-to-end lifecycle of the digital capital markets: pre-trade, primary and secondary markets, and post-trade.

Hydra X obtained its CMS licence in February 2022 from MAS to facilitate the provision of regulated financial services in this space to Hydra. With this approval, Hydra X graduated from the MAS FinTech Regulatory Sandbox to provide custodial services, including tokenised securities, after complying with the regulatory standards and licensing conditions set by MAS. At that time, Hydra X was the first company to have graduated early from the Sandbox before the deadline stipulated by MAS. Getting regulated is important for Hydra X to expand its services to clients looking to unlock the value of their assets through tokenisation. Providing access to regulated custodial services to foster confidence in the growing digital asset ecosystem is also important. The regulatory support MAS provides via the Sandbox framework has also played an important role in facilitating this development. It has allowed Hydra X to commercialise its technology in a live environment as one of the first movers in this space while providing sufficient regulatory oversight to encourage adoption among institutional clients. In this way, Hydra X was able to validate its solutions in this nascent space. The provision of independent, regulated financial services is a necessary cornerstone for the continued growth of the digital asset ecosystem. Hydra X continues to see increasing interest in the asset digitisation space and expects to play a bigger role in the development of modern financial markets.

Hydra X is uniquely positioned to address these gaps with its unique two-pronged approach: (i) it offers a regulatory-compliant, cloud-based, turnkey digital financial infrastructure that natively supports multiple market types and asset classes, and (ii) it provides complementary regulated financial services that are digitally enabled and pre-integrated with its tech infrastructure. In this way, Hydra X is a one-stop capital market service provider, subject to the oversight of a leading regional financial regulator, providing both technology and financial services.

As venture capital and startups grew in Singapore, some areas that became the focus of attention were developing secondary trading for private markets and enabling digital interface fundraising for startups.

Alta, previously known as Fundnel, was launched to address deep inefficiencies in the private capital markets and alternative investing. Alternative investing has typically been a fragmented market with high investment costs, illiquidity, and exclusivity, creating high barriers to entry. Alta sought to democratise alternative assets to address these challenges, making them more accessible while enhancing liquidity for investors.

Since its launch in 2016, Alta has grown to offer much more. On top of offering access and liquidity to private equities and funds, it operates Southeast Asia's largest digital exchange for alternative investments as a fund management arm, making it a true end-to-end marketplace for alternative investment.

In November 2022, Fundnel rebranded to Alta and acquired Hg Exchange. Founded in 2020, Hg Exchange graduated from the MAS FinTech Regulatory Sandbox with an RMO licence the following year. The member-driven private exchange was established by four firms: Fundnel, PhillipCapital, PrimePartners and Zilliqa.

Conceptualised as a private exchange to support the issuance and trading of both digital and non-digital capital market products, Hg Exchange benefitted from the innovative regulatory sandbox as it developed its blockchain-powered offering. In 2021, Hg Exchange launched the world's first asset-backed security tokens for rare whiskeys. It has since launched several new listings, which span a growing inventory of luxury assets, private equity, and private credit. It has expanded its member firm network to provide access to over a million investors worldwide.

Today, Alta is fully integrated with the exchange. It brings efficiencies for investors to trade alternative assets at smaller, fractionalised blocks, thereby enhancing liquidity in the private markets and investing in alternatives.

Since 2016, over its evolution to become an end-to-end alternative investment marketplace, Alta has completed over 1,500 transactions valued at more than USD600M. She has created global access for investors to invest over USD22B in mandated opportunities. Phillip Securities, Nomura Holdings, Binance, Integra Partners and Prime Partners are investors of Alta.

Singapore FinTech Nation has proven resilience and innovation amid the ever-evolving customer needs and market landscape. Singapore's unique approach to encouraging innovation for concepts and business models outside the governance purview of current regulations enables regulators to focus and prioritise in the spirit of garden innovation. As next-generation concepts like Web 3.0 and Defi become more mainstream and seek consumer protection, Singapore FinTech Nation must expand its scope to accommodate such future opportunities.

Chapter 3

SCALING INNOVATION — BLOCK BY BLOCK

Singapore gained independence in 1965 with a population of 1.8 million and a Gross Domestic Product (GDP) of less than USD1B. By many standards, it was an underdeveloped nation faced with social, geopolitical and economic challenges. Fast forward to 2023, 58 years since independence; Singapore is now home to thrice as many people and boasts a GDP of more than USD360B. From being an ordinary shipping port with no comparative advantage to becoming a global financial hub in less than two generations is no accidental feat.

Singapore has utilised its *kampung* (village) spirit as the DNA of its society and the secret of Singapore's success. The *kampung* spirit has unified the people of Singapore. It has inspired those residing in the city-state to face the difficult challenge and emerge victoriously as a community. In more ways than one, Singapore's success is attributed to the collective effort of its people, who have raised this country since its birth and now watch as it shines in front of a global audience.

Singapore is small. Most global cities are bigger than this little red dot that will house a 5.64 million population in 2022. Before it became a shipping and trading hub, the country was a small fishing port. Only gaining independence in 1965, Singapore was one of the youngest countries in the world and was highly underdeveloped by global standards at the time. Nevertheless, the community has united to build the nation over the last 50 years. The *kampung* spirit is the DNA of Singapore's society, galvanising the country into action to overcome emergent challenges.

FinTech *Choupal*

One unique feature of Singapore is the presence of social communities. One of the most popular communities in FinTech is called "FinTech *Choupal*". *Choupal* is a Hindi word to describe a central village square. It is a platform for discussion, debate and free speech in the village. FinTech *Choupal* was created in May 2015 as an experiment by Varun Mittal to bring people in payments together for discussion. It grew organically from a place to talk about challenges faced by startups to founders helping each other find resources.

The underlying principle of *Choupal* was that there needs to be a safe space for startups to dialogue without the pressure of feeling vulnerable. The expectation of always looking energetic and motivated wears down the most motivated and brave souls.

One of the critical turning points for this group was a drinks session hosted by Markus Gnirck, one of the original FinTech evangelists who came to Singapore to set up one of the first FinTech accelerators. In August 2019, he curated and brought together 15 people to join for drinks to share their experience generally. At the end of the session, only three people were in the room: Markus; the newly appointed Chief FinTech Officer at the Monetary Authority of Singapore (MAS), Sopnendu Mohanty (Sop); and Varun Mittal, founder of FinTech *Choupal*.

Globally, no regulator engages in such forums with startups, and MAS was no exception to that precedence. One of the biggest concerns was that the startups might criticise MAS, which may become an unpleasant chat. So Varun convinced Sop to join the WhatsApp group FinTech *Choupal* for five days, and if Sop did not see value in that, he would back off. Varun's persistence and willingness to push the boundary triggered off a world's first phenomenon, where regulators are talking to startups openly in private access, controlled WhatsApp group!

It is a simple WhatsApp group built as a bridge for startups and regulators to engage in real-time discussion, allowing each side to understand the views and needs of each other. Three days after the challenge, Sop called Varun to invite the rest of the MAS FinTech team to join the group as well, and since then, it has remained the cornerstone of the MAS FinTech dialogue.

As of 2023, the group remains an invite-only platform for grassroots community members with close to 300 handpicked participants. Though several attempts have been made to turn it into a broader outreach and broadcast platform, Varun has yet to do to moderate the quality of discussions. Everyone in the Singapore FinTech community can reach anyone within one degree of separation through *Choupal*, so everyone knows someone who is inside it, and they can get the help they need. An infamous feature about *Choupal* is the law of three strikes issued to members by admin if they violate any of the group's rules.

In the spirit of **Garden Innovation** of Singapore, inactive members are replaced by new people due to the governance and quality controls imposed on the group. The constraint has become the strength and driver of quality for the community.

Due to the growing interest and specialisation of FinTech in Singapore, Varun created two sister WhatsApp groups for the main FinTech *Choupal* group. One focuses on the ASEAN VC community, and the other on the InsurTech sector. Both groups operate on similar rules and invite-only structures and nurture grassroots engagement in the community. Creating such communities focused on specific interest sectors and moderated by the members creates a spirit of bonding and ties that extend beyond professional lives.

FinTech *Choupal* has been the birthplace of some of the most famous initiatives arising from the grassroots dialogue between startups and MAS. Some notable ones have been the creation of the Singapore FinTech Association (SFA), spinning off as a cousin of *Choupal* to bring together the investors for MAS Investor Summit and getting startups a seat at the table during the formulation of several regulatory policies. The group gained so much recognition that the *Times of India*, the largest newspaper of India, covered it, in addition to broad local coverage by the media. FinTech *Choupal* remains a safe zone for startups to make their voices heard.

In 2021, MAS institutionalised this kampung spirit, creating Elevandi, an independent legal entity set up as a non-profit organisation. As a result, Elevandi has become an important platform that connects the public and private sectors to support the growth of the FinTech ecosystem.[1]

Singapore FinTech Association

As Singapore witnessed the rise in the FinTech sphere and its collaboration with incumbent financial institutions (FIs), there was a need for a common platform to facilitate communication both within the space and with government regulators. While Singapore has several informal groups and meetup circles, none could claim to represent the community formally.

[1] https://www.elevandi.io/#ourstorys

In the early stages of the ecosystem development, Varun Mittal reflects on his conversation regarding the SFA's formation in FinTech *Choupal*, the WhatsApp group mentioned earlier. *"Upon my suggestion of forming a common association for Singapore-based FinTech startups, I received a very Singaporean reply, 'Do not suggest. Do it, and call us when you need help. When should we expect to hear back from you?'"*.

Varun recalls the sudden realisation of the colossal task at hand. However, he lauds the Singaporean *kampung* spirit, which he witnessed first-hand as all the relevant stakeholders banded together over several *kopi* chats and mapped out their next steps. The biggest challenges for SFA's first committee were to create a long-term governance structure that could outlive all the people in the room that day while ensuring that the voice of FinTech remains relevant in the financial community. During the early days, Varun recollects his journey to find a team with sound, legal and compliance standing: *"I was fortunate to get a legal firm and one of the Big 4 auditing firms since we wanted to ensure the highest level of compliance and governance. It was April 2016, and the Singapore FinTech Festival was six months away, and we decided that we would need to get the Singapore FinTech Association formed by November 2016"*. Working in an economy as unique as Singapore, SFA added a clause ensuring that at least half of its elected council, at all times, must be startups with revenue of less than SGD1M per year, thus guaranteeing the startups will have a place on the SFA Council. As a diverse global hub, it was also important to ensure that there is representation from local as well as international constituents. Safeguards were built into the nomination and election process to ensure fair representation of different nationalities and backgrounds. The number of large financial institution representatives was capped at 20% to ensure enough involvement but still space for startups to air their voices.

In the Singapore spirit of **Garden Innovation**, SFA was formed when community efforts and government support came together to create one unified platform to serve the community. SFA acts as a neutral non-profit platform for the FinTech ecosystem and continues to be a key milestone in Singapore's FinTech journey. Singapore understands that for it to be successful, Southeast Asia as a whole needs to succeed. Prosperity does not exist in isolation. SFA proactively takes upon that responsibility to build community-to-community bridges within the global FinTech ecosystem.

In its early years, SFA received no government grants. Like the startups it represented, it embraced bootstrapping with members' contributions, with some revenue from FinTech talent programmes to fund operations. It did not have any full-time staff for the first two years. Most of the work was undertaken by volunteers who carved out time to support the community. What started as a bootstrapped startup is a flourishing enterprise with five full-time staff, a multi-million-dollar budget, and a resilient global footprint. It is now one of the most successful FinTech associations worldwide.

SFA has excelled as a community for like-minded people to unite and socialise. One of the key members of SFA is Eddie Lee from SeedIn then. With the President, he approached one of the authors of this book to serve as SFA's Advisor in Talent Development. Dr Lillian Koh, who has taught for 17 years at the Nanyang Technological University, agreed and joined forces with SFA. She dedicated her time to training and researching needs and seeing to the successful implementation of the talent development programme for individuals keen to learn about what FinTech entails and to gain insights on how their expert domain knowledge could still be useful and relevant in this new world of digital transformation. Besides catering to this target segment of working adults, she also conducted talks, seminars and workshops for university and polytechnic lecturers and students in Singapore on demystifying FinTech. In addition, with various stakeholders like the Institutes of Higher Learning and industry leaders, conferences and hackathons were organised for youth in FinTech.

SFA was established to be the vehicle to interact with the regulators and represent the ecosystem of FinTech startups. If there was anything the FinTech community needed to lobby for, SFA provided the communication channel. Eventually, different verticals, like the RegTech and InsurTech subcommittees, were established for more specific conversations in the respective verticals.

SFA has grown from strength to strength over the years. However, there is still an opportunity for more exposure. There are overseas trips (to Cambodia, Philippines, etc.) in collaboration with Enterprise Singapore in search of expansion opportunities for members to operate their businesses there. Eddie has taken his experience in SFA to help build the ecosystem outside Singapore and set up Cambodia FinTech Association (CFA) in 2018. After the successful formation and the completion of his term in 2020, Eddie celebrated the succession of the new president and the new executive team to CFA. This example of Eddie's involvement in Cambodia shows how Singapore can leverage connections to create growth in the global FinTech ecosystem.

In a personal interview with Rob Findlay, one of the founding members of the SFA, he recalls the committee's journey and purpose. When Rob started, the FinTech space was unorganised, with individuals working all over the city, trying to find some coordination. MAS had a vision of turning Singapore into a hub for FinTech. Amidst this vision and the spotlight shining on the FinTech sector, Rob shared that everyone was clamouring to find their voice in the ecosystem. The next logical step was to create an independent group for startups and big players, an agency that voiced the government's ambitions but remained objective enough to question regulations. The aim was to build an agency that did not favour a particular investor or sector — to create a truly independent body that would become the first contact point.

The initial challenge was establishing what needed to be done together as a community and each player's role. Rob was involved in the formation, bringing structure to the organisation of SFA. Soon after, other individuals started taking on more central roles and became more committed to SFA. For example, Anna Haotanto is part of the SFA's founding committee and leads the Women in FinTech subcommittee.

The development of SFA happened very rapidly. Everyone assumed formal roles within nine months, and the FinTech ecosystem emerged.

SFA started as a platform for the industry, acting as a voice and bringing structure to the Singapore FinTech scene. Establishing SFA enabled easier communication with the government and simplified processes for new entrants to become established in the Singapore FinTech scene. In addition, the agency encouraged activity in the Singapore FinTech scene and joined forces with MAS in a complementary manner. MAS provided SFA with funding upon its formation, and both parties worked together to achieve a common objective of becoming the focal point of FinTech in the region.

> *"Innovation in FinTech is more about culture than about finance or banking. It is not just about technology, but about how to open one is towards change."*
>
> *Rob Findlay, 2020, in a personal interview, on the future of FinTech innovation*

As Singapore cements its position as a global FinTech hub, SFA continues to be a driving force in the industry, promoting further growth in the FinTech ecosystem. SFA was formed as a neutral, non-profit organisation, uniting community efforts and government support to create a unified platform to serve the FinTech community. Rooted in its mission to build community-to-community bridges within the global FinTech ecosystem, SFA has become a dynamic community including industry professionals, government stakeholders and international counterparts.

SFA's beginnings were humble. In its early years, SFA operated with limited staffing and funding, relying heavily on the support of its community members to drive its mission forward. Like the startups it represented, the organisation embraced bootstrapping, generating revenue through FinTech talent programmes to fund its operations. Today, SFA has grown exponentially into a flourishing enterprise, boasting almost 900 corporate members, a multi-million-dollar budget, and a resilient global footprint. SFA created an important role in COVID-19, helping manage the administration of COVID support and solidarity grants for the FinTech startups in Singapore.

SFA has come a long way since its early days, providing a platform for collaboration, advocacy, and innovation. It has played a pivotal role in transforming the future of FinTech across the region. In an interview with **Shadab Taiyabi**, President of SFA, he says, "We have made bold strides in building bridges across the FinTech communities in the region and putting Singapore on the map as a global FinTech centre. I am incredibly proud of the progress so far. Moving forward, we continue to commit to bolstering FinTech acceleration and innovation in Singapore and beyond." The SFA Executive Committee sets the strategic direction for SFA's activities related to advocacy, fostering business growth, facilitating access to capital and opportunities, and growing FinTech talent. Shadab highlights the key pillars of SFA in representing the FinTech ecosystem, building networks, and contributing to developing the FinTech industry in Singapore. It is a cross-industry initiative facilitating collaboration between all market participants and stakeholders. SFA brings together a strong community to foster collaboration, innovation and partnerships among members and the industry to strengthen Singapore's position as a global FinTech hub.

Khai Lin Sng, Vice President of SFA, says, "The FinTech talent pool will play a pivotal role in driving innovation and growth in the industry, and we aim to create a strong talent pipeline that can support the growth and sustainability of the FinTech ecosystem." The FinTech Talent Programme is a Career Conversion Programme by SFA that equips mid-career individuals with the skills and knowledge required for key technology roles within the FinTech industry, such as software testing and quality assurance. SFA has established 10 subcommittees spanning different FinTech areas: Payments, InsurTech, Web 3.0, Digital Financing, and Cyber Risk. These sub-committees provide a platform for members to champion and advocate for initiatives, drive conversations, and build resources for their respective sectors. For example, the Payments subcommittee actively engages with regulators to represent the Payments community in Singapore on current and future state regulations, market structure, and practices within the financial services sector. They also organise events to raise awareness and engagement, provide the latest market insights, and work with tertiary institutions in Singapore to develop talent and promote industry best practices.

RegTech is critical as the technological advancement in the "Fin" side of the equation needs to be balanced with an equally robust RegTech ecosystem. RegTech, in a nutshell, is the use of technology to address regulatory problems. In May 2019, a RegTech Sub-committee was formed within SFA to promote the invention and adoption of RegTech solutions in Singapore.

Beyond local efforts, SFA increases regional and global exposure for its members through mission trips. These overseas events help members stay ahead of the curve and make meaningful connections with international players and investors in the industry.

FinTech Nation

The mission and vision to establish Singapore as the leading Singapore FinTech Hub in the world led to the development of **Fintech Nation**, a not-for-profit grassroots platform to bring together the FinTech community, regulators, investors, startups and corporates. Started in 2020 with the development of the FinTech Nation book by Varun Mittal and Lillian Koh, it supports access and scaling talent, capital, policy and venture development in Singapore. It has awarded recognition to over 250 individuals through the Fintech 65 platform and invested in multiple startups through Fintech Nation Fund.

Singapore: The Fintech Nation, the first edition of this book, was created to document untold stories of how Singapore became successful as a FinTech hub. Therefore, the book's authors set out to develop a storyline of how and what made Singapore a successful FinTech hub and track historical development to identify common themes, attributes, and characteristics that explain how it arrived at its current state and possible impact on the future.

To achieve their goal, the authors analysed several hundred FinTech investment transactions to identify and prove the correlation between programmes undertaken by MAS to identify high-potential companies and their impact on success. In addition, they conducted 70 primary interviews, bringing together the stories and journeys of founders and enablers of the FinTech ecosystem, including access to capital, customers, talent, and policy initiatives which have made them and Singapore successful. They also analysed key regulatory policy decisions and the background of how some of the foundation blocks of Fintech Nation were set up and evolved.

These three key principles are the foundation of the Fintech Nation's success. The first principle, Right First, Fast Later, focused on the firm belief that in the long-term scheme of things, it does not matter who came first; instead, who did things the right way. As a result, Singapore's economic and FinTech policies are a unique example of balancing social welfare with economic development.

The second principle, Singanomics, delved into a unique economic system that lets market forces define most outcomes while retaining a nudge from public policy to support the navigation in the right direction. At the same time, a progressive government develops a broader structure of guidelines and policy investments to enable innovation and competition to develop further.

The last principle, Garden Innovation, was entrenched in a unique Singaporean view of the conciliatory approach of picking vital focus areas of innovation and providing all possible resources to nurture them like a compassionate gardener. Unlike the international model of advocating disruption, Singapore practises more Asian values of peaceful coexistence and respect for differences while aiming for long-term alignment.

Fintech Nation Fund

As an extension of the Fintech Nation Community, several FinTech founders, operators and angel investors came together to support other founders on their journey to build the next generation of companies in the Fintech Nation, creating a community structure of the Fintech Nation Fund (FNF). FNF stands out as a venture capital fund that strongly emphasises community connectivity and deep-rooted ties to entrepreneurship in Singapore. The fund is led by Varun Mittal, founder of Fintech Nation, and supported by a professional team from a leading Southeast Asian venture capital firm, ensuring entrepreneurs have access to top-notch guidance and support.

FNF invests in early-stage FinTech and embedded finance companies in Southeast Asia, focusing on sub-10M valuations and sub-2% ownership stakes. The fund has a unique investment approach, allowing for pro rata rights and board observer roles but no board seats, giving entrepreneurs the freedom to operate their businesses while benefitting from the fund's expertise and resources.

One of the key advantages of FNF is its open-ended fund structure, which allows for a long-term commitment to the growth and scaling of ventures with no hard exit dates. This approach will enable founders to focus on execution and building their businesses rather than worrying about exit timelines.

FNF is known for its lightning-fast decision-making process, with a commitment to providing funding within just five days. The fund is also committed to supplying entrepreneurs with industry terms without hang-ups, ensuring startups have the necessary resources to succeed. With an evergreen capital structure, FNF is in alignment to support the next generation of entrepreneurs in Singapore and beyond.

FNF offers a cheque size of up to USD500,000, making it an attractive option for entrepreneurs looking for early-stage funding. In addition, the diverse pool of deal leads brings expertise and experience to every investment, ensuring that the best opportunities are identified and nurtured.

The fund also presents a unique opportunity for FinTech entrepreneurs in Southeast Asia and Singapore to receive support and funding from a community of experienced industry leaders. The fund's investment approach and carry-only model ensure that the interests of the entrepreneurs and the fund are fully aligned. In addition, the diverse pool of deal leads brings expertise and experience to every investment.

Fintech 65

As Fintech Nation was born as a grassroots initiative to nurture and scale Singapore's FinTech ecosystem, it also embraces the role of community in talent development, nurturing startups and awarding recognition. Fintech 65 is a talent initiative from Fintech Nation. In collaboration with SFA and Elevandi, it identifies and recognises emerging and proven leaders across different categories like startups, corporate, product management and venture capital in Singapore. The number 65 is especially unique for Singapore, as it represents both the year of Singapore's independence and the international country phone code of Singapore.

Fintech 65 develops annual lists of 65 leaders curated by leaders from industry and academic institutions with an open nomination process for grassroots participation. The platform enables peer-to-peer learning and mentorship for young talents from experienced ones. In 2022, Fintech 65 focused on identifying leaders across five categories: Emerging FinTech Founders, Young Leaders in FinTech (aged 30 and younger), Women in FinTech, Women in Corporate, and Women Investors. Over 500 candidates submitted nominations, of which 250 were curated and recognised by industry leaders. In 2023, Fintech 65 focused on identifying leaders across risk, compliance, ESG, Web3, data and artificial intelligence.

MAS Grants

MAS set up the Financial Technology and Innovation Group (FTIG) in 2015 to oversee the development of Singapore's financial technology (FinTech) industry. FTIG's mission is to facilitate the growth and development of the FinTech industry in Singapore by providing regulatory support, encouraging innovation, and fostering collaboration between stakeholders. It also aims to promote the use of technology to enhance financial services and improve financial inclusion. Since its inception, FTIG has been actively supporting the growth of the FinTech ecosystem in Singapore through various initiatives such as the Singapore FinTech Festival, the Financial Sector Technology and Innovation (FSTI) scheme, and the Global FinTech Hackcelerator.

The FSTI scheme supports financial institutions, FinTech startups, and research institutions in Singapore to develop and test innovative FinTech solutions in a live financial sector environment. In addition, the scheme encourages collaboration between financial institutions and FinTech startups to enhance Singapore's financial sector's efficiency, competitiveness, and resilience. The initiative aims to strengthen Singapore's position as a leading FinTech hub in the region and foster the development of a vibrant FinTech ecosystem. The government's commitment to this project highlights the country's strong focus on innovation and its determination to stay at the forefront of technological advancements.[2]

The FSTI 1.0 scheme — an investment-funded research and development supporting the growth of FinTech startups in Singapore — committed SGD225M over five years from 2015 to 2019. By 2019, the FSTI 1.0 scheme supported over 500 projects, and the government found invaluable lessons in mature verticals, the ones that needed more assistance and those that could not achieve their objectives.

Despite the disruptive effects of the COVID-19 pandemic, the FinTech sector in Singapore has managed to maintain a relatively strong position due to the active involvement of the government in providing financial support to FinTech companies and its approach to job preservation and growth within the financial services industry.

The Singapore government has demonstrated a firm commitment to developing FinTechs and the broader startup ecosystem by implementing

---

[2] https://www.mas.gov.sg/news/speeches/2015/a-smart-financial-centre

various funding initiatives. One notable example is allocating an SGD125M package designed for FIs and FinTech firms. This comprehensive support package has three key components to drive growth and innovation.

Firstly, a SGD90M training allowance grant has been established to incentivise FinTechs and FIs to invest in the training and upskilling of their employees. This grant encourages the development of enhanced capabilities within the workforce, ensuring that Singapore remains at the forefront of financial technology advancements. Secondly, a SGD35M support package has been introduced to assist firms in adopting digital solutions. This initiative aims to promote the adoption of cutting-edge technologies by FinTechs and FIs, enabling them to upgrade their systems and implement digital tools that facilitate seamless business operations, such as document collaboration solutions and virtual conferencing platforms. Lastly, MAS has provided Singapore-based FinTech firms six months of free access to API Exchange and new digital self-assessment frameworks. By granting access to these digital platforms and tools, MAS empowers FinTechs to leverage the latest technologies and drive innovation in their respective domains.

The Singapore government demonstrated its unwavering support for the FinTech sector through these comprehensive measures. By providing financial assistance, training opportunities, and access to cutting-edge technologies, the government actively fostered a conducive environment for the growth and development of FinTechs, ultimately bolstering Singapore's position as a global hub for financial innovation. The take-up of the Digital Acceleration Grant (DAG) that was announced in April 2020 as part of the USD125M support package boosted the morale of the FinTech and financial services ecosystem. More than 350 FIs and FinTech firms applied for the grant to adopt digital solutions to strengthen operational resilience, improve productivity, and provide better management of risks and engagement with customers. The government also committed to ensuring talent remains strong with funding for interns and graduates. The Singapore government encouraged firms to continue hiring within the financial services sector through government-funded schemes, including a SGD100M fund to create training programmes to help interns and new graduates amidst a weak job market.[3] Under the programme, trainees will receive a monthly training allowance based on the scope and skills required for the traineeship lasting up to 12 months. The government funded 80% of the allowance and the trainee's host company funded the remaining amount.

The private sector also collaborated with SFA and MAS to support FinTech startups during the COVID-19 crisis. MAS, SFA, AMTD Group, and AMTD Foundation jointly announced the MAS-SFA-AMTD FinTech Solidarity Grant launch. This SGD6M grant aimed to support Singapore-based FinTech firms facing challenges due to the COVID-19 pandemic.

The grant aimed to help FinTech firms sustain operations, foster innovation, and facilitate growth. It complemented the SGD125M support package previously announced by MAS to strengthen capabilities in the financial services and FinTech sectors. AMTD contributed an initial SGD2M to support the Singapore FinTech ecosystem, and MAS added SGD4M from the Financial Sector Development Fund, bringing the total grant amount to SGD6M. The grant comprised the SGD1.5M Business Sustenance Grant (BSG) and the SGD4.5M Business Growth Grant (BGG). BSG provided eligible Singapore-based FinTech firms with a one-time grant of up to SGD20,000 to cover day-to-day working capital expenditures, such as

[3] Ministry of Manpower, $100 Million Set Aside to Provide Graduates with Traineeship Opportunities Amid a Pandemic-Hit Job Market, 24 April 2020, https://www.mom.gov.sg/newsroom/press-releases/2020/0424-$100-million-set-aside-to-provide-graduates-with-traineeship-opportunities

salaries and rental costs. This support aimed to help these firms sustain their operations and retain their employees.

BGG allowed eligible Singapore-based FinTech firms to receive funding for their first proof of concept (POC) with financial institutions on the API Exchange platform, with up to SGD40,000 provided. Subsequent POCs were eligible for SGD10,000 each, subject to a total cap of SGD80,000 per firm throughout the grant duration. BGG encouraged collaboration between FinTech firms and financial institutions, fostering innovation and creating growth opportunities. Both AMTD and MAS supported BGG. Additionally, BGG allocated funding for undergraduate intern salaries, capped at SGD1,000 per month per intern. This initiative aimed to support approximately 120 interns in the FinTech sector, assuming an average internship duration of three to five months. The objective was to encourage FinTech firms to offer internships and contribute to developing the local FinTech talent pipeline. FinTech firms meeting the eligibility criteria could apply for BSG and BGG. SFA conducted the administration and review of grant applications.

MAS launched the FSTI 2.0 scheme in August 2020, continuing the FSTI scheme introduced in 2015.[4] The objective of the FSTI 2.0 scheme remained consistent with its predecessor, aiming to drive innovation and transformation within the financial sector. The FSTI 2.0 scheme was built upon the success of its predecessor, promoting the development and adoption of innovative FinTech solutions in Singapore's financial sector. It focused on fostering industry-wide transformation and significantly emphasised promoting Singapore as a green finance and sustainability hub. The FSTI 2.0 scheme will focus on three key areas: accelerating technology and innovation adoption, strengthening the resilience of Singapore's financial sector, and fostering talent development.

[4] https://www.mas.gov.sg/news/media-releases/2020/mas-commits-s$250-million-to-accelerate-innovation-and-technology-adoption-in-financial-sector

Overall, the SGD250M commitment by MAS under FTSI 2.0 demonstrated its commitment to supporting the growth and development of Singapore's financial sector. By investing in technology and innovation, strengthening resilience, and fostering talent development, MAS aims to build a vibrant and innovative financial sector that can compete globally. The FSTI 2.0 aimed to foster a culture of innovation within the financial services sector by attracting financial institutions to set up research and development and innovation labs in Singapore. It focused on aiding the development of industry-wide technological infrastructure and improving the financial sector's efficiency and productivity through industry-wide projects.

Under the FSTI 2.0 scheme, various grant schemes were made available to financial institutions, FinTech startups, and research institutions to support their projects. The grant schemes included the Innovation Adoption Grant, which supported financial institutions to adopt digital solutions, covering up to 50% of qualifying costs with a cap of SGD1M per project. Another scheme was the Institution-level Projects grant, which facilitated collaboration between financial institutions and FinTech startups to develop and test innovative solutions. This grant covered up to 50% of qualifying costs, capped at SGD2M per project. Additionally, the Industry-wide Projects are grant-supported projects aimed to drive transformation in the financial sector, providing funding of up to 50% of qualifying costs, with a cap of SGD3M per project. The Talent Development grant aimed to nurture talent in FinTech, data analytics, and cybersecurity. It offered financial institutions and FinTech startups funding support of up to 70% of qualifying costs, with a cap of SGD1M per project.

Under the FSTI scheme, financial institutions and FinTech startups had access to several grant schemes for funding support. These schemes included the Proof-of-Concept (POC) grant, which facilitated the developing and testing of innovative FinTech solutions in a live financial sector environment. The grant covered up to 70% of qualifying costs, with a cap of SGD200,000 per project. The Proof-of-Value (POV) grant supported financial institutions conducting pilot trials for already developed and tested FinTech solutions. It provided funding of up to 50% of qualifying costs, capped at SGD1M per project. Furthermore, the Artificial Intelligence and Data Analytics (AIDA) Grant aimed to enhance financial institutions' operations and services by adopting artificial intelligence and data analytics solutions. It covered up to 50% of qualifying costs, with a cap of SGD1M per project.

Artificial Intelligence and Data Analytics (AIDA) Grant aims to promote adopting and integrating AI and data analytics in financial institutions. Furthermore, the Cybersecurity Capabilities Grant intends to strengthen the cyber resilience of the financial sector in Singapore and help financial institutions develop local talent in cybersecurity. Lastly, the Digital Acceleration Grant (DAG) supports smaller financial institutions and FinTech firms in adopting digital solutions to improve productivity, strengthen operational resilience, manage risks, and serve customers better. The DAG provides these smaller FIs and FinTech firms based in Singapore with 80% co-funding of qualifying expenses, including hardware, software, and professional services. The funding is capped at SGD120,000 per entity, ensuring that even smaller organisations have the means to adopt digital solutions and stay competitive in the rapidly evolving FinTech landscape.

In 2022, MAS announced the third generation of financial support with a new commitment of SGD150M for the next three years from 2023 to 2025 as the FSTI 3.0. The focus of the third tranche will be on areas such as AI, analytics, regulatory tech and cybersecurity, in addition to new areas such as ESG (environmental, social and governance) FinTech.[5]

[5] https://www.businesstimes.com.sg/companies-markets/banking-finance/singapore-fintech-festival-2022/mas-commit-s150m-fsti-scheme-over

Conclusion

The *kampung* spirit embodied by the people in Singapore has unified them in the face of challenges and adversity as a social community. A child (startup) in the village (FinTech arena) would find refuge in FinTech *Choupal*, which provides a safe space for startups to share knowledge and resources and have their voices heard by the regulators. In line with the development of the FinTech ecosystem, SFA was formed as a neutral, independent body to provide a unified communication platform for startups to interact with the regulators and to facilitate potential business expansion outside of Singapore. The recent COVID-19 pandemic has not derailed the FinTechs from their tracks, with the support from the government through its funding initiatives.

Chapter 4

DANCING WITH THE PHOENIX

Although Singapore can join the ranks of cities like Hong Kong, Shanghai, Tokyo, and London to become an established financial hub in the ASEAN region, the "hub" concept is common to Singapore. There are established hubs for almost all industries, which complement the work of industry regulators. In the case of the FinTech space, this hub is powered by the incumbents and a few bottom-up initiatives to facilitate dialogue between the FinTech startups, venture capitalists and regulators. So what differentiates the Singapore idea of the "hub"? After all, many countries use this concept to explain the synergy and convenience that arise from bringing all things relevant "under one roof". Perhaps the key difference lies in how the nation has used the "hub" as a launchpad for its FinTech aspirations.

The FinTech ecosystem is one of constant innovation, which rings true even more so for Singapore's dynamic market. Over the last few years, there has been an immense influx of new FinTech entrants. At the same time, the established financial hub in Singapore has pivoted to supporting and co-opting these innovations. The innovation lab is a cornerstone of this bridge between incumbents and FinTech disruptors. The recent proliferation of innovation labs in Singapore, from labs set up by local banks such as

DBS, OCBC and UOB, to those by global players like HSBC, Citi, UBS, and ING, is a sign of Singapore's evolution from a financial hub into a FinTech nation.

Community Hub

The creation of the FinTech hub in Singapore was driven by the pragmatic desire to solve problems and generate new ideas. It was not born out of lofty initiatives or meant to be a complicated notion. Instead, the "hub" was birthed through many informal and candid conversations about the country's favourite beverage: the *kopi*. Whilst it is tempting to think of Singapore Sling as the national drink of Singapore, it is coffee beans brewed in a sock, locally called *kopi*, which binds Singaporeans together. This humble beverage with at least 15 variations is the perfect catalyst for conversation. People from all walks of life huddle over their *kopi* in animated discussions at a corner coffee shop. Contrary to popular belief that artisan coffee consumed in air-conditioned comfort is the number one choice, nothing beats the humble local *kopi*. The power of a *kopi* chat in these heartland coffee shops or food courts can only be understood by having one on a humid afternoon in Singapore.

The FinTech community is fortunate to have set up several common spaces for founders across different sectors to build upon each other's ideas. The government set up one of the first in 2011 near the National University of Singapore (NUS) and the INSEAD campus outside the Central Business District. It was named Block 71, known as a start-up hub, and was a successful experiment. Currently, there are several Block 71-like establishments all over the world set up by Singapore government agencies. At the same time, the initial set-up has expanded to several buildings around the original building.

Over the years, a close-knit entrepreneurial community of startups, accelerators and venture capitalists has also emerged in true innovation hubs such as Blocks 71, 73 and 79. These communities are part of JTC LaunchPad @ one-north, a 6.5-hectare site set up in 2015 to provide a conducive environment for startups to grow. In addition, the area is close to public and private research institutes and tertiary institutions to facilitate collaboration between academia and industry.

DBS, the largest bank in ASEAN, has its innovation lab near the original Block 71. While Block 71 was perfect for developing technology-focused startups, it also attracted some initial FinTech innovation programmes. One of the challenges the original hub faced for financial services was the concentration of most financial services companies in the relatively nearby Central Business District.

Such FinTech hubs work to democratise the access and network to both new to the ecosystem and established participants. The proximity to customers, talents, investors and fellow startups creates a network effect that fosters creativity.

The second wave of FinTech hubs was set up around the main building of the Monetary Authority of Singapore (MAS), which was within a 2km radius area in which 90% of the financial services' head offices in Singapore, stock exchange, and more than 75 coffee joints were located. In addition, this second wave consisted of dedicated co-working places like Lattice80 (now called 80RR), 79 RR, JustCo, and several WeWork spaces and innovation labs from top global and local financial institutions.

80RR is home to the largest FinTech association in the world — the Singapore FinTech Association, with more than 860 FinTech companies domestically and a global network in more than 40 countries as of 2022. The success of 80RR is evident in scaling companies to the level where they require dedicated offices outside of initially shared office space. For example, Bambu, Jumper and Policypal are companies that started there and moved on to larger offices elsewhere in the city.

Another feature unique to the FinTech community in Singapore is the Innovation Lab Crawl. You may be familiar with pub crawls, where adventurous people go from pub to pub. Every November, Singapore hosts the Innovation Lab Crawl, where visitors to Singapore explore and experience over 40 innovation labs over two days. The elements of fun, openness and hospitality in the Lab Crawl strengthen the innovation DNA of the ecosystem.

To date, Singapore has more than 33 innovation labs. Most of them generate their network of innovation around them. So, in addition to having the highest per capita swimming pools in the world, Singapore also has the honour of the highest per capita FinTech innovation labs globally. No mean feat, indeed!

With a strong focus on collaboration, the Singapore PayPal Innovation Lab, established in 2016, is a one-stop melting pot for developers, students, and innovators. The PayPal Innovation Lab collaborates with government agencies, Institutes of Higher Learning, and Trade Associations & Chambers to help small and medium-sized enterprises (SMEs) overcome the challenges they face in the current business environment. It helps businesses go digital and use technology effectively. In addition, the lab aims to groom and upskill the next generation, which can help transform businesses.

PayPal wanted to build a positive corporate image as an accessible business in collaboration with the government. In addition, it wanted to learn from new entrants in the market to understand better the gaps that needed to be filled. Finally, PayPal understood that some of these companies were potential business partners. Helping them advance would eventually benefit itself in the long run, giving it access to a previously untapped market. It was able to do this through the Innovation Lab.

A challenge that PayPal faced was that most startups needed a concrete business structure in the early conceptual stages. As a result, it took much work for the startups to form long-term partnerships, but PayPal was able to help them source funding as best as possible.

Yoke Yong Lai, more commonly known as YY, was the Lead of the Startup and Incubation at PayPal from 2016 to 2020. He has been a part of Singapore's FinTech ecosystem since the early days. First, he worked for the Infocomm Development Authority of Singapore (IMDA), where he was involved with its technology adoption and startup funding programme. He then moved to NTU Ventures, a venture arm of Nanyang Technological University (NTU), working with the alums, students, and professors to review their business models and acquire capital and funding for startups. YY has been on the ground for many years and has seen first-hand how government schemes have developed with the FinTech industry. As a result of his experience, he was invited to join the PayPal Innovation Lab. Currently, YY is working as a Partner with Signum Capital, a technology and crypto-focused fund.

One of the first startups that YY's team worked with at PayPal was TenX, which enables customers to access crypto and facilitate their payments. The users can use their mobile app or debit card for transactions. Over the past few years, TenX has gained traction by getting consumers to utilise cryptocurrencies more effectively. It allows users to seamlessly spend their cryptocurrency without converting their funds from other cryptocurrencies such as bitcoin or stablecoin to fiat currency. With the opportunity to incubate this company, PayPal could connect clients with relevant investors, equip them with the necessary knowledge and tools, especially in risk management and compliance, and flourish in the industry. TenX, an alumnus of the first batch of FinTech-focused PayPal incubation programmes, went on to raise USD100M, becoming one of the leading blockchain companies in the region.

YY has seen the emergence of many blockchain startups in this space and has seen their products and services used more widely. An ecosystem that is being adopted across several fronts is Ethereum. An advantage of this market is that it is not bound by geography. Investments can easily be made globally, as anyone can tap into the blockchain community remotely. On the other hand, traditional venture capital funds are usually geocentric since there are expectations of meeting the founders and building relationships. YY sees real crypto and blockchain applications in the future and believes that the crypto sphere and other internet sectors will merge to provide disruptive products and services.

YY shares that the main attributes PayPal sought in FinTech startup teams are passion, genuine curiosity in the problem sets, and the ability to influence people. This is not limited to PayPal alone. If an entrepreneur is passionate enough and knows their business environment well, it creates a significant influencing power to get talents to join them and potential investors. Bringing that passion and curiosity across when talking about one's idea is more likely to convince investors to take a stake in the startup. This is also the key to attracting co-founders and other key team members.

When asked about his perspective on the current financial scene, YY sees startups filling the gaps in the market — they are spread out and present tremendous growth opportunities in the digitisation space. Crypto and blockchain's potential is still in its infancy. For startups expanding across the region into countries such as Indonesia and Vietnam, several untapped markets are waiting to be addressed.

Startupbootcamp (SBC) is a network of industry-focused startup accelerators. It was founded in 2010 and now operates globally with 20+ industry-focused programmes in key locations, including San Francisco, Amsterdam, Cape Town, Chengdu, Berlin, Dubai, Hartford, Istanbul, Rome, London, Melbourne, Miami, Mumbai, Mexico City, New York, and Singapore. Since launching, SBC has accelerated over 600 startups, of which 78% received funding. SBC startups received an average of EUR582,438 in investment.

To understand the FinTech market, SBC organised a FinTech Pitch Day in 2014. SBC saw roughly 375 applications. **Markus Gnirck**, the founder of SBC FinTech, shared that it was surprising to see how many FinTech start-ups are in the region.

Markus's journey in FinTech began in London in 2013 when he started SBC FinTech. It was the first community accelerator apart from Barclays. The accelerator brought together different banks and stakeholders when TransferWise and other big companies started. The programme was part of the SBC family.

When Markus first launched SBC in London, the media supported FinTech. Not long after the launch, Singapore came knocking. IMDA, which funded SGInnovate, had a new strategy to invest in different industry verticals to accelerate the early growth of startups. It was a fast and efficient approach in Singapore to anchor SBC in the country. Markus shares that they could bring many other partners (such as Thomson Reuters, RHB, CIMB, DBS, etc.) on board. SBC was then launched in Singapore in 2015 as the first accelerator for FinTech in Asia.

Samuel Hall was the Managing Director of SBC from 2016 to December 2019 and is currently the Partner and CEO of APAC at Rainmaking. As the previous MD, Sam believes accelerators are a useful tool for corporates. He likens the role of accelerators to the myth of Sisyphus.

> *"The boulder has been pushed up the hill by SBC. The issue is ensuring how the boulder is placed on the top of the hill and what action must be taken to prevent it from rolling back down. It is not the responsibility of any one stakeholder, but a joint responsibility that needs to be taken on by the FinTech ecosystem."*
>
> *Samuel Hall, 2020, in a personal interview*

The ecosystem needs to see what is preventing stakeholders from progressing. At the end of three years, the ecosystem should have moved on, and the accelerator should not be needed anymore. SBC, as an accelerator, is merely a facilitator to get things moving in a less mature market or a market in its early stages. The ecosystem needs to establish how to move on after an accelerator has done its job of getting the gears turning.

In progressing from the accelerator stage, the Singapore government has put resources into multiple aspects of the system. Apart from relying on the support from MAS, startups need to establish a true value proposition on their side. This will enable them to gain traction and seed funding. They must then maintain a forward outlook: "How do we scale series A?" and so forth. Demands and expectations in the industry grow year on year, as everyone is so used to seamless integration in every aspect of their lives nowadays.

As a result of the COVID-19 black swan event, the financial services sector has undergone a generational transformation during 2020–2022. More capital has been invested in FinTech, innovation and transformation. Sam believes the corporate ecosystem will drive the most change in the traditional financial services sector. Startups bring something new but need the numbers or the power to create waves. However, they must continue fueling the fire to push corporates in the right direction.

Volume does create growth, but individual returns may be less ideal. Sam uses the analogy of letting a thousand flowers bloom to describe the benefits of size. Collectively, however, the entire FinTech ecosystem in Singapore gains returns in the form of an international presence. As illustrated with the boulder analogy, sufficient mass means that if one individual stops pushing the boulder up the hill, there will always be someone who can step up and take that place.

Apart from SBC as a standalone accelerator, software company SAP also runs startup accelerators in FinTech. For example, SAP.iO Foundries are

SAP's global network of equity-free startup accelerators that help promising startups to integrate with SAP solutions and accelerate their entry into a curated, inclusive ecosystem whose offerings can be easily accessed and deployed by SAP customers. This is possible due to SAP's business as an enterprise software company that integrates technology such as artificial intelligence (AI) and machine learning into a large part of its business. This, in turn, helps customers innovate through partnerships.

Innovations by Singapore Banks

The OCBC Open Vault aims to redefine banking through co-innovation with global FinTech firms. It started with the announcement in June 2015 by MAS's FinTech and Innovation Group (FTIG) team. The formation of the FTIG was accompanied by funding to support FinTech initiatives. OCBC started the Open Vault with Altona Widjaja at the helm.

The Open Vault symbolises open innovation, and the vault represents the bank. Therefore, it is unnatural for a vault to be open usually. Coincidentally, at the venue itself, there is a vault that cannot be closed. At the Open Vault, OCBC gained much direct engagement with the FinTech players. They started engaging different parties, such as educational institutions, including a one-to-one initiative with the polytechnics in Singapore. On top of this, there was also significant outreach to local universities such as NTU and NUS. At the same time, OCBC positioned the Vault as a gateway for all FinTechs who wanted to collaborate and partner with OCBC. However, doing it piecemeal needed to be more scalable, leading OCBC to do an SBC.

As a result of the innovation lab and its community programmes like the accelerator, the seed for culture change in OCBC was planted. Consumer banking was the first segment that OCBC worked to innovate and digitalise. Back in 2016, other segments of OCBC were less involved. Some individuals were very sceptical, having experienced the dot-com bust. To them, FinTech seemed to be nothing more than a build-up to a repeat of the dotcom crash. In the initial days of the Vault, it took much work to get startups to propose their ideas. Over the first year, the Vault worked to get much engagement through bi-monthly meetings with various business units.

With MAS funding, OCBC created a programme for startups to experiment in a controlled environment and with a niche set of use cases to encourage involvement, kicking the conversation into full throttle. Back then, accelerator participants were consumer banking centric (i.e., wealth management, investments). It started targeting non-wealth management startups in its second year. OCBC also contracted startups to do proofs of concept (PoCs) and tried them out. However, it was not widely accepted due to the lack of publicity.

When asked about the future of FinTech, Altona said the answer lies in infrastructure. However, the key question remains: What power can push for infrastructure change?

One of the key outcomes of such experiments was the launch of the first wealth robo advisors in Singapore from a bank. OCBC RoboInvest was an automated, algorithm-based digital investment service for young and tech-savvy retail investors. It was developed with WeInvest, a FinTech startup formed through the Open Vault initiative. Beyond this, OCBC has made strides in the payments space by collaborating with Google Pay's peer-to-peer (P2P) funds transfer business and bringing it to Singapore. The bank also worked with Rapyd, a local FinTech startup, to launch Singapore's first instant mobile payments solution. In the SME space, OCBC targets to improve the overall banking system for startups by providing quick access to banking activities in Singapore after incorporation rather than waiting in the standard timeframe. This was possible by collaborating and implementing an application programming interface (API) between OCBC and Experian.

UOB fills out the three local banks that dominate the Singapore landscape. It recognised early on the potential of FinTech solutions in enabling it to accelerate its own innovation drive and business aspirations. So it initiated a concerted effort to support and partner FinTechs.

In 2015, UOB launched The FinLab, an innovation accelerator for early-stage, fast-growing companies looking to enter and accelerate growth in Asia. Notable FinTechs such as Turnkey Lender, CardUp, Transficc and AImazing have benefited from the mentorship, resources, and community that The FinLab brings. As a result, they have gone on to raise funds and grow their business successfully. The FinLab's programme also selected and deployed commercially viable ideas, such as Tookitaki's machine learning technology, to enhance UOB's Anti-Money Laundering Suite.

UOB's collaboration with FinTechs has led to some exciting initiatives at the bank. UOB is one of the first banks in the region to incorporate AI heavily into their banking processes, both for the benefit of the bank and its customers. For example, it was the first to use AI to personalise the digital banking experience for its customers in the region when it launched ASEAN's first digital bank, TMRW, in Thailand in 2019. In building this personalisation engine, UOB tapped into the digital engagement and data categorisation solutions of FinTech firms, Personetics and Meniga.

UOB also invested in Personetics in 2018 to extend its expertise by co-opting the knowledge of the fast-growing FinTech firms and sharing the bank's expertise. This shows the initiative in UOB to be more hands-on in working with innovative FinTechs and commitment to the growth of these firms.

Embedded finance which refers to the access to financial services (i.e., payments, lending, and investments) for consumer digital platforms, is fast gaining prominence in the financial services industry. The area of embedded finance is a strategic focus for UOB to leverage key partnerships with ecosystem players and FinTechs to "embed" the bank's offerings into these non-bank digital platforms. A good example of this partnership is the use of Avatec's[1] next-generation credit assessment solutions for alternative data scoring, which powers UOB's lending solutions to merchants on its partners' e-commerce platforms. As a result, merchants with financing needs on these popular e-commerce sites, such as Qoo10, can now apply for business loans directly on their platforms instead of going through the traditional loan application process.

Technology enables a fundamentally different approach to financial infrastructure than today's centralised systems. With the advancement of blockchain technology innovation, UOB sees asset tokenisation and Central Bank Digital Currencies as positive and constructive developments for the financial services industry. The bank is also actively working with partners, including FinTechs, to use this technology for their clients and business. For example, in June 2022, UOB was the first financial institution in Singapore to tap this innovative form of blockchain technology on Marketnode's digital asset issuance, depository and servicing platform as both an issuer and bond house.

Janet Young, who joined UOB in 2014, heads the Group Channels and Digitalisation and leads UOB's engagement and collaboration with FinTech ecosystems to help drive connectivity, performance, and customer experience. She chairs the bank's Innovation Workgroup, which focuses on raising employees' awareness of and interest in digitalisation. In addition, she ensures that UOB branch employees are equipped with digital capabilities to be future-relevant.

Having more than 25 years of experience in the banking industry, Janet believes that the banking sector holds a great deal of promise to develop further Singapore's global role. While FinTech is a vertical industry by itself, it is also a horizontal one that allows other industries to develop and

[1] Avatec is a UOB joint venture with Chinese FinTech firm Pintec.

innovate. In her opinion, FinTech in Singapore must take a more prominent role and become a mainstream field, as it has the potential to deliver greater impact and benefits to Singapore and the region.

One key area is Sustainable Finance — integrating environmental, social and governance considerations into financing decisions to achieve sustainable development outcomes. As a recognised financial and innovation hub, Singapore's financial sector can play a useful role in catalysing sustainable and green finance in the region. To this end, UOB continues to work closely with FinTechs and industry partners to explore the use of technology for accurate tracking, measurement and reporting of sustainability. In addition, the bank will continue to grow its suite of financial products for consumers, businesses, and investors to participate in sustainability efforts.

To support the sustainable growth of businesses, particularly SMEs, The FinLab has expanded its focus to assist these businesses on their digitalisation journeys in Singapore and across ASEAN through the Business Transformation Programme. The FinLab partners with numerous regional government agencies, including the Digital Economy Promotion Agency, the National Science and Technology Development Agency, the Office of SMEs Promotion in Thailand, the Malaysia Digital Economy Corporation, and communities such as Mums@Work. Through these partnerships, The FinLab has assisted over 4,000 SMEs by connecting them with the relevant tools, knowledge, and tech providers to digitalise.

To further support the growing number of SMEs needing digital skills, The FinLab partnered with NTUC LearningHub, NTUC U SME, and Ngee Ann Polytechnic to run the SME Digital Reboot Programme. This programme was created to uplift the digital capabilities of Singapore's SME workforce through relevant training programmes. The SME Digital Reboot Programme also aims to support SMEs in creating sustainable business tools to adapt to rapid changes in this age of digitalisation.

In 2019, The FinLab launched The FinLab Online, a digital platform to help SMEs and startups across ASEAN implement digital solutions to transform their businesses. In addition, SMEs can tap The FinLab's established regional network of industry mentors, tools, and resources, curated to address business needs and guide companies in sustainable digitalisation strategy planning.

Lastly, DBS, the largest bank in Singapore, took unique approaches to developing the FinTech ecosystem and embracing innovation. DBS is synonymous with finance in Singapore, and its journey in the FinTech landscape mirrors Singapore's journey. **Han Kwee Juan**, Managing Director and Group Head of Strategy and Planning for DBS, shares DBS's approach to the emergence of digital transformation.

Kwee Juan has been driving the bank's innovation and data agenda since 2019, which encompasses design thinking, reimagining customer journeys, agile methodology, data science and analytics, FinTech partnerships, hackathons, etc. Kwee Juan's portfolio also includes responsibility for developing and driving new business models through ecosystem partnerships to deliver banking solutions and convenience to corporate and retail customers in these ecosystems.

Kwee Juan recalls the emergence of FinTech in 2014: *"The world was already changing, FinTech was gaining traction, new entrants were coming into the market, and customer expectations were changing accordingly. In addition, the transition from analogue to digital was imminent, with the rise of Amazon and Alibaba being the most notable."*

DBS aimed to become an indispensable part of the ecosystem rather than merely existing within it. Their core approach drove this: engaging in the customer's journey. Kwee Juan states that DBS used its financial and technological facets in perfect harmony: *"Being a tech company, we had access to superfluous amounts of data, which we could use to create extraordinary solutions, with the help of our partners and ecosystem, with demonstrable financial progress and growth."*

However, according to Kwee Juan, the role of DBS transcends any traditional bank. Due to DBS's role as a major financial provider in Singapore, it regularly collaborates with other banks to detect fraud and money laundering transactions.

Post the financial crisis of 2008, traditional banking services have faced potential disruption by FinTechs through the process of unbundling banking services. Social media and new communication platforms have also led to a drastic change in customer expectations, whether the ability to bank digitally or customer acquisition more focused on digital presence rather than a physical branch around the corner son the street.

DBS coined its own acronym GANDALF, a protagonist in J. R. R. Tolkien's novels *The Hobbit and The Lord of the Rings*. The acronym from the DBS perspective incorporates the big tech giants such as Google, Amazon, Netflix, Apple, LinkedIn, Facebook, and D for DBS, thus placing themselves in the company of the global technology giants. DBS has focused on building a culture in which customers and employees feel they are part of, and engaging with, a tech company rather than a straightforward bank.

DBS created a GANDALF scholars' programme to encourage self-directed learning, where they get internal employees to learn new technology-related skills and apply them to the bank's transformational journey. DBS has made this a core tenet of its upskilling programme to retain talent and leverage new learning opportunities.

Kwee Juan shared that the other two vital elements of digital transformation are embedding the culture of DBS in customers and pushing customer-journey thinking throughout the organisation, creating a 27,000-startup culture that is customer-obsessed and data-driven, encouraging risk-taking and experimentation. These enable a learning organisation.

Global Banks in Singapore

The local banking institutions in Singapore have actively embraced FinTech, but Singapore is not just a local market but a global financial hub. To evolve into a full FinTech nation, global financial institutions must also embrace the innovation in the market and the local labs by DBS, UOB and OCBC operating in the city to bridge FinTech with financial institutions.

The labs sponsored by global institutions in Singapore feature different initiatives targeting their respective customer base. For instance, HSBC's Singapore Innovation Lab, one of the oldest dedicated spaces by a financial institution in Singapore, launched in 2015, focuses on HSBC's core business in the region: cash management, liquidity, trade and supply chain. As such, the lab focuses on innovations in the FX, cash flow, securities, and smart banking sectors.

On the other hand, institutions like ING are focused on their core trade finance business in Asia-Pacific. So, their lab works on innovations in global trade, including digitisation of supply chains, applications of blockchain ledger tracking or implementing the Internet of Things, and analytics to optimise trade flows and supply chains. They also act as semi-incubator by focusing on startups, scale-ups, researchers, entrepreneurs, and corporates.

Finally, UBS, focusing heavily on the wealth management sector, has developed its innovation lab, EVOLVE. It focuses on the wealth management sector but looks at solutions holistically. EVOLVE looks to leverage technology as a catalyst to drive innovation and to meet the needs of the clientele currently in Asia.

Tenant Banks

Tenant Banking is a Digital Bank model wherein risk management and regulatory reporting are the responsibility of the incumbent bank. Technology partners focus on customer acquisition, provisioning, and servicing. In such a setup, FinTech offers end-to-end consumer or business digital banking services without having its traditional banking licence. Instead, it operates on a lighter regulatory requirements platform like wallet, payments, or lending.

The capabilities would be a complete digital banking stack on the banks' infrastructure. However, per the regulations, customers may or may not be required to see the Bank powering the infrastructure for the FinTech.

Tenant Models of Licensing (Incumbents renting infrastructure to challengers) include the following:

- Account Issuance (DBS — Wise, Aspire, Revolut; CIMB — Matchmove, Spenmo, Sleek)
- Banking as Service (SCB — Nexus; Citibank — Spring; DBS — DBS Remit)
- Lending as Service (DBS — Funding Society; CIMB — Capbridge)

▸ *Account Issuance*

One of the foundational building blocks for FinTech startups and scaleups is building solutions to help customers trust that their money is safe and that they are not losing money. Such confidence and faith are the foundation of the financial services ecosystem. Singapore has very high standards for awarding bank licences to new players and has big aspirations to be a FinTech nation.

As a result, multiple incumbent Singapore banks embraced this opportunity to offer bank accounts to non-banks and FinTech startups to build their solutions. Such a service of providing the ability to issue bank accounts by a non-bank, leveraging the infrastructure of a traditional bank, is defined by us as "Tenant Banking — Account Issuance".

DBS has taken one of the most active positions to be one of the largest backend providers to non-banks with FinTech solutions. With the new partnership, Wise (formerly Transferwise) offers DBS Bank accounts to all retail and SME customers in Singapore to enable them to receive, store and transact beyond the limits imposed on non-bank payment service providers by regulations. Similarly, Revolut can assign a unique 15-digit virtual account number to each customer in Singapore. The customer transfers money to their virtual account from their bank, and the amount is reflected in their Revolut app, enabling its customers to top up their wallets via bank transfers.[2]

Additionally, FinTech providers like Nium, Railsbank, Rapyd and Walex have become service providers, allowing other businesses and FinTech to use DBS Account Issuance capability. FinTech startups like Volopay (Nium), Aspire (Walex), LytePay, TazaPay (Rapyd), and Singlife (Railsbank) leverage B2B FinTech providers who rely on DBS account issuance as the underlying infrastructure. Aspire has built a large SME focused offering leveraging infrastructure from DBS Bank and other FinTech solutions like Transferwise, Walex and CurrencyCloud.

CIMB is another forward-looking bank for leveraging FinTech to build scalable solutions. A few years ago, RHB, a Malaysian bank in Singapore, launched a travel card, a first of its kind undertaken by a traditional bank in collaboration with a FinTech company using CIMB infrastructure. It was pathbreaking for competing banks to collaborate on infrastructure like card issuing with FinTech as the bridge between them. CIMB has also collaborated with Matchmove to power several other FinTech companies

[2] https://asianbankingandfinance.net/cards-payments/more-news/revolut-singapore-enables-virtual-wallet-top-bank-transfer

like Spenmo, Sleek and Subtra with their account issuance infrastructure.[3] CIMB also launched its Virtual Account in 2020, digitising businesses' cash flow while competing directly with neo-banks.

Google Pay launched in Singapore in 2020 by partnering with three top banks to allow their customers to use their bank accounts to connect to Google Pay, thus paving the way for using contactless tap and pay and global online transactions. By integrating Google Pay with the fund's transfer service PayNow, DBS PayLah!, OCBC and StanChart, customers can link their bank accounts to the Google Pay mobile app to debit directly without needing a card.

▶ *Banking as Service*

Standard Chartered Bank (SCB) has been actively experimenting with new business models, such as Mox and Nexus, to meet the evolving needs of its clients.

SCB launched Project Phoenix (Singapore), a second digital-only bank in Asia through a joint venture with the National Trades Union Congress (NTUC) Enterprise. NTUC Enterprise is a unit within NTUC, a national confederation of trade unions and professional associations across Singapore sectors. In 2022, SCB launched Trust Bank after winning a licence to set up a digital-only bank in Singapore in collaboration with the NTUC.[4]

Mirroring its efforts in Hong Kong (Mox), SCB is accelerating its digital strategy in Singapore to compete with larger local rivals such as DBS Group Holding and non-bank challengers such as Grab Holdings and SEA Holdings. Mox is a new virtual bank created by SCB in partnership with

[3] https://www.straitstimes.com/business/banking/on-the-go-convenience

[4] https://www.itnews.asia/news/stancharts-trust-bank-to-replicate-mox-bank-backend-578919

PCCW, HKT and Trip.com, which provides a suite of retail banking services entirely digitally over its app. Mox brings an innovative touch to the traditional banking industry through a cloud-based bank built from the ground up with resilient infrastructure and rapid, cost-efficient development addition cycles. In addition, Mox was the first bank in the region to launch a numberless bank card.

With the shifting consumer behaviours due to the pandemic as a catalyst for the growth of online financial activity, more than 56% of Indonesian consumers now prefer online purchases and payment. An overwhelming 80% of the Indonesian market expects the country to go entirely cashless by 2025.

In that regard, SCB launched its "Banking as a Service" solution, Nexus, in Indonesia. Nexus allows other digital platforms and ecosystems, such as e-commerce, social media, or ride-hailing companies, to offer financial services such as loans, credit cards, and savings accounts co-created with SCB to their customers under their brand name.

SCB, in collaboration with Indonesian e-commerce platform provider, Bukalapak, launched innovative financial offerings on its e-commerce platform. Bukalapak, an online marketplace that competes with Shopee, Tokopedia and Lazada, has about 100 million users and 13.5 million sellers in Indonesia. Bukalapak has successfully pulled in more than USD100M from Microsoft, GIC and Eland Mahkota Teknologi as part of the ongoing fundraising round. In 2022, this collaboration took a step further with the launch of BulaTabungan, combining Bukalapak's all-commerce platform and the nexus technology.[5]

The second partnership Nexus has forged in Indonesia is with an established beauty and personal care e-commerce platform, **Sociolla**. Such a strategic

[5] https://scventures.io/bukalapak-and-standardchartered-launch-bukatabungan/

partnership opportunity allows SCB to reach the unbanked and expand its customer base in the world's fourth most populous country, where the e-commerce adoption rate is the highest globally. Furthermore, the strategic addition of banking service is a significant added value to complement the integrated beauty ecosystem compliment continuously.

Backed by the same global financial institution, SCB, Autumn maintains institution-grade security measures to protect potential clients' financial and health information. Autumn is a digital wealth, health and lifestyle solution that aims to harness the power of technology to integrate wellness with wealth management, making meaningful retirement accessible to more people.

Citibank has streamlined its business in the ASEAN region by selling consumer banking portfolios for all markets except Singapore. Globally, Citibank has been collaborating with FinTech and offering banking as a service under their platform Spring, with FinTech companies like Stripe, as global marque clients. As a result, the digital payments market is expected to grow from USD96.19B in 2022 to USD111.11B in 2023.[6] In 2022, the Asia-Pacific market was the largest region in the digital payments market.

Citi launched Spring by Citi in Asia-Pacific in 2021, a full-stack payment processing unit, a business that processes over USD4T daily across the globe.[7] Spring by Citi enables digital commerce for clients by providing streamlined access to locally relevant payment methods worldwide. The platform helps customer-centric institutions build seamless payment experiences that increase sales conversion while mitigating risk.

---

[6] https://www.thebusinessresearchcompany.com/report/digital-payments-global-market-report#:~:text=The%20global%20digital%20payments%20market,least%20in%20the%20short%20term.

[7] https://asianbankingandfinance.net/trade-finance/news/citi-apac-appoints-former-ey-partner-head-spring-citi

With Japan's increasing foreign resident population, Japan's Seven Bank collaborated with DBS Bank to tap into DBS's digital remittance system, DBS Remit, to provide more robust outbound distribution capabilities for its retail customers. The average cost to remit money from Japan is 9.56% of the sum sent abroad, and Seven Bank currently charges 4.1%. With DBS Remit, Seven Bank can decrease its fees to under 3%.[8]

▸ *Lending as Service*

In 2016, DBS Bank partnered with P2P lending platforms such as Funding Societies and MoolahSense to expand funding sources to small businesses. Traditionally, smaller enterprises have a track record of being ignored by big banks due to the low-risk appetite of the banks, which limits the amount of lending to SMEs. Hence, this partnership allows DBS to refer their SME clients to these P2P lending platforms. In turn, the P2P lending platforms will recommend borrowers with higher credit history and have completed two fundraising rounds to DBS for larger commercial loans. With DBS's partnership with Funding Societies and MoolahSense, traditional and alternative financing providers can work together to provide the funding small businesses will require.

In 2019, World Bank Data showed that more than 38% of Indonesia's population is unbanked or has no banking services, while more than 60% have access to smartphones. Therefore, it presented an opportunity for DBS Bank to bridge the gap through the Ecosystem strategy. As a result, the bank collaborated with Home Credit Indonesia to reach out and serve more people.

Through this collaboration, DBS can provide financial services to the Indonesian public through a joint financing scheme. When customers apply

---

[8] https://www.straitstimes.com/business/banking/japans-seven-bank-to-tap-dbs-money-remittance-network-in-new-deal

for a loan with Home Credit, there will be a bundling banking programme wherein a DBS bank account will be available to them.

This strategic partnership provides fast and easy financial solutions for the unbanked in Indonesia, further increasing the coverage of quality financial services for everyone.[9]

CapBridge collaborated with UOB and CIMB Bank Berhad in 2019 to strengthen the private equity market in the region by offering a more comprehensive range of capital solutions to high-growth companies in Singapore, Malaysia, and Indonesia.[10]

In contrast to the traditional private equity model, where there is a typical lock-up period of more than five years, this collaboration facilitates the trading of listed private equities at the convenience of the investors. In addition, through CapBridge's affiliate exchange (1X), a regulated private securities exchange platform, the banks' clients can be exposed to a more extensive investor base. It also creates a new asset class of tradable private equities to provide flexibility and alternative liquidity business financing.[11]

In collaboration with Grab, Citibank developed Citi Quick Cash using Grab's API-enabled lending capability. It enables existing Citibank credit card customers to apply for a personal loan on Grab by converting their credit limit into a cash loan payable on a monthly instalment. With Grab's

[9] https://www.dbs.com/newsroom/Bank_DBS_Establishes_Joint_Financing_Cooperation_with_Home_Credit

[10] https://capbridge.sg/press-release-capbridge-and-uob-sign-agreement-to-provide-companies-across-asia-with-access-to-private-capital/

[11] https://capbridge.sg/press-release-cimb-capbridge-collaboration-facilitates-companies-access-to-private-capital-through-investment-platform-and-blockchain-enabled-securities-exchange/

API connectivity, customers can access a quick, easy, and secure banking system with CitiBank.[12]

Consumer Internet Partnership Models

Singaporean banks and insurers have demonstrated a keen interest in the financial services ambitions of consumer internet companies and have consequently pursued strategies that involve collaborating with FinTech firms while maintaining a competitive edge in other areas. Specifically, banks have identified areas where partnerships with FinTech are most advantageous. These collaborative efforts take on various Consumer Internet Partnership Models, such as investment partnerships (including those between DBS-Carousel, GE-Axiata, Singapura Finance-Matchmove, and MUFG-Grab), commercial partnerships (such as those between UOB-Grab, UOB-Shopee, DBS-Chope, Fave, and DASH), and joint product partnerships (such as those between DBS-Cardup and OCBC-Pace).

Investment

With the changing consumer behaviours, traditional banks have been increasing their participation by raising their investments in the FinTech ecosystem to offer a wider variety of digital financial products and payment services.

Some examples are the DBS-Carousell and Singapura Finance-MatchMove collaboration. The banks have been leveraging digital technology and innovation from their technology counterpart to seamlessly integrate banking into their customers' lives. In addition, Carousell raised USD85M

[12] https://www.citigroup.com/citi/news/2020/201221a.htm

from its Series C funding, with DBS jumping on board as a new investor in 2018.[13]

Spark Systems, a Singapore-based financial technology startup, successfully attracted strategic investors and raised SGD15M from tier 1 global banks and strategic Southeast Asia-focused investment firms, such as Citi, HSBC and OSK Ventures, in 2020. The funds raised will further enhance Spark Systems' in-house technology capabilities, increasing the performance to build the next-generation high-speed trading platforms.[14]

In addition to banks investing in FinTech startups such as Grab, non-traditional investors such as Hyundai, Microsoft and Booking Holdings invested almost USD3B into Grab. Since Series H, Grab has raised more than USD6B from investors, a record-breaking figure for a Southeast Asian startup.[15]

In Grab's aggressive expansion plan, Grab announced a debt financing deal of USD700M to finance the growth of its vehicle fleet in 2018.[16] In addition, Grab managed to secure a SGD500M facility from HSBC Singapore to finance its Grab Car business.[17] The debt financing deal was oversubscribed by 250%, evidencing a strong appetite for debt facilities for non-traditional companies and the market's belief in Grab as Southeast Asia's leading FinTech platform.

In 2020, Great Eastern invested USD70M in Axiata Digital's financial services business, allowing GE to leverage Axiata's network and digital

[13] https://www.marketing-interactive.com/carousell-secures-us85m-in-funding-dbs-jumps-on-board-as-new-investor

[14] https://fintechnews.sg/40380/wealthtech/spark-systems-s15m-round-includes-investments-from-hsbc-citi-and-osk/

[15] https://techcrunch.com/2018/11/06/grab-hyundai-250-million/

[16] https://www.grab.com/sg/press/others/grab-closes-us2-billion-term-loan-facility/

[17] https://www.businesstimes.com.sg/companies-markets/grab-secures-s500m-facility-from-hsbc-for-vehicle-fleet-financing

capabilities to grow and reach new unbanked customer segments in the ASEAN region.[18]

UOB, in collaboration with Pintec, launched Avatec.ai in 2018, a digital solution that helps financial institutions increase efficiency and accuracy in potential customers' credit quality assessment. In future, UOB will offer the solution to other industry verticals like point-of-sale financing in e-commerce, retail, and travel.[19]

Commercial

UOB, in a strategic alliance with Grab, accelerated the use of digital services among ASEAN's growing base of digital consumers. Under the partnership, UOB became Grab's preferred banking partner in ASEAN, which enabled UOB to deliver financial services to Grab's ASEAN-wide user base.[20]

This strategic alliance allowed Grab to offer various payment solutions from UOB's holistic suite, such as payments, analytics, real-time insights, foreign exchange, and wallet top-ups.[21] In addition, the parties are also exploring embedding more features within Grab's mobile app, allowing users to enjoy a fully digital and seamless banking and payments experience.[22]

---

[18] https://www.greateasternlife.com/sg/en/about-us/media-centre/media-releases/collaboration-with-axiata-digital-in-fintech.html

[19] https://www.uob.com.sg/web-resources/uobgroup/pdf/newsroom/2018/media-release-uob-and-pintec-join-forces-to-launch-next-generation-digital-credit-assessment-solution.pdf

[20] https://www.uobgroup.com/techecosystem/news-insights-uob-and-grab-better-together.html

[21] https://www.grab.com/sg/press/others/uob-and-grab-announce-strategic-regional-alliance-to-accelerate-the-use-of-digital-services-among-aseans-consumers/

[22] https://www.businesstimes.com.sg/companies-markets/uob-launches-partnership-network-to-simplify-digital-payments-rewards-redemption

Joint Product

Banks and FinTechs identified the merits of collaborating to serve specific market segments where joining forces would be beneficial for the both of them.

DBS collaborated with a local FinTech company, Cardup, to enable businesses to pay significant, recurring business expenses such as salaries and rent and help their customers pay them using credit and debit cards. The joint proposition allowed SMEs to extend their payables by up to 55 days, interest-free. As a result, SME recipients will get paid on time, while SMEs can defer the actual cash outflow until their card bill is due almost two months later.[23]

All the local banks in Singapore embarked on a programme to help SMEs digitise collaboration with an extensive SaaS and FinTech solutions suite. Through these digitalisation programmes, SMEs can enjoy cost savings to seize more significant growth opportunities in the digital economy.

DBS Bank partnered with IMDA and Enterprise Singapore to launch the DBS Start Digital Pack, helping small businesses start their digitalisation journey. It aims to digitalise essential business functions such as Accounting, Human Resource Management, Marketing, Collaboration and Cybersecurity.[24] Furthermore, in partnership with IMDA, UOB launched BizSmart, a suite of digital solutions to help SMEs stay competitive by increasing work efficiency, productivity and cost savings. In addition, OCBC Bank, in collaboration with Enterprise Singapore and IMDA, developed the SMEs Go Digital Programme. This programme started several initiatives, such as

---

[23] https://www.dbs.com.sg/sme/day-to-day/payments/dbs-x-cardup?pk_source=typed&pk_medium=direct&pk_campaign=bookmarked

[24] https://www.imda.gov.sg/-/media/Imda/Files/Programme/SMEs-Go-Digital/Start-Digital-Pack/Start-Digital-solutions_14May2021.pdf?la=en

Start Digital, Industry Digital Plans, and various digital solutions to help SMEs seize growth opportunities in the digital economy.

With the OCBC and Osome collaboration, SMEs can access professional expertise and cutting-edge technological tools to increase the efficiency of their business processes. Some of these packages include Xero and Talenox, the popular accounting software. Through these digitalisation programmes, SMEs can enjoy cost savings to seize more significant growth opportunities in the digital economy.[25]

In the initial phase of FinTech growth, banks and FinTechs saw each other as competition. Over the years, financial institutions like banks and startups have recognised the value and merits of co-existence to achieve growth and success. In several cases, the lines have blurred with financial institutions launching their FinTech ventures and offering infrastructure as a service. In contrast, FinTechs have either got banking licences or invested in regulated banks. The next phase of collaboration between banks and FinTechs will bring more opportunities and options for consumers benefiting the ecosystem as a whole.

[25] https://www.asiaone.com/business/osome-ocbc-bank-help-smes-save-s1080-accounting-hr

Chapter 5

DEMOCRATISING ACCESS TO BUILD

As a small country which is a success-focused welfare state, the government understands that there needs to be substantial public investments in developing foundational infrastructure. Some emerging technologies need significant upfront investment, and the country needs investment from the government to build these blocks. As a derivative of **Singanomics**, there is a unique approach to the government's role in creating and regulating competition. Singapore set off to build multiple pillars of equalisers to ensure that FinTech can focus on creating value in line with the knowledge economy traits of a developed nation, with the state providing the building blocks.

Recent investments in digital infrastructure have been particularly effective in enabling digital finance during this COVID-19 period. MyInfo has helped to streamline customer due diligence and improve the onboarding experience, removing the need for customers to visit a bank branch or conduct face-to-face verification physically. PayNow has enabled individuals and businesses to make e-payments and receive government disbursements such as Care and Support payouts swiftly, securely and conveniently.

Electronic payments have also taken off since the COVID-19 crisis. As of the end of 2022, FAST and Paynow had 292 million transactions, with a total volume of transactions in Singapore amounting to around SGD380B with an average size of SGD1,304. This was more than half the total amount of transactions conducted in 2020. The transactions included corporate users from active businesses, credit and debit cards, and other forms of e-payment. In addition, digital banking has become the norm.[1]

GovTech Bedrock

Adopting tech across ministries and government agencies was to help Singapore residents achieve digital access, literacy and participation so that the country could seize new opportunities in an increasingly digital world as a Smart Nation.

Singaporeans must be digitally enabled to participate in and benefit from these projects. Singaporeans, especially those at the highest risk of being excluded, such as older people and those in the lower-income segments, should have four fundamental digital enablers — a mobile device with network connection, internet access, a bank account with card facility and national digital identity.

The Smart Nation plan by Singapore aspires to deliver a Digital Government that uses data, connectivity and computing decisively to re-engineer business processes, re-architect technology infrastructure, and transform services for the citizens, businesses and public officers. Furthermore, a Digital Government automates processes to better serve its citizens with a personal touch that enriches the user experience.

[1] https://www.mas.gov.sg/-/media/mas/sectors/payments/h2-2022-retail-payment-statistics.pdf

In the spirit of **Singanomics**, the Smart Nation plan aims to ensure that every consumer and corporate entity receives e-payment options pre-filled with government-verified data and digital solutions for wet ink signatures to ensure end-to-end digital transactions.

The foundation of digitisation, transparency and authenticity is identity. So the government built a standardised centralised identity to ensure all public and private enterprises can leverage the identity infrastructure to bring digital services to the doorsteps of all residents.

> *"Our vision is for Singapore to be a Smart Nation — a nation where people live meaningful and fulfilled lives, enabled seamlessly by technology, offering exciting opportunities for all. We should see it in our daily lives where networks of sensors and smart devices enable us to live sustainably and comfortably. We should see it in our communities, where technology will enable more people to connect more easily and intensively. Finally, we should see it in our future where we can create possibilities for ourselves beyond what we imagined possible."*
>
> *Prime Minister Lee Hsien Loong*[2]

Singapore is one of the most progressive nations, with its government leading the way in digitalisation. It has a unified national ID system which works

[2] Prime Minister Lee Hsien Loong's speech at Smart Nation Launch, 24 November 2014. See more at https://www.smartnation.gov.sg/whats-new/speeches/smart-nation-launch#sthash.0uFcUwNU.dpuf

across all government departments, and all the information about a citizen's life is available to them on any device at any time of the day.

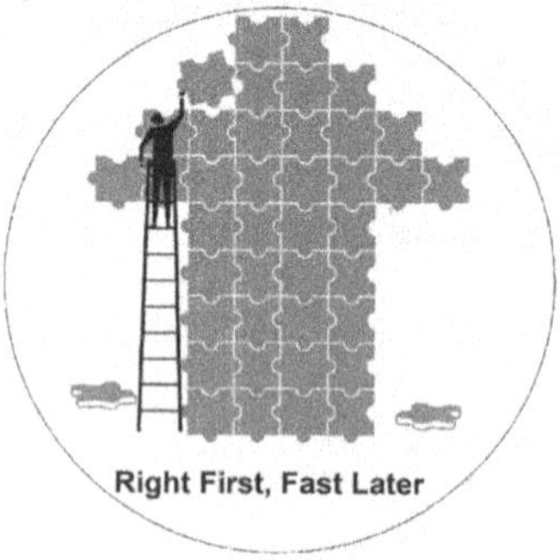

The depth of insights ranges from necessary information like income tax and retirement money to obscure ones such as vaccination plans for children. All this information is available to every resident of Singapore free of cost. In addition, residents have a right to access and share this information with any service providers they want to seek services from across all walks of life.

The identity system, coupled with a full consent and trust management framework, gives enormous power to innovators to create solutions and capabilities by leveraging this infrastructure. However, in line with the Singaporean concept of **Right First, Fast Later**, Singapore believes the government needs to solve the fundamental problems around ensuring that data is available in a standard format across different departments.

The standard format data is also connected to a unified identity-setting platform for developing future use cases and scenarios. As a small market, Singapore could be more attractive for private enterprises to build underlying core infrastructure. Due to their size, the investment returns are much more attractive in neighbouring markets. Digitisation is a key enabler, not an end goal. Being "digital to the core" is about using data, connectivity and computing decisively to transform the way the government serves its citizens and businesses and the way it enables public officers to contribute fully to their work.

The real Digital Government is one that "Serves with Heart" and makes digital empathy its core operation mission. The aim is to automate work where possible and provide a personal touch engagement that enriches the engagement experience between the government and the citizens.

The digital medium allows us to build stakeholder-centric services that cater to the needs of the individual. It enables policies, facilities and infrastructure to be better designed through data and evidence-based policymaking rather than by agencies' functional boundaries or the limitations of our human resources.

Different agencies have set up data-sharing processes and controls for efficient data-driven policymaking and service delivery. It involves tackling legislative, policy, capability and technical challenges simultaneously.

The Singapore government recently formalised data sharing and safeguards in the public sector through the Public Sector Governance Act in 2018, which provides the legal means by which data is shared safely, responsibly, and appropriately.

Agencies can use government-verified data to provide services to citizens without requesting additional documents and sensitive information online. At the same time, personal data will be protected through robust safeguards, including access control, and de-identified when used for analysis and policy design.

In the spirit of **Singanomics**, the government has set measurable targets for all facets of Digital Government, such as public servant familiarity. This has been done via tools, seamless digital transactions and ensuring all government services are available digitally.

The government aims to provide end-to-end digital services to its citizens across all walks of life. For example, filing one's income taxes is fully digital, and our citizens can access library resources without having to access the library physically. Citizens can access their health records, educational documents, tax filings and other departments with a few clicks on a smartphone.

Achieving the Key Performance Indicators will require significant improvements in delivering digital services and new tools and platforms. While technology can be the catalyst, it will require a holistic re-engineering on the government's part of how it provides solutions and conduct the execution of civil services.

The government's digital platforms are open for private companies to participate in to enable new innovative B2B and B2C services. GovTech builds digital platforms to connect citizens, not just to build a community but also to support crowdsourcing for solutions and services.

To provide users with a single digital identity to transact with the government and private sector more securely and seamlessly, the government has developed a National Digital Identity (NDI) system extending from the SingPass platform. As a next step, the government launched the SingPass Mobile, an app allowing citizens to transact more quickly using one's fingerprint or a user-determined passcode. With increasingly digitised transactions, the government hopes to ensure that everyone has an equal opportunity to benefit from using technology.

With most of its team working remotely and its completely digital processes, Sleek, a homegrown start-up, was well-placed to thrive in a global pandemic. Sleek boosted its client portfolio twofold and posted a yearly recurring revenue of USD10M in early 2021. Sleek was founded in 2017 by **Julien Labruyere** and **Adrien Barthel** to respond to the cumbersome process of starting and growing a business. Julien recalls his early battles with opening bank accounts and sending invoices and paperwork. Together, they created a one-stop platform for new companies to register and operate seamlessly.

Its founders envisioned a company that:

- Maximises digital tools to allow companies to be operation-ready in days;
- Reaches a global market. They operate headquarters from Singapore and have expanded their services to reach Australia, Hong Kong and the United Kingdom;
- Integrates with local regulators such as the Accounting and Corporate Regulatory Authority (ACRA) and Inland Revenue Authority of Singapore (IRAS) for greater automation and smoother processes; and
- Employs the best talent. In a global race for the best brains in the industry, they know their company is as good as the talent they have.

The local FinTech landscape has grown tremendously since the Monetary Authority of Singapore (MAS) started the FinTech and Innovation Group (FTIG) in 2015. Firms that were traditionally not FinTech have moved naturally and instinctively into FinTech. Singapore's local regulators have supported the extension of FinTech for partnerships and payment rail service providers. There are exciting opportunities for collaboration with the Singapore FinTech Association (SFA) to build and enhance the FinTech community, especially regarding payments FinTech.

Launching its business account in 2021, Sleek expanded its product offerings to better serve small and medium-sized enterprises (SMEs). Specifically, in Singapore, the new services launched in 2022 facilitate processes such as bookkeeping, expense management, and payments and collections, to name a few.[3] Given this status, Sleek is uniquely positioned to be a trusted advisor to businesses, especially small companies, wanting to start their journeys. They understand how daunting the process can be, and by providing direct and personalised services, Sleek tailors its services to fit the needs of each client.

[3] https://fintechnews.sg/62751/virtual-banking/sleeks-foray-into-singapores-dynamic-sme-digital-finance-space/

Sleek maximises its service potential by:

- Building its digital technology solutions. It is not subject to third-party vendors' terms and can provide direct service to clients. This sets Sleek apart and makes it a powerful brand;
- Having its core system of payments and transaction services while integrating that with local payment rail providers in some countries; and
- Having unique insight into real-time data on client cash flow cycles and being able to advise clients on the data and its predictions.

FinTech companies frequently face the issue of personalisation and achieving that against the backdrop of digitalisation approaches while considering the scalability of services and high-level innovations. Personalisation means having access to client data to understand each client. The key, Julien believes, is empowering each client to understand and trust the processes. While much of Sleek's backend processes are automated, the human touch is still key to managing front-end inquiries. This helps to foster trust in the relationships that Sleek builds with clients. Ultimately, Sleek remains competitive, ensuring its innovations and products meet clients' needs.

MyInfo

MyInfo is a "Tell Us Once" service that allows users to automatically fill in personal details on online forms instead of repeating them or submitting supporting documents. It is part of the NDI project. Although designed initially for government agencies, MyInfo is now used by most banks and FinTechs in the country. It saves customers the hassle of providing certain supporting documents, such as proof of residential address. After the MyInfo pilot with banks, 50% of eligible customers chose to use MyInfo over existing options. As there was potential for businesses and developers to use MyInfo for even more digital services, the MyInfo Developer & Partner Portal was made available in November 2017. Presently accessible to Singapore citizens and residents with a Singpass account, MyInfo helps users manage their data, simplifying their online transactions.

Under the Go Digital Programme, SMEs can first refer to the sector-specific digital roadmaps to determine the digital solutions for each growth stage. Next, they can consult digital specialists at the SME Digital Tech Hub if they need expert help to appreciate digitalisation better before they embark on it. Then, when they are finally ready to get started, they can select from a list of proven digital solutions pre-approved by the Infocomm Media Development Authority or embark on industry-led pilot projects to achieve new growth.

The future is digital, and Singapore's approach to facilitating the FinTech ecosystem is a testament to this belief. The private sector has seen multiple investments from the government, and their efforts have created a culture of financial inclusion. Singapore has actively encouraged all forms of competition, but at the same time, the government can intervene when the effects of competition get detrimental to the ecosystem. As a result, it has allowed the industry in Singapore to flourish within a mutually beneficial infrastructure.

> *"Data is the lifeblood of a digital economy and a Digital Government. As the custodian of a vast amount of data, the Government takes its responsibility of securing the data and preserving individuals' privacy very seriously."*
>
> *Prime Minister Lee Hsien Loong*[4]

[4] November 2019. See more at https://www.smartnation.gov.sg/why-Smart-Nation/secure-smart-nation#sthash.b2QgqWuE.dpuf

MyInfo and its suite of solutions like Singpass have uses beyond financial services, and it was the backbone of Singapore's COVID response with the tracking of social access and vaccine distribution leveraging the technology.

SGFinDex

Singapore has taken a unique approach to open banking compared to most regulators worldwide. In comparison, regulators worldwide focused on pushing financial institutions to open the application programming interface (API) for consumption by FinTech and using API as an instrument of democratisation access to data.

In the true spirit of Singanomics, Singapore focused on defining business and social needs before nudging financial institutions to open API. Some of the unique social attributes of Singapore are the ageing population, the need for holistic retirement and financial advice, and the average customer having more than three different bank accounts and multiple insurance policies.

It was identified that an ideal use case for Open API would enable customers to access their financial, insurance, tax, retirement and mortgage holdings in one place to create effective holistic financial advice.

SGFinDex is the Singapore Financial Data Exchange, a Singapore government initiative and collaborative effort among financial institutions and government agencies. It allows individuals to view their consolidated personal financial data using their Singpass (National Digital Identity) conveniently and securely on any financial planning application they choose.

SGFinDex has been helping individuals to better understand their financial situation by providing a consolidated view of their financial data. This can help them to make more informed financial decisions, such as saving for retirement or investing in their children's education. It makes it easier for individuals to manage their finances by allowing them to access their financial data from a single platform. This can save them time and effort, and it can also help to reduce the risk of fraud.

SGFinDex uses Singpass for user authentication to ensure security and retrieves data only with user consent. Users have control over which participating entities can access their data. The user's identity must be verified when personal financial data is retrieved. The retrieved data is encrypted, and only the authorised financial planning application can decrypt it, ensuring enhanced security measures.

SGFinDex is the world's first public digital infrastructure to utilise a national digital identity and a centrally managed online consent system. It enables individuals to access financial information through applications from various government agencies and financial institutions. Strict safeguards are in place to protect data privacy and ensure the security of personal financial information. SGFinDex does not read or store data; it only transmits encrypted data packages.

Cybersecurity

Cybersecurity is of utmost importance to Singapore as a nation that has embraced digitalisation. Most of Singapore's residents possess banking accounts, mobile phone subscription plans, and internet access. In addition, the COVID-19 pandemic has further driven the transition towards digital payments. While Singapore has consistently maintained a robust reputation in terms of cybersecurity, ranking sixth in the Cybersecurity Index in 2018, it is not immune to cyberattacks.[5] Singapore's financial sector, which is largely centred around a digital infrastructure,

[5] International Telecommunication Union, "Global Cybersecurity Index 2018" (2019) 62 https://www.itu.int/dms_pub/itu-d/opb/str/D-STR-GCI.01-2018-PDF-E.pdf.

is highly vulnerable to cyberattacks. As of June 2022, Singapore became home to 1,150 FinTech companies. This means that any cyberattack on large or small firms could have extensive effects on the financial system of Singapore.[6] Smaller firms are especially vulnerable as they are often less prepared to fend off cyberattacks than larger firms. Therefore, there is a need to impose appropriate cybersecurity regulations to ensure that firms can protect themselves from cyberattacks, reducing the likelihood of major disruptions to the financial system of Singapore.[7]

> *"[Cybersecurity] is not a race that we can win alone. However, a rising tide raises all boats, and collaboration between governments, businesses, academia and individuals across multiple fronts will be crucial to our success."*
>
> *David Koh*[8]

According to Anton N Didenko,[9] Singapore has a solid international reputation in cybersecurity. However, as Singapore's financial sector is largely centred around a digital infrastructure, it is an area highly vulnerable to cyberattacks. Therefore, there is a need to impose appropriate cybersecurity regulations to ensure that firms can protect themselves from

[6] Monetary Authority of Singapore, FinTech and Innovation, https://www.mas.gov.sg/development/fintech

[7] Anton N Didenko, "Cybersecurity Regulation in the Financial Sector: Prospects of Legal Harmonisation in the EU and Beyond" (2020) Uniform Law Review 4.

[8] Keynote Address by Mr David Koh, Chief Executive, Cyber Security Agency of Singapore, at the 3rd Annual Billington International Cybersecurity Summit, 21 March 2018, https://www.csa.gov.sg/news/speeches/the-3rd-annual-billington-international-cybersecurity-summit-keynote-address-by-ce.

[9] Anton N Didenko, "Cybersecurity Regulation in Singapore's Financial Sector: Protecting FinTech 'Ants' in a Jungle Full of 'Elephants'" (2020) UNSW Law Research Paper No 20-45, https://ssrn.com/abstract=3679678

cyberattacks, reducing the likelihood of major disruptions to the financial system of Singapore.

Singapore's Cybersecurity Bill, which aims to strengthen the protection of Critical Information Infrastructure (CII), was passed into law on 5 February 2018. The Bill provides a framework for regulating CII and formalises the duties of CII owners in ensuring the cybersecurity of their respective CIIs. It also provides the Cyber Security Agency of Singapore (CSA) with powers to manage and respond to cybersecurity threats and incidents, establish a framework for sharing cybersecurity information with and by CSA, and protect such information. Another objective of the Bill is to establish a light-touch licensing framework for cybersecurity service providers.

On ASEAN regional cybersecurity cooperation, S Iswaran, then Minister for Communications and Information, and Minister-in-Charge of Cybersecurity, discussed the deepening of cybersecurity cooperation on building a rules-based cyberspace, focusing on our regional norms implementation work plan and strengthening our regional cyber resilience through CII protection.[10]

API Strategy

Singapore firmly advocates for the idea that we should establish new laws only when the current rules prove insufficient to handle emerging situations and scenarios that have evolved since the initial regulations were put in

[10] Opening Speech by S Iswaran, Minister for Communications and Information, Minister in-Charge of Cybersecurity, at the 5th ASEAN Ministerial Conference on Cybersecurity (live virtual broadcast), 7 October 2020, https://www.mci.gov.sg/pressroom/news-and-stories/pressroom/2020/10/opening-speech-by-mr-s-iswaran-at-the-5th-asean-ministerial-conference-on-cybersecurity

place. When it comes to fostering the growth of FinTech, one of the primary concerns is ensuring access to APIs that allow the development of solutions for accessing the financial infrastructure. Unlike many other global FinTech hubs, Singapore has chosen not to impose mandatory open banking laws. Instead, it has encouraged banks to take the initiative in finding ways to implement these regulations.

Regulations are set with the societal context in mind and based on their cultural, societal, financial and technological landscape. Countries focus on deciding an appropriate approach for themselves and work towards implementing regulations that facilitate growth and innovation based on local contexts. They also aim to do it in the best possible way consistently. Hence, Singapore takes a balanced approach where the regulations and financial institutions collaborate through planning for the necessary actions to be taken, and financial institutions are expected to follow through.

In Singapore, the government is pacing the implementation speed to ensure that open banking and the adoption of APIs will be sustainable for the next generation. Singapore has a very in-depth API playbook. Secure, scalable, safe, and sustainable are the critical 4Ss that are the focus of Singapore's approach to API adoption. In Singapore, regulators and financial institutions have drafted an agreed roadmap that goes down to the granular level to ensure the ecosystem is aligned. While each financial institution can take a slightly different approach, speed and priority order, at the end of the day, all the financial institutions have the same end goal and framework.

The consensus-driven attitude is evident in creating the API Playbook, which reviewed and analysed over 400 APIs and worked on standardising and defining best practices and formats for financial institutions to follow. Ideally, a sustainable API solution should also be able to connect seamlessly with all financial institutions. In addition, minimal customisation should be needed to integrate the whole system into one. Several of the largest financial institutions in Singapore have published APIs use cases, and global banks based in Singapore also opened APIs without a mandate.

Regulators in Singapore work with financial institutions to chart the pathway of API adoption together. Singaporean regulators acknowledge the many possibilities for the adoption, but they are flexible and allow financial institutions themselves to prioritise which ones are most relevant.

The Singaporean approach has its critics, primarily FinTech providers and soon-to-come digital banks who want more Europe-like regulations that mandate the opening of API by the financial institutions to promote competition. However, the needs and context of Europe were very different, where many banks had to be given bailouts from public money and, thus, a need to increase competition and repetition of a too-big-to-fail situation after the 2008 crisis. Fortunately, none of the banks in ASEAN needed a public money bailout in recent history. On the other extreme, Singapore has been fortunate to have its three local banks consistently rated as among the strong banks in the world. As a result, under the Singanomics model, state intervention is utilised to support the financial sector to embrace innovation and competition sustainably.

One of the challenges in a country with an ageing population is ensuring financial literacy and preparing them for retirement solutions. Multiple government departments came together to solve this problem by defining a situation where they needed banks to open API, creating a concrete case for Open Banking. Identifying a clear use case with many social goods attached to it motivated the large banks to agree on standards and launch the world's first nationwide retirement and financial health solution. While some startups and Western observers are unhappy with this approach, it aligns with the **Singanomics** innovation model. The current scope of these APIs is limited and is likely to improve further in the coming years. The

Garden Innovation approach in API Banking avoided the Balkanisation of non-interoperable API standards between the banks.

Another product unique to Singapore surrounds the concept of "The Last Sandwich Generation", another issue to be solved with Open Banking or API Banking. As part of the Financial Planning Digital Services (FPDS), consumers can pull their data across financial service providers, including retirement savings, bank balance, wealth management solutions and other financial products to give them a holistic view of their financial health. This is very different from the Western concept of account aggregation. The FPDS is driven by helping the community improve and prepare for the future. Steadfast focus on building strong foundations instead of uncoordinated API offerings looking for problems to solve; Singapore uses technology to solve the issues on hand.

Percipient is a data technology company based in Singapore to help organisations reduce the complexity of their data architecture by enabling hyper-accelerate connectivity between data sources that currently do not talk to each other or cost too much to integrate. This can be data sources that are legacy and modern, structured and unstructured, real-time or batch. So, for example, data from the Internet of Things, blockchain and APIs can be easily, safely and cheaply managed using UniConnect, all without requiring yet another copy of the data.

Following a more than two-decade-long career in business roles at global banks and asset management, Navin Suri turned into a technopreneur in 2014. Having worked at Citibank, BNY Mellon in Hong Kong, and Nomura Asset Management in Taiwan, Navin was determined to re-imagine enterprise data management. So he co-founded Percipient in 2015 with two ex-colleagues and a team of young passionate developers to enable source and location-agnostic data unification using the latest data virtualisation and big data technologies. After 20 months of research and development, Percipient launched UniConnect, its flagship data integration platform.

Navin, and his co-founders at Percipient, entered the industry with specialised domain experience in banking technology and found Singapore's regulator, MAS, to be very progressive and welcoming to new ideas and change. In a conversation with the authors of this book, Navin states that it is due to the MAS's openness that Singapore has gained the global visibility it enjoys today. For example, the Singapore FinTech Festival (SFF) is the world's largest FinTech festival and making Singapore synonymous with the word "FinTech" on a global stage.

> *"Singapore as a market itself is too small to be noticed by the global financial industry; however, with the help of its regulator, it has positioned itself extremely well as a gateway to ASEAN. It provides global corporations with the necessary footing in the region to target larger markets in the ASEAN, potentially catering to more than 600 million people."*
>
> *Navin Suri, 2020, in a personal interview*

Navin shares that he had heard of the ease of doing business in Singapore, but what he experienced surpassed his expectations. It took him three hours to incorporate his company online, and his Personalised Employment Pass application was approved soon after its filing, allowing him to start working in Singapore immediately.

The company successfully raised seed funding in April 2017, including investments from several global corporate technology leaders. In October 2017, Hewlett-Packard partnered with Percipient to develop a next-generation data integration platform by leveraging Percipient's UniConnect platform. In addition, the Percipient signed a strategic partnership with Intel Corporation in November 2017, enabling it to gain early access to Intel roadmap technologies. The Percipient's teams are based in Singapore, India and the US. In 2022, Navin became an advisor to the board at Elevandi, which organises the SFF.

Payment Rails

One of the foundational use cases and first consumer touchpoints for adopting FinTech is payments. As a result, some countries allowed private companies to build critical payment infrastructure, enabling them to achieve the necessary scale.

Another challenge was the advent of many non-interoperable QR codes in the country, with a few of them supported by global FinTech players from China. This created a huge challenge for merchants to manage the complexity of helping many modes.

In the *kampung* spirit, MAS, and the Association of Banks in Singapore (ABS), brought together different ecosystem constituents, including service providers, startups, banks and infrastructure vendors, to plan out the future of payments. The infrastructure was built as a national project to create a level playing field and ensure smaller companies are included. Local payment switches and schemes were entrusted to ABS, and managing the local QR payment system was assigned to Network for Electronic Transfers (NETS), a company jointly owned by three local banks. Instead of spending years deliberating and lobbying, swift and strong actions were taken to appoint custodians for each initiative with overall monitoring from the regulators. However, it is not that there were no hiccups and dissatisfaction along the way.

Several countries went through challenges of wallet e-money providers building walled gardens and restricting competition from smaller players. Singapore wanted to prevent a repetition of a China model in which private players had too much control over retail payment that it could stifle competition.

Singapore addressed it through its unique approach to a "level playing field" by ensuring in the Payment Services Act that if a specific payment service provider becomes dominant and subsequently non-interoperable, MAS reserves the right to step in to ensure interoperability. Regulators work to ensure that the various players have the freedom to work within their frameworks. If one or two parties do not align with the rest of the team, the regulators have the power to ensure things are in place, but such enforcement measures are only taken as and when needed. The law has made provisions as to when enforcement measures will be triggered. Such an approach encourages an innovative environment for adoption through co-creation without a mandated system seen in other markets.

One might assume that a bill like the Payment Services Act may threaten innovation, especially when firms wish to keep their services proprietary. However, this is not the case, as interoperability and integration allow smaller players to freely build products and new technology. Large firms need more power to use their scale to impede innovation.

Ultimately, MAS protects user rights and information by ensuring technology risk management is in place (via know your customer [KYC] and anti-money laundering [AML] regulations). Trust from consumers is prioritised, and MAS has seen to it that checks and balances are in place and consumers have faith in the system.

InstaReM is a FinTech company offering digital cross-border money transfer services, also known as remittance services, to individuals and businesses. The company aims to be recognised as a Singaporean headquartered global FinTech company. Today, it has offices on six continents and 10 different offices across the globe.

InstaReM is unique because it is a hotspot of many different products. They provide not only remittance services but can also give you an account number, a credit card or a foreign currency account. These are brought to customers on a single platform, Nium, while most other platforms provide only one or two services. In 2021, Instarem rebranded itself, launching a first-of-its-kind consumer debit card.[11]

Prajit Nanu, co-founder and CEO of Nium, set his heart on becoming an entrepreneur in 2006, but it was in 2013 that that dream would become a reality. That year he was tasked with organising a party for a friend at a resort in Thailand when he faced issues trying to send and collect money across borders. First, the resort requested him to send money to their account via bank transfer. Second, a simple transaction for less than USD1,000 requires extensive documents. Gathering and submitting these documents would have taken him much time and effort. There had to be a better way. Luckily, he found a friend based in Thailand who could help him make the transfer. Later, his friend revealed that he had been sending money to India every month, and his bank was charging a fortune for the service and was even taking an FX spread on top of it. This pushed Prajit to look at solutions to this gap in the remittances industry and started InstaReM — Nium's first consumer-facing service. Instarem processes billions of transactions each year for millions of consumers worldwide.

Core to the success of the Instarem service is the advanced global payments platform upon which it is delivered. That platform is Nium. Today, the Nium platform connects businesses to various payment services through one API. Banks, payment providers, travel companies, and aspiring global corporations can embed services to send and receive funds in local currencies and issue physical and virtual cards globally through this one connection.

[11] https://www.instarem.com/blog/news/press-releases/leading-cross-border-payments-platform-instarem-unveils-new-brand-image-and-singapore-mobile-app/

In addition, Nium has simplified the global payments infrastructure's complexity, making it easier for businesses to embed financial services in weeks versus months.

Success will be driven by two recent strategic acquisitions, including the acquisition of travel B2B payments leader, Ixaris, which added comprehensive virtual card issuance capabilities to the Nium platform, as well as the acquisition of Wirecard Forex India Private Limited, which gives Nium greater reach into India's booming payments market. In addition, a capital infusion of USD200M in a Series D round led by Riverwood Capital in July 2021 has propelled Nium to "unicorn status" with a valuation above USD2B. The funds will expand Nium's payments network infrastructure, drive innovative product development, attract top industry talent, and acquire strategic technologies and companies. With revenues split almost equally across EMEA and APAC, Nium plans to accelerate growth in the United States and Latin America, with Prajit personally moving to the United States in 2021, eyeing a potential public listing on a US exchange.

> *"We started Nium with the modest goal of taking out regional complexity in cross-border payments. Today, our sights are set higher. We believe we can be a catalyst to increase global commerce by removing some of the payment friction that traditionally held businesses back. The Nium platform simplifies the B2B payments experience by enabling critical financial services to be easily embedded — helping today's local market players become tomorrow's global giants."*
>
> *Prajit Nanu, Nium's Co-founder and CEO,*
> *in an interview with authors*

Rapyd started as a mobile payments company but soon realised that a much bigger problem existed that needed to be solved. So in 2016, the team at Rapyd decided to build an e-wallet product that would allow a consumer to withdraw cash from an ATM in any country without a bank account. They started with a single country but found that it required integration with seven different systems and local services, on top of managing licensing and regulatory requirements — practices that were not scalable globally. As commerce is becoming increasingly cross-border and, at the same time, more local, this proved to be a real barrier to innovation.

Today, Rapyd helps businesses create great local commerce experiences anywhere. It builds the technology that removes the back-end complexities of cross-border commerce while providing local payments expertise. Global e-commerce companies, technology firms, marketplaces and financial institutions use its FinTech-as-a-service platforms — Collect, Disburse, Wallet and Issuing — to seamlessly embed localised FinTech and payments capabilities into their applications in a simple way. Rapyd has also built the Rapyd Global Payments Network that lets businesses access the world's largest local payment network with over 900 locally preferred payment methods, including bank transfers, e-wallets and cash in more than 100 countries.

Joel Yarbrough is Rapyd's current APAC Vice President and MD of Rapyd Ventures, the venture arm of Rapyd. Joel worked in PayPal's Global Product Strategy team and then with Grab, where he ran payments. He left Grab in 2018 on the week the company bought out Uber and started at Rapyd two months later.

The payment space can process things faster without new technology. It requires a mindset to make it simpler. Rapyd's job is to provide a smooth waterline to hide what is happening under the hood. Rapyd leverages technology to make it simple for others. It is not about championing technology over finance or vice versa but using the available technology to improve finance.

Rapyd's focus is on simplicity. Joel shares that the key focus of his team at Rapyd is on making payments easy for both large companies going global and small companies looking to expand. They work with everyone, with the singular aim of creating a smooth waterline for everyone to interact and build solutions. Rapyd has to pick the right technology to lower the switching costs for partners. Its involvement in technology manifests in a strong identity platform that utilises machine learning and transaction integration models.

Rapyd interacts across the board as a business with old management systems, popular systems such as Visa and Mastercard, and even with new APIs. In the centre of it all, Rapyd has built a business model that allows them to work with all these different complex situations (i.e., licences, bank partnership relationships, clean interface, etc.). Technology is used for leverage, but the ultimate delivery focuses on simplicity. Rapyd has a global universal infrastructure that applies beyond Singapore. As of 2022, it collects money from over 500,000 locations and disburses money in over 190 countries. The company has successfully built a network that takes them to all these countries with one integration. This network comprises remittance companies, payment gateways, banks, and issuers, all licensed actors in this FinTech ecosystem. Joel shares that his staff handle the tough stuff behind the scenes, allowing them to promise partners that their barriers to entry to enter new markets are very low once they have done the initial integration.

The future of Rapyd holds the soft launch of a new product — a risk management product focused on securing the transaction environment across a diverse set of countries and payment methods. Rapyd has already added consumer credit platforms to the payment side of the business, opening the credit side to give enterprises better access to working capital. Their aim remains to achieve interoperability at a very low cost.

Joel shares that till early 2010, the financial services industry focused on consumer protection and macroeconomic stability. Now, the focus is on innovation with a commercial mindset. In Asia, regulators look at each other and compete, build on each other's standards and move faster. The consistent cooperation and collaboration between regulators help everyone move forward in the right direction.

Joel rightfully points out that Singapore's key strength beyond FinTech is the trade: What can Singapore do in the payments landscape to leverage this? What does this look like across different sectors? Currently, there are possibilities to extend PayNow beyond the Singapore dollar. This would significantly amplify the shipping, aviation and financial sectors.

The main thing needing improvement in Singapore is that the country cannot pick one company as a poster child for FinTech success. Joel highlights Paytm in India and asks, who would be the Paytm of Singapore? The success in Singapore could be the ecosystem itself. However, how would one measure the ecosystem's success in this case? Another disadvantage is market size. Entrepreneurs would rather take 5% of Indonesia than 50% of Singapore. Therefore, the market size must be considered by startups when deciding where to base their businesses.

> *"How do we create a larger virtual market outside our physical size? If there is interoperability between markets, how does Singapore position itself as a key hub amongst these larger markets?"*
> *Joel Yarbrough, 2020, in a personal interview, on Singapore's focus in the years to come*

Founded in 2015 with a millennial name, FOMO Pay is a B2B company in the mobile payment space. Behind FOMO Pay are two accomplished young men featured on Forbes 30 Under 30 Asia 2018. Co-founder Zack Yang of FOMO Pay is also a member of the invitation-only Global Innovators Community created by the World Economic Forum. He also sits on the Forbes Finance Council as Council Member. In 2021, he became a venture partner with Teja Ventures and co-chaired FinTech Investment.

When asked about the interesting name, Zack shares that FOMO Pay aims to create a "Fear of Missing Out" for clients in this niche digital payment market; today, FOMO Pay is widely recognised by industry players such as hotels, financial institutions and airline.

The company started as a mobile payment aggregator. Along the way, it had to pivot and adapt its business model. Then, in 2017, the Singapore government invited FOMO Pay to join the Singapore Quick Response Code (SGQR) task force under MAS. This was a year-long project where the company could work with Visa, Mastercard, UnionPay, American Express and local banks.

When FOMO Pay started, Zack believed the company's main competitors were the local banks. However, he learnt that banks would take much longer to establish a digital payment platform due to regulations and restrictions. That was when he realised that this opportunity was really for FOMO to capitalise on. Instead of presenting itself as a FinTech player, FOMO Pay positioned itself as an enabler, working with all the banks and financial systems. It opened its ecosystem to include the banks through partnerships. FOMO Pay's product is used by banks, while the brand name is under the bank. Banks can save effort and time in the product development stage through this symbiotic relationship and quickly enter the mobile payment stage.

Zack is researching the FinTech landscape in Singapore compared to other markets. He believes that what Singapore has are only government support and talent. As a neutral third party, Singapore has the unique advantage of being able to represent itself as a gold standard for other countries. Take for example, the SGQR Standard. Singapore becomes a learning point when other countries establish national QR code payment standards.

In the future, Zack wishes for the world to become more connected. He believes strongly in the power of learning from other countries. He envisions an open banking standard with an open API structure. Different financial systems in different countries could even become interoperable. That is the future he believes in and what distributed ledger technology is trying to promote. This vision was realised in 2022 when FOMO Pay integrated Alipay+, to provide one-stop digital payments and marketing solutions for businesses in Singapore. Merchants can now accept cross-border digital payments globally, becoming more interconnected.

> *"Singapore itself runs like a startup."*
> *Zack Yang, 2020, in a personal interview, on Singapore as a FinTech nation*

Blockchain

Blockchain technology enables innovation across the financial services industry and transforms how we do business. Given its efficiency, security and transparency, applying blockchain technology in capital markets will open new possibilities in fundraising and investing.

Blockchain technology is designed for public networks to operate in a decentralised manner in the absence of a trusted central party. Fulfilling the controls' requirements can help alleviate contention around ownership structures yet provide sufficient trust between participants to transact on a common platform. Moreover, it creates a possible path forward for implementing a common international settlement platform on which central banks and banks can participate and directly settle transactions.

Another equaliser which knowledge-based economies such as Singapore had to ace was blockchain. Early on, Singapore realised that blockchain would have a role to play in the future of financial services, even though the same end-state opportunities needed to be visible. The nation's commitment towards this technology was evident in Temasek joining the Libra project in May 2020.

Aligning with the nation's focus, MAS also identified blockchain as a core focus area of innovation and, as an example of Garden Innovation, committed significant resources and bandwidth to launch Project Ubin in 2016. It is a collaborative effort between MAS and the financial industry to explore using blockchain and distributed ledger technology (DLT) to clear and settle payments and securities. In addition, the project seeks to develop simpler and more efficient alternatives to current systems based on central bank-issued digital tokens. Project Ubin comprises several phases, each aiming to solve pressing challenges faced by the financial industry and the blockchain ecosystem.

Phase 1 of Project Ubin saw the partnership between MAS and R3, a DLT company and a consortium of financial institutions, to conduct inter-bank payments using blockchain technology. In addition, Deloitte produced a report, *Project Ubin: SGD on Distributed Ledger*, which introduced DLT and provided an understanding of the prototype developed.

Phase 2 of Project Ubin saw MAS and ABS lead the consortium in successfully developing a software prototype of three different models for decentralised inter-bank payment and settlements with liquidity savings mechanisms. The consortium included financial institutions and technology partners, with the source codes and technical documentation made available for public access under Apache Licence, Version 2.0.

Phase 3 of Project Ubin saw MAS and Singapore Exchange (SGX) collaborate to develop Delivery versus Payment (DvP) capabilities to settle tokenised assets across different blockchain platforms. Anquan, Deloitte and Nasdaq were appointed technology partners for this project. They demonstrated that DvP settlement finality, inter-ledger interoperability and investor protection could be achieved through specific solutions designed and built with blockchain technology. In addition, MAS and SGX jointly published an industry report, *Delivery versus Payment on DLT*, which provides a comprehensive view of automating DvP settlement processes with smart contracts.

Phase 4 of Project Ubin saw the Bank of Canada (BoC), the Bank of England and MAS jointly publishing a report that assesses alternative models that could enhance cross-border payments and settlements. The report, *Cross-border Interbank Payments and Settlements: Emerging Opportunities for Digital Transformation*, examines existing challenges and considers alternative models that could improve speed, cost, and transparency for users. MAS and BoC subsequently linked their respective experimental domestic payment networks, namely Project Jasper and Project Ubin. They announced a successful experiment on cross-border and cross-currency payments using central bank digital currencies (CBDCs). MAS and BoC jointly published a report, *Jasper-Ubin Design Paper: Enabling Cross-Border High-Value Transfer Using DLT*, which proposes a blueprint for other central banks to follow.

In Phase 5 of Project Ubin, the collaboration between BoC and MAS continued from Phase 4 to examine alternative models for cross-border payments using blockchain and CBDCs. However, this phase focused on developing the multi-currency payments model. The Phase 5 network has connectivity interfaces allowing other blockchain networks to connect and integrate seamlessly. It also has features that support use cases such as DvP with private exchanges, conditional payments, escrow for trade, and payment commitments for trade finance. Phase 5 aims to improve cross-border payments' efficiency, security, and transparency and promote interoperability between blockchain networks. The continued collaboration between BoC and MAS in Project Ubin demonstrates their commitment to exploring the potential of blockchain and digital currencies to transform the financial industry.

Project Ubin is a multi-year multi-phase project exploring blockchain and DLT to clear and settle payments and securities. The project has made significant progress across its various phases, with each stage successfully addressing pressing challenges faced by the financial industry and the blockchain ecosystem. The source codes and technical documentation are available for public access. In addition, the project has demonstrated the potential of DLT in enhancing the efficiency of settlement processes.

MAS has launched Ubin+, an ambitious initiative to advance cross-border connectivity in wholesale CBDCs. Ubin+ builds on the success of Project Ubin (2016–2020) and draws on the learnings from MAS's participation in Project Dunbar and the multi-currency corridor network collaboration with Banque de France (BdF).

Ubin+ consists of several projects, including Project Cedar Phase II, which focuses on maintaining connectivity across heterogeneous digital currency networks. This project was a collaboration between the Federal Reserve Bank of New York's New York Innovation Center and MAS. It aimed to enhance designs for atomic settlement of cross-border cross-currency transactions, leveraging wholesale CBDCs as a settlement asset.

Another key project under Ubin+ is Project Mariana, a partnership involving MAS, BdF, Swiss National Bank, and the Bank for International Settlements

Innovation Hub's (BISIH) Eurosystem, Switzerland and Singapore Centres. This project explores the use of automated market makers (AMMs) to automate foreign exchange and settlement of Swiss franc, Euro, and Singapore dollar wholesale CBDCs. In addition, Project Mariana aims to explore the design and application of AMMs for wholesale CBDCs and investigate if a supra-regional network could work as an efficient and trusted hub for cross-border settlement.

In addition to the above projects, Ubin+ will study business models and governance structures for cross-border foreign exchange settlement and develop technical standards and infrastructure to support cross-border connectivity.

Interoperability of platforms and atomic settlement of currency transactions is the foundation to secure seamless settlement of currency transactions. At the same time, it is important to establish policy guidelines for the connectivity of digital currency infrastructure across borders.

Ubin+ will significantly reduce settlement risk, a key pain point in cross-border cross-currency transactions, and strengthen Singapore's capabilities to use digital currency-based infrastructure for cross-border transactions. In addition, MAS is working with competent, like-minded partners to accelerate central banks' collective progress to an optimal future state of digital infrastructures.

In a groundbreaking development that could transform the global financial system, MAS has released its highly-anticipated report titled *Project Dunbar*. The report delves into the potential of blockchain technology, specifically DLT, to revolutionise the resilience and efficiency of the financial system. It proposes implementing a decentralised, interoperable network allowing financial institutions to conduct seamless transactions while retaining control over their data and assets.

The project comprised developing two prototypes for a shared platform enabling international settlements using digital currencies issued by multiple central banks. The forum will facilitate direct cross-border transactions between financial institutions in different currencies, significantly reducing costs and increasing speed. However, the project identified several challenges in implementing a multi-CBDC platform shared across central banks and proposed practical design solutions to address them.

Led by the Bank for International Settlements (BIS) Innovation Hub's Singapore Centre, Project Dunbar was a collaborative effort between the Reserve Bank of Australia, Bank Negara Malaysia, MAS, and the South African Reserve Bank. The project demonstrated that financial institutions could use CBDCs issued by participating central banks to transact directly with each other on a shared platform, potentially reducing reliance on intermediaries and processing times for cross-border transactions.

The project's findings support the G20 roadmap for enhancing cross-border payments, particularly in exploring the international dimension of CBDC design. In addition, the report proposes practical solutions for addressing critical issues such as governance, trust, and shared control. The findings from Project Dunbar provide a solid foundation for future work in this area, says Michele Bullock, Assistant Governor (Financial System), Reserve Bank of Australia.

The successful completion of Project Dunbar is a testament to the importance of central bank collaboration in supporting the development of next-generation payment infrastructures, notes Fraziali Ismail, Assistant Governor, Bank Negara Malaysia. The project marks a key milestone in advancing the efficiency of cross-border payments globally, adds Sopnendu Mohanty, Chief FinTech Officer, MAS. Rashad Cassim, Deputy Governor of the South African Reserve Bank, states that the project highlighted the possibilities of using multiple CBDCs issued on a shared platform for international settlement, paving the way for further exploration and investigation.

Central Bank Digital Currencies

A CBDC is virtual money backed and issued by a central bank. As cryptocurrencies and stablecoins have become more popular, the world's central banks have realised that they need to provide an alternative — or let the future of money pass them by. As of 2022, 105 countries are exploring the possibility of CBDC.

CBDCs can offer a range of advantages. They can play a central role in advancing the digital assets revolution in a regulated, lower-risk and — crucially — accessible way, helping make financial markets more efficient and available to all global citizens. CBDCs can also give the central banks more effective, future-oriented tools to implement monetary policy and help shape the future of digital money[12] in more direct and innovative ways while keeping pace with technological change.

> *"What is important is that central banks have come to realise the extent of the transformations already happening in digital currencies and that they see the importance of embracing a significant role in bringing about this change. We hope this paper provides a useful and thought-provoking example of one promising approach."*
> *Joseph Lubin, Founder and CEO of ConsenSys, Co-Founder of Ethereum*

Seventy per cent of the world's central banks are contemplating some degree of prototyping or analysis surrounding CBDCs. There needs to be an open platform that will serve as the delivery rails for these assets. The Libra system can support this public sector innovation and help bridge that gap.

[12] A ConsenSys white paper (2020), Central banks and the future of digital money

The key is to build blockchain-based payment systems and tokenised versions of assets, whether CBDCs or stablecoins. This will produce an economic breakthrough, effectively empowering individuals to have more control over what Chief Strategy Officer and Head of Global Policy for Circle Dante Disparte calls the 4 "S"s of money: how individuals spend, send, save and secure their money. The concept of universal free banking as a basic human right becomes an important first principle to the Libra project and these types of projects in general.

Approximately 1.7 billion people need access to the financial system. In addition, there are more than 260 million economic migrants worldwide. This powers the remittance and payment systems. It costs 7% for these individuals to send money back home through a largely analogue and manual process. During the pandemic, the inability of the Fed Fund to dispatch direct payments to people in need in real-time has proven a vulnerability in the current system. Libra's cross-border payments can lower the cost of and speed up these processes while effectively protecting these consumers.

In Singapore's case, Dante sees that a single regulator is responsible for the entire financial system. Comparatively, regulators in other countries have a sense of parochialism due to their fragmented nature. In addition, regulators try to portray a tech-neutral outlook but may not display this impartiality in practice. What Dante encountered in Singapore with MAS is a commitment to innovation, and a real commitment to tech-neutrality, focusing on the activity and figuring out how to create an enabling environment for that activity regardless of the standards that are used.

FinTechs have sometimes attempted to work around the system, taking the path of least resistance. Unfortunately, as a result, they have learnt the hard way the necessity of regulation. The unique proposition of combining our deep knowledge and expertise in the regulatory and compliance fields with the smart use of available technologies allows us to offer very cost-effective solutions for smaller and medium-sized organisations and larger-scale corporations from both the financial and non-financial sectors. These sectors include banks, insurance, publicly listed companies, casinos, e-payments, blockchains, FinTech startups, brokerage, corporate service providers, payments and remittances, precious stones and metals dealers, accounting and audit, and law firms.

From a currency selection point of view, more than 50% of the world's population is subject to a hyperinflationary currency environment. As a result, only a few currencies are stable, with independent long-range central banking being a part of the currency environment, with sufficient liquidity in secondary markets. This liquidity is necessary to ensure that a stablecoin arrangement has adequate liquidity and a sovereign guarantee. In 2022, Singapore continued to protect users by proposing further measures to mitigate cryptocurrency risks.

Project Orchid is a multi-year, multi-phase exploratory project initiated by MAS to examine the various design and technical aspects of a retail CBDC system for Singapore. While there is no urgent need for a retail CBDC in Singapore, the project aims to develop the technology infrastructure and technical competencies necessary to issue a digital version of Singapore dollar cash and explore the potential use cases for programmable money in Singapore.

The project adopted FinTech Nation's Right First, Fast Later principles to undertake a phased approach to embrace new technologies. It balances innovation and potential risks a retail CBDC could pose to the financial system's stability. The first phase, purpose-bound money (PBM), explores the potential use cases for a programmable digital SGD and the required infrastructure. PBM is a protocol specifying conditions for using an underlying digital currency. PBMs are bearer instruments with self-contained programming logic.

The project developed best-in-class insights and provided an in-depth analysis of the usage patterns of PBM under different scenarios, which can be useful for individuals and institutions looking to establish programmable digital currencies.

Phase 1 of Project Orchid features four trials that test the use of PBM for disbursements to selected individuals, issuance of commercial digital vouchers, funds disbursement from government agencies without requiring recipients to have a bank account and managing learning accounts. The trials involve various banks, government agencies, and private companies, including DBS Bank Ltd, GovTech's Open Government Products Division, Temasek, StraitsX, Grab, OCBC Ltd, the Central Provident Fund Board, United Overseas Bank Ltd, and SkillsFuture Singapore.

Overall, Project Orchid is a comprehensive and innovative initiative aimed at advancing the financial infrastructure in Singapore and exploring the potential of programmable digital currencies. The project's multi-phase approach, user-driven focus, and collaboration with various stakeholders, including government agencies, private companies, and financial institutions, demonstrate its commitment to driving innovation and enhancing financial inclusivity in Singapore.

Use Case	**Interaction Patterns (Transfer of value)**	
GOVERNMENT	**Government to Person**	**Person to Government**
	E.g. Government Disbursement	E.g. Pay Taxes
COMMERCIAL	**Corporate to Person**	**Person to Corporate**
	E.g. Corporate Vouchers, rewards points	E.g. Commit to spend
INDIVIDUAL	**Person to Person**	
	E.g. School Allowance, purpose bound donation	

Asset Tokenisation Use Cases

MAS recognises the potential benefits of these emerging technologies, such as increased efficiency, access, and financial inclusion. However, it acknowledges possible financial stability and integrity challenges such as market manipulation, fraud, and cyber threats. Therefore, as a testament to the spirit of "Right First, Fast Later", it seeks to balance innovation and risk management by promoting responsible experimentation and informed regulation.

Project Guardian is a collaborative initiative with the financial industry that seeks to test the feasibility of applications in asset tokenisation and DeFi while managing financial stability and integrity risks. The project aims to develop and pilot use cases in four main areas: open, interoperable networks, trust anchors, asset tokenisation, and institutional-grade DeFi protocols.

Project Guardian aims to carry out industry pilots with financial institutions and FinTechs to develop good asset tokenisation use cases for financial services. It will allow the industry to identify opportunities to unlock economic value and surface potential risk management issues. The initiative also aims to study tokenised asset transactions' regulatory and risk management implications and promote oversight and accountability by developing technology standards to support interoperability across the digital asset ecosystems.

Project Guardian collaborates with MAS, financial institutions, and technology providers to achieve its objectives. MAS works closely with these partners to develop policy guidelines, technical standards, and governance frameworks for digital assets and DeFi. MAS also provides funding support for industry pilots to test the feasibility of various use cases, such as asset tokenisation, cross-border payments, and trade finance.

Several pilot projects are underway, including an initiative led by DBS Bank Ltd., JP Morgan, and Marketnode to explore potential DeFi applications in wholesale funding markets. The project aims to carry out secured borrowing and lending on a public blockchain-based network through the execution of smart contracts. Another pilot project explores the issuance of tokens linked to trade finance assets, intending to digitise the trade distribution market. Finally, HSBC and UOB are working with Marketnode to enable native digital issuance of wealth management products, enhancing issuance efficiency and accessibility for investors.

Project Guardian represents an innovative and collaborative effort by the financial industry to improve financial stability and integrity and promote the safe development of the ecosystem using industry experiments and research as a reference.

Conclusion

The concept of digital payments, at first glance, appears simple. Still, digital payments must remain simple, elegant and intuitive for mass adoption across all customer segments, including semi-skilled foreign workers to high-net-worth individuals and millennials who are mobile-first and mobile-only. The different pieces of the jigsaw puzzle, such as E-KYC, blockchain and digital currency, are available today, and FinTechs are racing to formulate a solution to market. This would be reiterative as customers share feedback and financial institutions refine their solutions and products. Still, the consumer stands to benefit from financial services tailored to their lifestyle and life phase and holds high expectations that these services are to be fast, safe and at low costs. CBDCs could simplify and reduce the cost of cross-border remittances while forming the basis for more efficient, more secure interbank payment networks.

Chapter 6

SUSTAINING NETWORK EFFECTS

Singapore's domestic market is small. However, it has positioned itself as "*The Gateway to ASEAN*". The proximity between Singapore and its neighbours has led several global businesses and investors to establish Singapore as their base to cater to the broader ASEAN market, including Malaysia, Indonesia, Vietnam, the Philippines and many others. This web of networks has allowed Singapore to overcome its limitation of being a relatively small market, and its roots are visible in Singapore's internal landscape. The FinTech Sandbox is a prime example of the positive network effects, which allow for effortless B2B transactions, and financial inclusion to develop in the ecosystem.

Orchestrate Network Effects provide a comprehensive examination of the pivotal role network effects have played in propelling Singapore towards its status as a FinTech nation. This chapter explores how Singapore has harnessed the power of collaboration, trust, and open platforms to cultivate a thriving FinTech ecosystem. It highlights the government's proactive approach, supportive policies, and strategic partnerships that have fostered an environment conducive to FinTech innovation. By orchestrating network effects, Singapore has successfully attracted startups, financial institutions, government agencies, and educational institutions to collaborate and drive transformative advancements in FinTech, ultimately cementing its position as a global FinTech hub.

Monetary Authority of Singapore Programmes and Spin-offs

Keeping with the spirit of capitalism and the public good, several projects that began as MAS-led and funded initiatives have transitioned into independent entities with their management teams and external investors. The focus has been creating sustainable, long-term platforms to drive innovation and progress in the financial industry. For example, Project Ubin has developed multiple blockchain-based platforms, including Project Dunbar, which focuses on creating a decentralised platform for trade finance. Another platform, Partior, is designed to streamline cross-border payments using blockchain technology. These platforms have become independent companies with management teams, funding, and business models. These platforms continue to work closely with MAS and other industry stakeholders but also have the flexibility to pursue their strategic objectives and goals. This approach reflects Singapore's commitment to fostering a vibrant and innovative financial ecosystem that benefits both the private sector and society. By creating independent platforms that can drive long-term progress, MAS is helping to create a sustainable future for the financial industry in Singapore and beyond.

▸ *Elevandi*

Elevandi is a non-profit organisation that aims to advance FinTech in the digital economy by fostering an open dialogue between the public and private sectors. Founded by MAS, Elevandi focuses on building a global knowledge and collaboration platform that brings together the international financial and FinTech community to address pain points in the workings of the financial system.

Since its inception in 2016, Elevandi's flagship event, the Singapore FinTech Festival (SFF), has become the world's largest gathering of the global FinTech ecosystem. The festival attracts over 60,000 people from over 130 countries and serves as a platform for showcasing new ideas, technologies and solutions.

To further its mission, Elevandi has created a range of initiatives to connect people and drive collaboration, including monthly events such as the Green Shoots Series, which brings together the global FinTech community to discuss critical topics trending in FinTech and the digital economy.

Elevandi also has a deal-making programme called Elevandi Connects, where investors and start-ups explore new investment opportunities. In addition, Elevandi has a platform called Oxygen by API Exchange (APIX) that offers masterclasses, panels, podcasts and research content from industry experts dedicated to promoting worldwide knowledge sharing for financial institutions, FinTechs and tech enthusiasts.

Elevandi's purpose-driven roundtables, the Elevandi Forums, bring together the public and private sectors to advance developments and issues within the FinTech industry. These forums aim at addressing pain points and identifying opportunities for innovation in finance to improve the well-being of individuals, economies and societies.

Elevandi has also collaborated with the Switzerland government to convene leaders, investors and founders in Zurich for the invite-only Point Zero Forum. The World FinTech Festival, another partnership with public and private sectors in markets worldwide, expands Elevandi's mission and reach.

Elevandi's education initiatives, such as certificates and mentoring programmes, upskill and reskill the global FinTech community in collaboration with academic and industry partners. Finally, the Elevandi FinTech Insider Report, an annual report on digital advancements for the global FinTech industry, synthesises knowledge from Elevandi's activities with the public and private sectors.

Elevandi aims to become a world-class knowledge platform with fresh insights from initiatives connecting people, including SFF, Green Shoots Series, Inclusive Fintech Forum, and Point Zero Forum. By driving collaboration, education, and new sources of value at the industry and national levels, Elevandi is advancing the development of FinTech in the digital economy.

▸ *Synfindo*

Synfindo is a FinTech company, backed by LemmaTree (a Temasek entity) and Mastercard, with a mission to enable growth for the financial services industry through innovation and digitisation. It owns and operates the APIX platform which was initially built and operated by MAS, International Finance Corporation (part of the World Bank Group) and ASEAN Bankers Association.

APIX serves as a pioneering solution aimed at overcoming the challenges faced by financial institutions (FIs) in the search for FinTech collaborators. This collaborative innovation platform acts as a centralised hub, bringing together the finest FinTechs and innovators from over 90 countries. Its primary objective is to empower FIs in accelerating their innovation journey. By leveraging APIX, FIs gain access to a vast network of global FinTech companies, enabling them to swiftly discover, test, and evaluate innovative solutions. To facilitate this process, APIX hosts innovation challenges and hackathons, allowing FIs to explore and assess potential partnerships seamlessly.

APIX offers numerous advantages to FIs seeking to embrace innovation. Firstly, it serves as a comprehensive repository of FinTech companies, eliminating the cumbersome and time-consuming process of individually sourcing and evaluating potential partners. FIs can now discover and connect with the most suitable FinTechs through a single platform, streamlining the collaboration process significantly. Furthermore, APIX enables real-time testing and evaluation of FinTech capabilities, allowing FIs to make informed decisions promptly. The platform's global reach ensures access to a diverse range of FinTechs, fostering a rich ecosystem of collaboration and knowledge-sharing.

APIX has emerged as a game-changer for the financial services industry, revolutionising the way financial institutions approach innovation and collaboration with FinTechs. The platform's success is evident through its adoption by major global banks, insurers, and regulatory bodies as their go-to platform for driving innovation.

With APIX, FIs can navigate the complex landscape of FinTech partnerships more efficiently, paving the way for enhanced growth and competitiveness in the rapidly evolving financial industry.

Proxtera

Proxtera is the commercialisation of the Business sans Borders initiative led by MAS and the Infocomm Media Development Authority. The company's vision is to create a global, open ecosystem of micro, small, and medium enterprises (MSMEs) via trusted credentials and enable business-to-business (B2B) cross-border trade through services for financing and fulfilment. The company acts as a neutral hub connecting B2B marketplaces, service providers, and trade associations digitally to simplify and amplify trade for SMEs. Proxtera has a network of 18 platforms across Asia and Africa, connecting 400,000 SMEs.

In early 2023, Proxtera announced the successful first close of its Series Seed funding round, which Ant Group, CerraCap Ventures, and EDBI led. The investment will support the development of the company's innovative digital cross-border trade and financial services enabled by trusted credentials. CerraCap Ventures also led Proxtera's previous investment round in 2020.

Proxtera has launched the SME Financial Empowerment programme, the Emerging Markets Currency Exchange, and the Ghana Integrated Financial Corridor to help SMEs easily find competitive forex rates for exotic/illiquid currencies. The company is poised to develop and release more digital products to cover the end-to-end digital trade journey for B2B trade.

Proxtera's mission is to simplify and amplify trade and increase market access for SMEs using technology to grow and scale. It is closely aligned with its investor Ant Group, making it easy to do business anywhere, as shared by **Jia Hang**, Regional General Manager for Southeast Asia Ant Group. He adds that Ant Group is pleased to join other investors and partners in contributing to this collaborative effort to enhance the global SME community's digital capacity and open ecosystem.

Overall, Proxtera's Series Seed funding round and continued growth in the digital trade and finance space demonstrate the company's commitment to providing greater access to finance, FinTech, payments, and other relevant services that support businesses, employment, and local economic development for SMEs.[1]

COSMIC

Safeguarding Singapore's financial centre by preventing money laundering, terrorism financing and proliferation financing is one of the key priorities for MAS and government agencies. In the spirit of "Right First, Fast Later",

[1] https://technode.global/2023/03/17/singapores-proxtera-closes-seed-round-funding-from-ant-group-cerracap-ventures-and-edbi/

MAS conceived an industry consultation process to design a shared industry utility embracing the industry, consumer and regulatory viewpoints to create a long-term solution for the challenge. Utilising the **Singanomics** spirit, financial institutions like banks get support while actively participating in building the platform.

MAS has unveiled a new digital platform named COSMIC, which stands for "Collaborative Sharing of ML/TF Information & Cases". It will enable FIs to securely share information on customers and transactions that cross material risk thresholds to combat money laundering, terrorism financing and proliferation financing. The COSMIC platform is co-created by MAS and six major commercial banks in Singapore, including DBS, OCBC, UOB, SCB, Citibank, and HSBC. It will have strong security features to prevent unauthorised access to information and will be under the management of MAS. MAS will also provide legislation permitting information sharing by FIs only for combating financial crime. COSMIC's regulatory framework will specify the types of information to be shared and the circumstances under which information sharing will be permitted or mandated.

The initial phase focuses on three key financial crime risks in commercial banking: abuse of shell companies, misuse of trade finance for illicit purposes, and proliferation financing. The six banks involved in COSMIC's development will participate in sharing information during this initial phase. MAS plans to progressively extend COSMIC's coverage to more FIs and focus areas and make some sharing aspects mandatory. MAS will also use the platform to detect illicit networks operating in the financial system and target these activities for timely supervisory intervention.

The COSMIC platform is a collaborative initiative between MAS and the major commercial banks in Singapore to facilitate information sharing among FIs to combat financial crime. The platform's unique features include a centralised structured format for information sharing that allows for seamless integration with data analytics tools, making it easier for FIs to collaborate and scale up their efforts to detect and disrupt illicit networks.

KYC Utility 2.0

In 2018, MAS piloted a centralised know your customer (KYC) utility to help streamline and automate KYC processes for small and medium-sized enterprises to engage with financial institutions. The centralised KYC utility idea was first proposed in 2017 and was meant to allow financial institutions to identify and verify potential customers' details seamlessly. The e-KYC utility would have allowed a more efficient way of checking against sanctions and blocklists. In addition, it could have fundamentally changed how banks labour through documents to block illicit funds from money laundering or terrorism financing activities from being channelled through the banking system in Singapore. However in 2018, the Association of Banks in Singapore put the project on hold as the technology was too expensive to implement.

> *"The economics did not work out: our proposed solution would cost more than the savings that banks would be going to get out of it. We tried, failed, will learn, and will do better next time."*
>
> *Ravi Menon, on the centralised KYC utility project*[2]

MAS then announced plans to resurrect the project in 2019.

In the initial days, the inability to make one's startup work was looked down upon, and people would use names like "pivot" and "transition" to accept failure. Over the last few years, thanks to emerging successful startup founders owning up to their mistakes and failures, the stigma associated

[2] Ravi Menon in a speech at the Singapore FinTech Festival 2018, 12 November 2018.

with startups not becoming successful eventually faded. Several founders successfully transitioned from startups to other startups or corporates while bringing their valuable lessons to the other side.

API Exchange

Singapore is obsessive about planning, which is easily attributable to the *kiasu* aspect of Singaporeans' personalities. However, as the number of FinTech startups started growing, there were challenges around these solutions' reliability, scalability, discoverability and sustainability. While debating on how to tap into network effects, Navin Suri, a former banker turned FinTech entrepreneur, and Sopnendu Mohanty, Chief FinTech Officer at MAS, came up with the blueprint for FinTechs to operate in a controlled sandbox environment to prove their solutions to the financial institutions while growing their coverage to as many markets as possible.

Singapore is geographically a small market for direct-to-customer applications due to its small population. Hence, at the onset, it was clear that there needs to be a concerted effort to nurture and scale the FinTech sector by finding them customers regionally and globally. Furthermore, since most of Asia's headquarters of financial institutions are based in Singapore, there was a significant focus on B2B FinTech solutions to cater to business needs for digital transformation and innovation.

On the global APIX marketplace, financial institutions and FinTech firms can discover and connect efficiently and cost-effectively. The APIX sandbox allows financial institutions and FinTech firms to collaboratively design experiments to validate digital solutions in different scenarios via APIs. APIX facilitates financial institutions' adoption of APIs and enables them to rapidly deploy new digital solutions to underserved markets in ASEAN and other parts of the world.

"MAS is encouraged by the strong support from the industry and regulators for the AFIN industry sandbox. The sandbox will facilitate broader adoption of FinTech innovation and enhance financial access for a wider population. In addition, the joint platform for experimentation between banks and FinTechs allows regulators to understand financial innovations better. This will, in turn, encourage policy harmonisation and partnerships to make ASEAN an even more conducive market for businesses and investment."

Sopnendu Mohanty[3]

This infrastructure was built before the world thought about any pandemics and lockdowns. It became the lifeline of the FinTech sector in the aftermath of COVID-19. APIX became a single point of enabling a new wave of proof of concept (POC) projects to be sponsored through government grants. Over 600 startups signed up for the process, representing over half of the FinTech companies currently in Singapore. Multiple corporates have joined the initiative to procure solutions from the startups through APIX and have embraced the opportunity provided due to a slowdown in the overall business.

ASEAN Financial Innovation Network (AFIN) is a not-for-profit entity based in Singapore. The charter of AFIN is to speed up the collaboration process between financial institutions and FinTechs. APIX, the API exchange, is AFIN's first product. APIX came into existence as a minimum viable product launched in 2018 during the Singapore FinTech Festival (SFF). Since then, AFIN has spent much time taking feedback from potential users, members and customers.

[3] Joint Media Release, "ASEAN Financial Innovation Network to support financial services innovation and inclusion", 16 November 2017, www.mas.gov.sg/news/media-releases/2017/asean-financial-innovation-network-to-support-financial-services-innovation-and-inclusion

When the idea for AFIN was in the early stages, Rachel Freeman was with the International Finance Corporation (IFC), which is one of the shareholders of AFIN. IFC was heavily involved in financial inclusion and financial services but felt that they could do more to deliver impact. Banks were also moving towards digitisation. The IFC needed a way to help the ASEAN banks digitise without having to go to each bank on a personal level, which would have been inefficient and time consuming.

Singapore FinTechs also needed help in terms of obtaining user volume, as Singapore provides a relatively small consumer base for businesses. There was a need for a vehicle that could help these Singapore FinTechs expand into the wider ASEAN region.

This manifested in the creation of AFIN. One major challenge was getting all regulators on board. ASEAN Bankers Association needed to create AFIN as MAS and IFC were unable to do so due to restrictions. On top of this, every country's banking association had to approve the creation of AFIN. Education had to be provided to get these countries on board, in partnership with Percipient and Fidor Solutions. AFIN was also endorsed by Queen Máxima of the Netherlands, lending credibility to the project.

APIX, at its core, is a public sandbox. It is a global FinTech marketplace. AFIN has signed Memorandums of Understanding (MoUs) with almost 12 FinTech associations globally, and they continue to add to the numbers. They have been able to create a pipeline of nearly 1,000 FinTechs today by reaching out to them through MoUs with the associations. A core aspect of the AFIN platform is the API catalogue. All the FinTech companies who are onboarded get the opportunity to display their products and capabilities. Besides the API endpoints, startups can now upload their pre-built solutions (called the solutions catalogue) on the APIX platform. One can run the whole solution on the APIX platform. This allows the startup to showcase its end-to-end solution capabilities.

Manish Diwaan, Managing Director at APIX and AFIN from 2019 to 2022, shares that their collective vision at APIX is that, at some point in time, FinTech startups will start using the APIX solutions catalogue for their solutions, similar to how working professionals have networked through LinkedIn. Besides providing the technology, APIX has built a vast and vibrant community of like-minded people who talk about technology, want to solve problems, help other people solve problems, and grow together as a community. Hence, it is known as the APIX community platform.

AFIN started with three public utility board members (IFC, MAS, ASEAN Bankers Association), with Mastercard and AMTD joining in 2019. Manish shares that their initial members were all regulators, policymakers, and an umbrella of associations of banks, with a limited view on the actual market dynamics and the ground realities of things, which was very important for what AFIN was building. As such, they implemented a strategic advisory council. AFIN became their eyes and ears to the market, helping to take APIX to the next level. On the advisory board, there are infrastructure service providers like AWS, Credit Bureaus and BNY Mellon. ASEAN countries, including Cambodia, have also increased their involvement, with the National Bank of Cambodia director-general Chea Serey joining the advisory board in 2021.

The Institute of Banking and Finance Singapore

The Institute of Banking and Finance Singapore (IBF) was appointed the Jobs Development Partner (JDP) for financial services in October 2020 by the National Jobs Council chaired by then Senior Minister Tharman Shanmugaratnam. As JDP, IBF works closely with MAS on furthering the jobs and skills agenda for the financial services sector.

Since 2018, IBF is the appointed programme manager to administer Professional Conversion Programmes (PCP) by Workforce Singapore for the financial industry. As at August 2021, about 50 financial institutions are on the programme and have committed to reskill close to 6,000 individuals through PCP. In addition, to help expand the pool of technology talent for the financial services sector, IBF launched the Technology in Finance Immersion Programme (TFIP) in 2019 to help early/mid-career professionals' transit into technology roles in the financial services sector. Trainees were trained and placed into in-demand areas such as Data Analytics, Artificial Intelligence, Cybersecurity, Cloud Computing and Software Engineering. This was well received and over 2019 and 2020, the programme assisted close to 260 trainees gain skills and experience in leading financial institutions. TFIP was further expanded in 2021, with financial institutions committing to host up to 450 new trainees and IBF also launched new tracks to address other in-demand areas such as Digital Marketing, UX Design, Agile IT Project Management, Business Analysis, and Technology Product Management.

On the skills development front, MAS and IBF introduced enhanced course fee subsidies in April 2020 to help finance professionals enhance their skills during the pandemic downtime. This resulted in more than 60% increase in training participation year-on-year. The scheme was further extended in 2021 to keep up the training momentum and help entrench the continuous learning and upskilling culture as the sector transforms. As the national accreditation and certification agency for financial industry competency in Singapore under the Skills Framework for Financial Services, IBF encourages all finance professionals to be constantly aware of job role changes and continuously upskill to stay relevant.

IBF Chief Executive Officer, Ng Nam Sin, says, "IBF understands that while skills upgrading is an individual effort, employers and the government also have a role to play in supporting the deepening of capabilities, especially in growth areas. As the JDP for the financial sector, IBF will continue to guide financial services professionals and job seekers in their skills upgrading journey and continually expand our course offerings with in-demand and future skills courses for a competitive financial sector workforce in Singapore." To this end we can see the tremendous support accorded by IBF in this journey for FinTech space as well.

International Hubs and Bridges

Built on trading foundations, Singapore has always consistently focused on building international bridges and collaborations. As a small local market, internationalisation is the founding DNA of many businesses. Moreover, as one of the most developed countries in GDP per capita, it is an effective talent magnet, increasing the need to build sustainable relations with its neighbours. It encourages these relations at all levels, including government, regulators, private sectors and industry associations.

Wai Lum Kwok joined the Financial Services Regulatory Authority (FSRA) of the Abu Dhabi Global Market (ADGM) in June 2015. He headed the Capital Markets division from 2019 to 2021, responsible for authorising and supervising financial market infrastructures and capital markets intermediaries. The division also regulates the offering of securities and collective investment schemes. In 2022, he became the Senior Executive Director of the Authorisation division. Wai Lum, a Singaporean from MAS, also spearheads FSRA's strategy and efforts to support the supervision of innovation in FinTech and the development of the FinTech ecosystem in ADGM. He shares his observations of Singapore as a FinTech hub from the perspective of someone abroad looking in.

MAS is experienced in developing ecosystems, from developing the financial hub in Singapore and now into the FinTech space. It collaborates across different ministries to push forward the agenda that gets set. In this case, the push in FinTech starting in 2015 came because of the Chief FinTech Officer and his novel approach to setting up a regulatory sandbox to bridge relationships between startups, regulators and incumbent banks. They set up a comprehensive set of rules and regulations for the FinTech sector; however, legacy regulations are creeping into new sections of FinTech, such as asset management. However, MAS has been very agile in adjusting for the regulatory creep, which has been impressive for a matured financial sector like Singapore.

One key stumbling block Wai Lum sees in Singapore would be legacy issues. Singapore is a matured hub for financial services, and these legacy regulations may cause friction with the disruption occurring in the FinTech space. Singapore has been very agile in this regard by being progressive on the regulatory front. It works well with the startups, incumbents, and other ministries, to adjust rules and regulations pragmatically. However, it takes a lot of time, and changes tend to occur over years compared to Abu Dhabi that is building from the ground up and is not mature yet.

Singapore is viewed as the hub for FinTech in Asia. On a global scale, the UK used to be the leader, but at this point, many feel Singapore has taken that crown due to the Brexit turmoil. Plus, Singapore is more agile in adjusting to the new requirements of FinTech within the existing financial framework. A key competitive advantage that Singapore has compared to other jurisdictions is attracting talent and a strong fiscal position. These two factors combined allow Singapore to come up with progressive and agile schemes to attract talent while being able to fund through ample fiscal reserves.

Thomas Krogh Jensen has a storied career in financial services, and insurance, and has been serving as the CEO of Copenhagen FinTech since 2016. He is also a board member of the Danish IT Society (Dansk IT), Digital Hub Denmark, Disruption Task Force via the Ministry of Industry Business and Financial Affairs, and the Danish Entrepreneurship Commission. He draws some comparisons between the Singaporean and Nordic FinTech landscapes.

He was first exposed to the Singapore FinTech landscape by attending the annual SFF. Having met world leaders at the festival, including Narendra Modi of India and Justin Trudeau of Canada, he realised that Singapore had leapfrogged in showcasing FinTech proficiency. Since then, he has been actively involved in bridging the Nordic and Singapore ecosystems and sees both value and challenges shared by both systems.

MAS has done a great job of being liberalised and proactive in the FinTech space. The Chief FinTech Officer is the key player here, having signed the first MoU internationally between MAS and Denmark. MAS has been a guiding star for the Danish/Nordic FinTech landscape and thus shows the first signs of Singapore's leadership in this space. The success at MAS inspired the regulatory sandbox in Denmark. This demonstrates a strong culture of collaboration not just within teams but across borders. The following year, Denmark sent a large delegation to the FinTech festival, and it opened their eyes to how big the opportunity is globally. Once again, MAS and the Singapore landscape led the way by example.

The highly collaborative culture, digital infrastructure and a human-centred design thinking approach have allowed the Nordic landscape to flourish in this space. This is the takeaway from the Nordic countries as to what could be a competitive advantage beyond just building an ecosystem.

Singapore's strengths are the planning, data-driven approach to innovation and sector growth. Rather than following what much of the world does, which is to go after everything, Singapore tends to focus on key verticals. As a result, it seems to have the most payoff or a competitive advantage. This is mainly due to the political and bureaucratic system in place here, which is something that other countries aim to emulate.

The key hubs are London, New York, Hong Kong and Singapore. But over the past few years, Singapore has leapfrogged the other centres outside New York. London has lost its crown due to the Brexit issues. Nevertheless,

Singapore's approach has been a huge success over the past few years. The approach of having both a grassroots initiative and connecting with the global community of FinTech has been the lynchpin to this growth, differentiating Singapore from the more hub focus of New York and London.

In the future, he envisions three big global hubs — the US, China and Singapore. The US and China would be more closed and regional focused, while Singapore stands to be the key area for ASEAN and potentially into Europe through collaboration.

Singapore is different from the Nordic landscape in the number of homegrown startups. The Nordic landscape, as mentioned earlier, is nearly 90%, but with Singapore, it is considerably lower. While this is a weakness for Singapore, it also speaks volumes for the openness and willingness for the ecosystem to co-opt startups from the region and the world. The sentiments in the industry are that digital transformation initiatives will accelerate due to the pandemic. FinTech will play a big role in not just innovating the current financial landscape but also helping to expand the reach of the financial services industry. The big relief packages will create a need for more open banking, expansion of reach and reduction of friction in transactions, all of which can be addressed via new FinTech developments.

For over six years, Francesca McKee has led UK–Singapore FinTech engagement at the British High Commission in Singapore. Her FinTech career started in 2015 when Chris Woolard, then Head of Innovation & Strategy at the Financial Conduct Authority (FCA) (the UK regulator), came to Singapore. The ecosystems on both sides were relatively nascent — the FCA's pioneering sandbox would not launch for another nine months. Chris and Francesca met with MAS's then newly appointed Chief FinTech Officer, Sopnendu Mohanty. They also toured OCBC's new Open Vault, saw Aviva apply the finishing touches to its Digital Garage, and met new Singaporean FinTech startups like Bambu over at Block 71. Since 2020,

Francesca has moved to a new role as the Head of Financial Services, Asia Pacific, in the Department for International Trade.

The landscape quickly shifted as FinTech became the topic of every conversation on the future of financial services. The UK and Singapore swiftly became global FinTech hubs — and this became a key element of their government-to-government cooperation.

The FinTech ecosystem went into overdrive from there. Francesca has attended every SFF over the last five years. There are now almost 50 UK FinTechs with presence across the Asia-Pacific, with unicorns such as Revolut, Greensill and Rapyd growing their businesses quickly in the region. Transferwise, one of the first UK FinTechs to spot the opportunity in Asia, has gone from their one expansion lead in Singapore in 2017 to over 100 people across the region today, with plans to grow further. Likewise, Singaporean FinTechs have expanded into the UK — like Bambu.

MAS has also demonstrated a wealth of thought leadership and foresight on future trends within FinTech — for example, through its "green FinTech" focused hackathon and support for digital trade. However, sometimes even when the regulators are doing the right thing and creating an enabling environment for FinTechs, financial institutions can retain a cultural resistance to working with these newer community members. The Global Financial Innovation Network (GFIN) works with the financial services sector to share case studies on how they have managed this in the UK to encourage more openness to partnerships within this innovative sector. Initiatives like the FCA-chaired GFIN, of which three of its founding members are from Asia (including Singapore), are critical to facilitating greater openness and cross-border cooperation.

With its growing, young, tech-savvy and underbanked population, Southeast Asia has immense potential for FinTech growth. Many regulators around the region are making great progress through their own FinTech offices, sandboxes and other initiatives. As one of the world's leading FinTech hubs, the UK is keen to share its experience with the region.

The "Prosperity Fund ASEAN Economic Reform" programme helps drive these discussions and support the development of FinTech ecosystems across the region. For example, the UK government is working on P2P regulation with Indonesia, eKYC frameworks with Thailand, and crowdfunding regulation with Vietnam, and are exploring ways to bring regional regulators together with our UK counterparts to discuss trends and ways to support FinTechs. To supplement this, they launched the "UK-SE Asia FinTech Series" in 2020 to bring UK FinTechs into the region to form closer partnerships with this rapidly growing market.

Singapore continues to be an attractive option for UK FinTechs looking to expand into the Asia-Pacific, with a progressive regulator and high ranking in ease of doing business. In addition, given the wealth of opportunities across the region, many UK FinTech firms use Singapore as a regional hub, so there is a growing role for Singapore to act as a channel to the rest of Southeast Asia and the Asia-Pacific through various FinTech initiatives. Some are underway, but there is scope for more, potentially in partnership with the UK.

She expects increased interest from UK FinTechs in Singapore and vice versa, in the coming years, given the acceleration of digital trends post-COVID-19. There is particular interest in FinTech solutions that support a green and sustainable recovery — including those targeting financial inclusion (e.g., InsurTech), sustainable finance, greater transparency and clarity around regulation (RegTech).

In conclusion, while we keep emphasising the importance of cultivating symbiotic relationships and fostering a virtuous cycle of growth, it is important to adopt a holistic perspective, illuminating the multifaceted aspects of network orchestration that extend beyond mere technological connectivity.

One of the most remarkable aspects of the discussions in this chapter, is the significance of creating a common purpose and shared values that resonate across all participants in a network. We stress the need for continuous adaptation and learning, encouraging network orchestrators to embrace experimentation and the evolution of their ecosystems.

Hence, the critical role of trust, transparency, and inclusivity in nurturing network effects will be necessary ingredients to power up collaborations and open platforms in driving innovation.

Chapter 7

FUELLING INNOVATION — VENTURE CAPITAL

The FinTech ecosystem in Singapore has witnessed substantial growth and investment activity since 2015, making it an attractive destination for venture capital firms and investors seeking opportunities in the sector. The venture capital landscape in Singapore's FinTech sector has experienced remarkable growth and transformation. The proactive initiatives taken by the Monetary Authority of Singapore (MAS) to foster FinTech innovation and development have played a pivotal role in positioning Singapore as a leading global hub for financial technology.

Landscape

Since 2015, Singapore has emerged as a vibrant hub for financial technology (FinTech), fueled by the proactive efforts of MAS. In 2015, MAS established the Financial Technology and Innovation Group to oversee the development of the country's FinTech industry. This marked the beginning of Singapore's FinTech journey, which has since witnessed remarkable growth and investment activity.

In 2022, FinTech investments in Singapore reached a significant milestone, with a total value of USD4.1B across 250 deals in mergers & acquisitions (M&A), private equity (PE), and venture capital (VC). This figure represented a year-on-year increase of 22% and marked the highest investment in three years. It is worth noting that this achievement came after a record high of USD5.62B in 2019, just before the outbreak of the COVID-19 pandemic.

The rise of FinTech funding in Singapore has been impressive. In 2015, the total funding in the sector amounted to USD299M. Fast forward to 2022, and the total equity funding for FinTech in Singapore reached an astounding USD3.4B. This represents an increase of 11.2% from the previous year and a staggering 11.6-fold rise compared to 2015. The Payments cluster accounted for the largest share of funding, with USD1.1B invested.

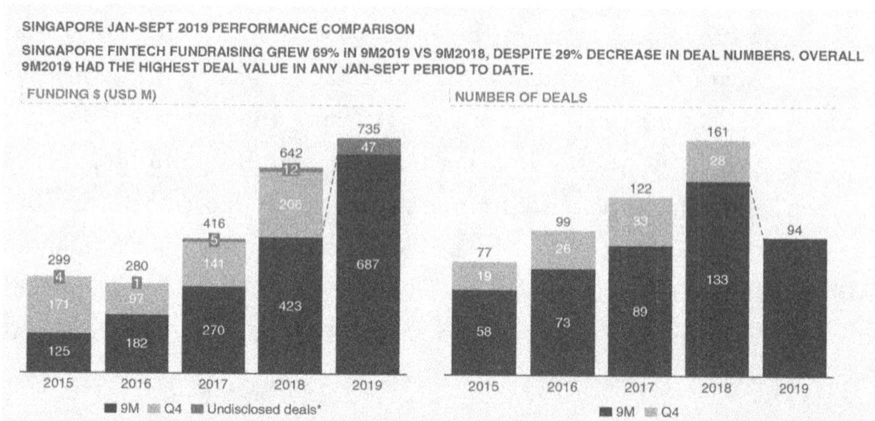

Note: Investment values referred to only deals with amount reported by CB Insights, Pitchbook, Tracxn and undisclosed venture capital transactions data provided by the MAS and deals volumes referred to all deals.

Disclaimer: There might be variations in historical numbers in new releases of the Fintech Watchtower as Accenture Research performs historical review of the previous data in every release which include, not limiting to, adding/removing deals from database based on relevance.

Source: Accenture Research analysis on CB Insights, Pitchbook and Tracxn databases.
*Undisclosed venture capital transactions data was provided by the MAS.

As of April 2023, there were 1,113 FinTech firms in Singapore and they continue to dominate the FinTech equity funding landscape in ASEAN, accounting for 74% of the total equity funding in the region during that period. The Financial Infrastructure and Trading & Investments clusters in the ASEAN equity funding were solely comprised of Singaporean investments, further underscoring the country's leading position. This demonstrates the concentration of FinTech activities and investments in Singapore, solidifying its position as the leading FinTech hub in Southeast Asia.

The success of Singapore's venture capital landscape in the FinTech sector can be attributed to several factors. The supportive regulatory environment, robust infrastructure, access to a diverse talent pool, and strong government support have all contributed to creating an ecosystem that attracts investors and entrepreneurs alike.

Singapore today is one of the top FinTech hubs in the world based on Fintech Ranking from a range of global consulting firms, and for Singapore to sustain and improve its position, it needs to prepare for the future.

The Global FinTech Marketplace report 2022–2027 has come up with the following findings:

- The global FinTech market will reach USD225.1B by 2027, growing at a 12.9% compound annual growth rate (CAGR).
- The largest software segment, with 47% of the global market share.
- The digital payments segment is the largest solution, with 94% of the global market.
- The US, UK, China, Germany and India are the largest countries in the global FinTech market.
- The Americas is the largest region, with 76% of the global FinTech investment market.

As of August 2020, the capital markets space counts 2,160 FinTechs that have attracted USD10B of equity funding. Trading and investments account for 90% (USD9.1B) of the cumulative equity financing amount raised by capital markets in FinTechs globally. Unlike other FinTech sub-clusters that have grown significantly in the last five years, the CAGR has been -5%. This is predominantly due to a sharp drop in funding in 2019, as equity financing amounts fell by 38% to USD696M. On the other hand, over the past circa 20 years, FinTech companies in primary markets have attracted about USD900M, of which approximately 50% was raised in 2018 and 2019 alone. Direct issuance and trading account for about 80% of the total cluster funding and include companies facilitating connections between market participants and mainly supporting pre-IPO companies to issue traditional or tokenised securities.

Singapore counts approximately 350 capital markets in FinTechs, representing about USD2.9B of equity funding to date (April 2022). As of then, this sector also experienced the highest number of acquisitions of Singapore-headquartered FinTechs among all FinTech clusters, at 27. This makes up just over one-third of total such acquisitions across all clusters.

Venture Capital

Singapore became independent only in 1965 and did not have a well-established professional venture capital (VC) industry. Learning from Israel and Silicon Valley, Singapore's leaders figured out that to attract the best founders across the region, Singapore will need to develop its homegrown VC. One where we can have a generation of successful founders who have exited the business, and the capital can start to flow back into the ecosystem. It is a chicken-and-egg problem that Singapore must crack while ensuring it aligns with the **Singanomics** principle of rewarding performance.

Early in the journey, Singapore understood that it needed to develop a base of local VC players backing local FinTech players to create a "Venture-Loop" effect. Singapore needs its homegrown leaders to build the next generation of entrepreneurs and venture funds. To foster this, the government created a massive programme to kickstart FinTech and startup innovation.

In June 2015, MAS committed SGD225M over five years for the following four purposes: innovation centres, institution-level projects, industry-wide projects and PoC scheme. In addition, the government introduced the Angel Investment Tax Deduction Scheme to encourage angel investment activity.

In December 2017, MAS announced a SGD27M Artificial Intelligence and Data Analytics Grant under the Financial Sector Technology and Innovation Scheme. In 2017, nearly USD2B capital was made available to the FinTech startups at SFF.

In 2020, MAS announced another USD125M FinTech fund to help startups in light of the COVID-19 challenges, in addition to USD258M committed to the overall startup sector.

FinTech firms in Singapore had raised SGD462M in equity funding in the first half of 2020, 19% higher than over the same period of the previous year, along with SGD188M in mergers and acquisitions. The fact that this was achieved during the COVID-19 crisis demonstrates investors' confidence in the long-term value FinTech firms will create in Singapore. As of September 2021, there were 1,350 operating FinTech firms in Singapore, which remained the highest among Southeast Asian countries since 2017. In addition, Singapore announced a scheme where the government would become a limited partner in VC funds on a 1:1 match basis. The government would match every dollar for the VC raised from the private sector up to a predefined amount. Some of the most known VC funds in Singapore are the output of this programme, Early Stage Venture Fund (ESVF), and led to the creation of Jungle Ventures, Tembusu Partners, Monk's Hill, Walden International and Golden Gate Ventures. These measures have been so successful that Singapore ranks top in attracting more venture capital investment per capita in 2022 than all other countries receiving over USD1B.

Two unique things about these investor and founder networks were the magnetic effect of this to attract international talent on both sides of the equation and the creation of another "Invented in Singapore" concept called "Co-Founder VC".

Most of the VC and founders in Singapore were first-timers, so they were learning on the job, making mistakes together, and building resilience through the challenges they faced.

> *"I chose to build Instarem (now Nium) in Singapore because the country offers business-friendly support from the government, widespread access to venture capital, an entrepreneurial community, and access to some of the world's best talent. While Singapore has incubated several world-class companies, such as ours, the startup ecosystem is still nascent. For it to compete on the world stage, we need to nurture and mentor new founders as they establish new ventures. I've personally invested my time and resources in being a source of knowledge for founders, openly sharing my failures and successes, in the hope that someone in the community applies to learn from me to build what could be the next big thing."*
>
> *Prajit Nanu, Founder and CEO, Nium*

Across Southeast Asia, there has been an increasing focus on inclusivity, meaning access to credit is required. However, there currently needs to be more meaningful access to credit at low prices in Southeast Asia. The current presence of loan sharks in Singapore may signal market failure. With a strong digital identity and digital distribution of financial products, and a focus on lowering transaction processing costs, this credit problem can begin to be fixed. There is also the problem of bureaus: bureaus only serve the existing market, not the emerging market. How do you fill this emerging market with no data? How do you create data to serve this market?

Joel Yarbrough says this is the problem to solve — ensuring everyone is included in the market.

A co-founder is more than a partner. They are a sounding board for ideas, someone you can continuously nudge for business opportunities or introduction, someone who would fight with you at the front lines, but more importantly, someone you can feel safe being candid with — regardless of good or bad news. With a co-founder mentality, the staff at Vertex Ventures pour their hearts into the business. They continually think of ways to work with the management team to help push their portfolio companies forward.

Vertex takes a unique approach to building relationships with its portfolio companies. It chooses a small number of companies to invest in and puts in much effort to help them from start to end. Vertex gets involved in the company's recruitment, business development and growth processes. It strives to be very hands-on and help shift the company's direction. Vertex pushes for input but always leaves it to the founders to decide. It takes a very active approach to the development and growth of the startup.

> *"One of the most fulfilling moments in my VC career was when InstaReM's founder, Prajit, introduced me to his friends in a unique, most heartfelt manner. He mentioned, 'Vertex is our Series A round investor, but beyond that, he is also a co-founder of InstaReM'."*
>
> *Genping Liu, 2020, in a personal interview*

Traditional metrics of benchmarking VC by frequency of deals are less preferred for a relationship-first Asian culture, where depth and intensity of involvement in sales are critical to developing long-term relationships. For example, Vertex famously was the first institutional money in the most useful super app in ASEAN, Grab. The commitment was showcased by a single-line comment by Grab Founder Anthony Tan, "Vertex believed in me when nobody else did".

Grab started in 2012 as a mobility platform and has since successfully transformed itself into a simple app, providing localised services such as ride-hailing and deliveries (food, packages and groceries) to users in Southeast Asia. In 2018, Grab launched Grab Financial Group (GFG), its FinTech division, offering mobile payments and financial services (lending, insurance and retail wealth management) across the region. Today, Grab has over 205 million mobile downloads, which means roughly one in three people in Southeast Asia have downloaded its app.

Reuben Lai, then Group Senior Managing Director, Head of Grab Financial Group, states in his interview that the motivation behind Grab's foray into financial services was based on the insight that existing banks and financial institutions did not optimally serve its driver-partners, merchant-partners and consumers. So what exactly are these gaps?

Reuben cites several examples: "Firstly, some of our drivers cannot get loans to buy cars to drive on Grab due to the fluctuating nature of their income. Secondly, most transactions are still cash-based as existing e-wallets do not have a strong value proposition for customers. Finally, many customers are under-insured as policies are difficult to understand, and pricing tends to be high and rigid".

To solve the gap in financial services for the underbanked, GFG has to use technology to achieve three objectives. Firstly, to increase accessibility through fractional pricing. Secondly, it offers greater convenience by embedding financial transactions into everyday life. Thirdly, to create more trust via radical transparency. GFG has experienced early success. It has helped to open more than 1.7 million bank accounts for its customers. GrabPay is one of the most popular e-wallets in the region. Through its GrabPay platform, GFG has sold more than 20 million micro-insurance policies. It is also one of the fastest-growing FinTech lenders by disbursals today.

On the back of this early traction, GFG launched GrabInvest, after Grab acquired Bento in February 2020. The company intends to make retail wealth management and investment solutions more accessible and convenient to its ecosystem of users, driver-partners and merchant-partners.

Reuben says, "Our customers work hard for their money, yet inflation erodes this hard-earned money if they leave it in a savings account. The launch of GrabInvest brings us closer to democratising access to affordable financial solutions that will help them reach their financial goals faster".

What are the challenges facing FinTechs in the region? According to Reuben, the large number of innovative FinTechs in Singapore allows the nation to serve as a hub to address the wider Southeast Asian market. In his opinion, the main competition FinTechs in Singapore face would be from international firms, which may choose to expand into the region and compete. Reuben states that adopting a hyper-local strategy is the key to overcoming this challenge.

Finally, Reuben stresses the need for a vibrant financial services ecosystem. He likens this to almost being like a tribal community, where FinTech firms and financial institutions work together and leverage each other's strengths to serve customers better and grow the overall market. This concept of cohesion is much needed in the industry and could enhance the general industry in the long run by sharing/exchanging ideas for mutual benefit.

Integra Partners, formerly Dymon Asia Capital, is Singapore's leading early-stage venture firm. Integra Partners invests in early-stage companies that leverage technology to drive access and affordability of financial services, insurance, and digital health in Southeast Asia. Since its founding, Integra Partners has partnered with 18 founders to solve difficult problems in credit, payments, FX, investments, and deep technology areas such as cyber security, quantum computing, and distributed ledgers. Christiaan Kaptein is a partner and member of the investment committee of Integra Partners.

Chris shares that Singapore's strength lies in a friendly and open jurisdiction to investors whilst maintaining a robust MAS regulatory framework for VCs. In addition, it enjoys the strategic advantage of being an easily accessible travel hub, positioning it as an attractive area for corporates. Proper corporate positioning has resulted in big companies such as Facebook, Google, Visa and Mastercard headquartering their APAC offices in Singapore.

Chris sees that the industry is moving into FinTech 2.0. He believes that the roadmap for this upgraded version of FinTech will be payments, banking, and insurance. The industry requires a real-time payments system, digital know your customer (KYC), onboarding, and digital identity to achieve this. All of these factors are present in Singapore. Governments and regulators are also paying more attention to open banking in the face of COVID-19. The pandemic has shown that there are still many points of failure in the value chain that can be eliminated by employing digital financial services.

Over the years, the end of human labour has been predicted many times. Upskilling is the key. The workforce must upskill to continue to add value. This will create overall wealth, increasing everyone's share of the pie. Chris feels that the basis of this is to educate the entire population, focusing more on those who need it the most and not just on those who can get there themselves.

With FinTech 2.0, FinTech will become an embedded ingredient in businesses. This is already happening today. For example, when customers need a loan, they apply for a product with a banker in a branch. Chris shares that the industry now sees that a customer is no longer required to go to a bank branch to get a loan. FinTech will likely be the future of financial services, although these transitions could take a few decades to complete.

From his perspective, Chris feels that Singapore banks are well on their way to becoming digitised. As observed in Singapore, the typical global trend is that consumer banking goes first. However, in the banking sector, there is still room for improvement. Some examples include an extremely high FX fee on credit card transactions and the need to digitise other small and medium-sized enterprises (SMEs) and wholesale banking slowly.

Chris' wish list is to see regulators and governments across the region trying to solve the most critical pain points. From an infrastructure point of view, Singapore needs to build certain crucial aspects. Some examples include a European-style open banking system with real-time payments, interoperable banking systems, low or zero-cost digital identities and digital KYC systems.

> *"You can build the most advanced car, but if there's no road to drive on, what's the point?"*
>
> *Chris Kaptein, 2020, in a personal interview*

Wong Joo Seng, one of the portfolio founders of Integra Partners, shares the differences between Singapore and Silicon Valley. In Silicon Valley, some VCs specifically focus on a narrow vertical within technology. Singapore has yet to have that level of scale, so VCs here must remain broad and develop a depth of knowledge in all verticals.

Integra Partners Asia Capital portfolio companies align with Chris' view of FinTech 2.0. Integra Partners' main aim is to increase the access to and affordability of financial services, with a significant focus on B2B2C to reach out to consumers indirectly.

Chris shares that this is an exciting time for Integra Partners and the industry. He predicts that they will see a lot of more exciting companies to partner with within the coming years. For example, many companies are entering the SME banking space, which is still an underserved market.

Currently, Integra Partners is in the process of adding HealthTech to its portfolio. Now, it is only involved in the finance and insurance spaces. Integra Partners' investment thesis is that finance, insurance, health and education will be the key points to address in Southeast Asia. Healthcare has relevant financial services synergy. Chris shares that the critical question in healthcare will always be: Who will pay for it? Insurance and credit are vital aspects. Thus, it makes sense that in 2022, Integra Partners made an offer to Singapore O&G, a healthcare services provider.

The team at Integra Partners connects with SMEs by having a robust online presence, being on the ground and travelling to talk to different SMEs. Chris shares that, ultimately, the VC is investing in the people, not the idea. He says having brilliant people with a plan is better than vice versa. VCs also look at the market size and the competition in the SME market before making investment decisions.

Apis Partners is a private equity asset manager focused on financial services in growth markets. It mainly focuses on private equity, financial services and investment banking. Some companies listed on their investment portfolio are Hero FinCorp, CodaPay, Tutuka, Qlink, EPS, Baobab, and the DPO Group. In 2019, the firm raised USD550M with total commitments of USD563M, including the GP commitment, exceeding the initial target fund size of USD400M. Investors committing to this funding round include global banks, insurance companies, development financial institutions, funds of funds, pension funds, sovereign wealth funds and family offices across major global investor markets in the US, Europe, Africa, the Middle East and Asia.

This is the second growth fund by the firm, and this "Fund II" will support companies with innovative business models adapted to local conditions and addressing a large portion of the unbanked or underbanked populations.

Nigel Lee started in the FinTech sector in 2000 with Electronic Data Systems and has seen the evolution of financial services firsthand. In 2022, Nigel will be a Senior Advisor to Apis Partners in Singapore and the APAC Senior Vice President for the Terminals, Solutions & Services Global Business Line.

When Nigel came to Singapore in 2010, there was a real dearth of VCs in Singapore. But ever since then, there has been a surge of investment in the country, leading to several firms eyeing the region as an untapped market. There are three things that Nigel sees that set Singapore apart from other players in ASEAN: the competence of its workforce, a massive influx of international capital, and a structured legal system.

BEENEXT is a VC firm investing in startups from India, Southeast Asia, Japan and the US. The VC has seen five exits and focuses on early-stage and seed capital. It currently has just shy of USD350M worth of assets under management.

Dirk van Quaquebeke is a Managing Partner at BEENEXT. He has lived in Asia since 2009, building and investing in early-stage tech companies for over 15 years. He actively participates in over a dozen company boards and has led investments in over 50 companies, such as Trusting Social, Bank Open, FleetX, YAP, Cropin, and Zenius. Before BEENEXT, he founded and led the company builder Alps Ventures Pte Ltd. Out of which more than a dozen incubations and investments were made; he headed an active operating role in three different ventures.

BEENEXT is a VC headed by experienced entrepreneurs aiming to support the next generation. It uses technology as a conduit to reach more people in a much more affordable manner, reshaping what is considered possible and what is not. At the start, it invested in payments and marketplace successes. Over time, its portfolio has expanded to over 180 countries.

As an early-stage investor, BEENEXT has minimal data on the founder and company traction. Dirk shares an analogy on surfing. While anticipating the next set of waves, you, as an investor, will sit and wait. You wait for the right surfer: a domain expert who can tell you what he is building, why he thinks a massive market dislocation is happening, how that will play out, and why. The right surfer will bring the investor to a sport with geographical and geophysical advantages at the right time. He will then share why it is the right place and time. Sometimes, the waves are evident to investors and are visible. The last aspect is the choice of the board. The board is likened to the decisions a founder has made for his company up to that point, which will either make or break the company, determining whether the founder and his startup can start surfing again. The best spots that amaze Dirk are consistent, beautiful waves of significant size where there is no competition. These are the hardest to find, and caution must still be exercised. One never knows why there is no competition — is there a rift under the sea or dangerous rocks? There needs to be a careful analysis of market dynamics under the surface.

Many VCs meet potential startups through their connections or networking events. Funding is provided, and the VCs may monitor the progress of the portfolio company. What makes BEENEXT unique is its Founder First approach. BEENEXT establishes a strong partnership with startup founders to serve their portfolio companies to the best of their ability.

The VC also carries this hands-on, vibrant spirit into building a strong startup community amongst its portfolio companies. When a founder partners with BEENEXT, the founder partners with the entire BEENEXT community. BEENEXT provides opportunities for co-creation, inclusive growth, knowledge exchange, mentorship and capital support. One way in which this is done is through the BEE Global Camps. The BEE Global

Camps break down barriers to networking by bringing all founders together in a transparent, intimate space. The camps work to get everyone forward together. BEENEXT started the journey of BEE Global Camps back in 2014 in Singapore and has continued this tradition since then. The next stop was in 2015 in Bali, in 2016 in Bangalore, in 2018 in Ho Chi Minh, and, most recently, in 2019 in Tokyo.

Dirk feels that Southeast Asia is fragmented. As a European, he has seen the emergence of a shared common currency and the breaking down of European borders. Dirk feels that Southeast Asia is very early in this process regarding infrastructure and removing friction between edges. He believes the jury is out as to whether this is a good model or not as well. This lack of free movement within Southeast Asia presents a difficulty for FinTechs looking to expand. Dirk believes that the next wave in the region is cross-border commerce and trade financing. International types and connectors are starting to be built, which also shows in BEENEXT's investments.

He splits FinTech into categories. The first is tech and data: it does not touch the physical world, is pretty innovative, and sees the most real innovation. The next category is tech-enabled services (e.g., Grab, GoJek). These are breakthrough innovations from a business model and engineering proof-of-value. This is where engineering of how the historical flow of products should be redesigned occurs. Businesses learn how to align incentives between themselves as new and existing market players. This leads to massive new alignment for market disruption. Most are not breakthrough ideas, usually with new platforms providing marginal improvement.

Dirk stresses the importance of perseverance in a founder. A founder who shows progress and how he has bounced back from challenges and setbacks is a founder who will attract investment. The founder also needs to offer an ability to pivot when needed. The product must also not be a passion sale — someone other than the founder must be able to sell it. At the same time, the product must be scalable as well. Especially in the early stages, a founder's story and the nuances of the founder can make or break one's development.

To be successful in the startup space, a business must identify the problem and figure out how to solve the problem in a way that genuinely relieves the pain of the individual user to the point that the particular user is willing to pay for it.

Plan Exit

Chain Reactions — Onwards

Singapore embodies the transformation from a backwater fishing town to a world-class financial hub today. The startup ecosystem grew from strength to strength. The potential of the ecosystem is clear.

Most Asian exchanges have stringent listing requirements, which can amount to relatively high costs (versus opportunity) and more extended pre-listing preparation. However, the evolution of the listing process is under progress by leading Asian exchanges such as the Singapore Exchange (SGX). SGX initiated a consultation round earlier in 2021, leading to special purpose acquisition companies (SPACs) listing later in the year. With interest from local and regional family offices and other institutional funds, this should increase the potential for Southeast Asian technology startups to list.

The largest trade sale exit in Southeast Asia has been USD140M,[1] according to the "Singapore FinTech Landscape, 2020 and Beyond" report by Oliver

[1] http://review.insignia.vc/2021/01/12/4-big-questions-on-southeast-asia-exits-in-2021/

Wynman and Singapore FinTech Association, the largest exit in Singapore is USD80M.[2]

In the ASEAN region, the common approach to exiting a startup is to either sell it before reaching a valuation of USD100M in Southeast Asia or to hold on until surpassing the benchmark of USD800M to USD900M. This trend is not limited to ASEAN countries alone. In Israel's startup ecosystem, a significant majority of companies opt to sell before reaching valuations of USD300M. Israeli entrepreneurs and their ecosystem have recognised that it is more advantageous to sell within the range of USD200M to USD350M, reinvest the proceeds, and pursue new innovations.[3]

A combination of new capital investment in growth companies, an increase in secondary transactions and regional unicorns acquiring startups brought the exits to new heights. In this second edition, we discuss the impact of the pandemic on the exit scene and the rise of SPACs in Southeast Asia.

▸ *Special Purpose Acquisition Companies in Southeast Asia*

The rise of SPACs has increased the interest of institutional investors in Southeast Asian tech startups. In addition, increased interest from late-stage investors (private equity), secondary buyers and SPACs, and the public market's favour for technology companies augur well for the startups. American and European tech companies will buy a startup for the technical capability to acquire and integrate it. If a startup can grow beyond that, it might go straight to Initial Public Offering (IPO) on the New York Stock Exchange. Israel, as a startup nation, has figured out that this is what it will be good at, and that is how it will play the game — recycling.

---

[2] https://www.oliverwyman.com/content/dam/oliver-wyman/v2/publications/2020/dec/singapore-fintech-landscape-2020-and-beyond.pdf

[3] https://www.calcalistech.com/ctech/articles/0,7340,L-3907659,00.html

That is because the same team may differ from the right people to scale it from zero to 10, 10 to 100, and 100 to 1,000. There are other problems to solve. In Israel and Southeast Asia, the public markets have a different depth than American and European markets. Both regions do not have large institutional investors and pension funds who will take those longer passive positions.

The public markets in Southeast Asia have limited liquidity and maturity, as a result of which even the most prominent private companies refrain from listing in Southeast Asia. All the new IPOs and SPACs you hear about are going to Hong Kong or the US because we need a larger public market. You cannot have a USD500M outcome with the ASEAN stock platforms, so if you do not sell before USD150M, you will have to wait for the long haul.

However, ASEAN has witnessed several SPAC deals setting the stage for several such companies to go public. Globally, more than 10 SPACs were listed in 2021, including several focused on Southeast Asia. Moreover, from 2020 to 2021, capital raised by Southeast Asia scaleup and SPACs had more than doubled.

Grab is one of the most high-profile announced SPAC mergers in ASEAN, with an expected value of USD40B. Across ASEAN, more than 10 companies are looking to list in public markets in 2021 and 2022 through the SPAC route.

Bulk IT UP

One of the critical challenges for ASEAN FinTech startups has been scaling large-scale exits. Historically, public markets across ASEAN and Singapore have yet to see many prominent technologies and FinTech companies go public since the critical size needed for a successful listing is non-trivial.

One of the strategies undertaken and currently being successfully executed by ASEAN players has been to acquire companies not just for expansion into new geographies and products but sometimes to create combined entities to achieve economies of scale.

Grab has been the most prominent example of following this strategy by acquiring Uber's business in Southeast Asia and consolidating its regional leadership in ride-hailing, which became the foundation for its financial service business. Grab later acquired several FinTech companies across ASEAN to become Singapore's second most valuable technology company after SEA Group. Since 2012, it has made eight acquisitions and 18 investments. In 2021, Grab was listed publicly as one of the world's largest SPAC deals.

Another notable shining star has been Singlife acquiring Aviva with support from private equity player Tarrant Capital IP, LLC (TPG), thus creating a large Singapore insurer. Singlife acquired Canva earlier to build up the payments side of its business. The largest listed insurer in Singapore is Great Eastern, with a market capitalisation of nearly SGD10B. For any new digital-first or challenger insurance to create a meaningful outcome, they must make a significant enough size worth listing in public markets.

Nium has been another example of acquiring global assets to become a global player of scale. For instance, Nium acquired Wirecard India's help, Ixaris in Europe and Rayo in the US. In 2022, Nium also acquired Socash, enhancing the provision of its services in emerging markets.[4]

Razer merchant solutions acquired MOL money in Malaysia in 2018. In 2022, it also received PT E2Pay Global Utama, based in Indonesia, to become one of the most significant payment players in the region.[5]

---

[4] https://www.nium.com/newsroom/nium-signs-definitive-agreement-to-acquire-alternati ve-payments-network-platform-socash

[5] https://merchant.razer.com/v3/news/razer-fintech-acquires-indonesias-e2pay/

▸ *Boost UP Team*

Startup journeys are challenging, and players must see the fruits of their hard work and success. Typically, people must see wealth creation and outcomes along the journey for an ecosystem. Founders must think through and manage many moving pieces so as to balance their interests and those of team members, their families, and investors.

Different founders have different perceptions of what success means for them. Though not all founders are motivated primarily by money, most care about their equity's value. For example, one category of founders aspires to run a startup for five to seven years and sell for USD50–120M. In such cases, the founder can achieve USD10–30M as an outcome for them and their team. The other category of founders is open to running a startup for 10 to 15 years, achieving unicorn valuation wherein a founder's shares are worth USD50–100M.

Raising venture capital increases the financial resources to execute its visions, the perceived value of a startup, and the implied wealth of its founders.

Every subsequent round of funding for the startup reduces the number of potential buyers. Depending on the region, sector and timing, startups also need help finding buyers, limiting the real wealth of their founders with investors pushing for liquidity to their investments on them.

Increasing valuation also exposes the startup to the risk of raising money in a down round, implying a lower valuation than the previous financing round. In the event of such a down round, founders do face the highest dilution, reducing the odds of their financial outcome being life-changing.

Another assumption of fundraising in consequent funding rounds is that the ultimate buyer, whether corporate acquisition or listing in public markets, will pay a significant premium to generate financial returns for founders, employees, and previous investors. Until when the startup's final exit happens, all the valuation and metrics are virtual and create limited impact for founders.

The ideal outcome for founders to secure life-changing financial consequences is to raise as limited funding as needed instead of as much as available to control their dilution and increase the odds of achieving optimum economic results for their team. It does not mean the founder should sell super early or raise a specific number of funding rounds. It just means that a final balance determines the outcome of a challenging startup journey.

A USD10M payout from a USD50–70M exit in five to seven years of the startup journey would be life-changing for founders and their families. Such medium-sized outcomes may be better potential optimisation from a venture capitalist perspective.

One school of thought for founders is to maximise the pie size without worrying about their share. At the same time, the other school of thought focuses on optimising the percentage of the pie, which in most cases, is a better predictor of overall financial returns for founders. The hard choice for founders is to navigate between these choices, aligning their team and investors and staying the course even in the face of lucrative distractions.

The VC model works best when the startups have outsized returns, and their incentives are aligned to maximise the shots at a home run. For many startups and scaleups, raising more money to pursue bigger, bolder goals is possible, depending on financing terms, which may come with attached strings like preferred liquidation, minimum returns, personal guarantees, founders' warrants, etc.

In most cases, Investor Capital is a one-way street, and more capital often increases the pressure. However, in VC terms, the scale of exit and reporting requirements is rising only in one direction, and founders should be exceedingly confident before adding more stress. A simple rule of thumb is that every additional investment round reduces the pool of potential acquirers and outcomes by half.

Most investors have placed liquidation preferences that give them capital protection in most cases. As a result, they are the first in line to receive any financial benefits if the startup goes through a liquidity event, favourable or unfavourable to founders. Since every new round reduces the probability of exit due to fewer players who can acquire the startup, it is imperative to pick the best fit for the founder, team, investors, and families.

The teams at startups hail from diverse backgrounds. Amongst them, one of the most vulnerable segments is the one that has given up stable corporate jobs to join a startup to build and scale something from scratch. In addition, their family responsibilities increase during the journey of starting up, thus changing the focus to short-term cash availability and long-term wealth-building through the startup's stock.

While taking such decisions, founders have to also factor in how long the journey will be and the scale of impact on the teams. Some of the startup employees have also taken salary cuts, and the challenger's enthusiasm in some cases starts to wane after a few years start.

Founder and team families often under-focus on the struggles and sacrifices made during a startup building. The working hours, benefits, net disposable income of the household and vacations are just some fronts where families adjust. Therefore, it is imperative to ensure that families share the vision and believe in the goals. Startups must consistently keep the tribe together and identify ways to get everyone behind the same idea. If the families are proud of the journey, it acts as a confidence booster and emotional stabiliser for the teams to give their best to the concept and company.

Several companies in Singapore took proactive steps to ensure they could share the fruits of success along the journey instead of just waiting for one final milestone day.

Matchmove, one of the oldest FinTech companies in Singapore, went through a few iterations and thus became a poster child for the resilience and perseverance of local FinTech companies. During their last fundraising round in 2020, they offered their staff to sell USD2–3M worth of shares to incoming investors as secondaries to ensure the team members serving the longest with the team could realise some of the fruits of labour.

M-DAQ, another pioneer of FinTech, was one of the earliest FinTech companies in Singapore to enable early shareholders and some employees to get liquidity during the investment round, which brought ANT Financial and EDBI as investors to the company.

Stashaway also enabled SGD2.5M for employee buyback to help early employees get liquidity, thus showing people that liquidity events can come in phases instead of one big day of revelation.[6]

FinTech Exits

The ability of a startup ecosystem to achieve certain key objectives determines its success. These objectives include generating meaningful outcomes for founders and employees, creating and nurturing venture investing as an asset class, generating employment opportunities for local talent, and recycling capital through exits that enable operators to become investors.

[6] https://www.businesstimes.com.sg/garage/stashaway-to-buy-back-up-to-s4m-in-employee-options-with-upcoming-fundraise

Several unique attributes in Singapore's FinTech landscape contribute to its potential for achieving these outcomes. However, Singapore faces certain limitations regarding the maturity of its public markets, and the primary mode of financial exits in its early stages has been trading sales and acquisitions.

Singaporean startups and their outcomes divide into three categories. The first category, Young Cubs, comprises fast-moving young companies that either find an acquirer from Southeast Asia or prefer to join a larger peer for easy access to capital and distribution. Most deals in this category are under SGD100M valuation. The second category, Asian Tigers, consists of companies with regional scale and leadership, typically valued between SGD300–600M. The key financial exit route is through acquisition by North Asian financial institutions from China, South Korea, and Japan. The third and final category, Global Leaders, consists of companies with global aspirations and scale, usually valued beyond SGD1B. These companies have offices beyond ASEAN and aspire to undertake an IPO in the US.

While Singapore has achieved success in all three categories, most financial or strategic exits occur in the first category of Young Cubs, contributing to almost 90% of the total outcomes. These transactions enable founders and investors to move quickly, recycle capital, and build newer ventures inside or outside the acquiring entities. There has been only one transaction above SGD1B in Singapore, an InsurTech merging with an incumbent with support from private equity investors. Singlife acquired Zurich Singapore and Canva in their growth phases and later merged with Aviva Singapore.

In the second category of regional leaders, Asian Tigers, there has been only one exit till now, wherein Ant Group acquired the Southeast Asian payment provider 2C2P. The acquisition aims to expand Alibaba and Ant Group's presence in Southeast Asia's fast-growing e-commerce market. 2C2P currently operates in eight countries, including Thailand.

Singapore's FinTech ecosystem's success hinges on its ability to generate outcomes that benefit founders, employees, and investors, create jobs for local talent, and recycle capital through exits. Although the country faces certain limitations, most financial or strategic outcomes occur in Young Cubs' first category, allowing stakeholders to move quickly and efficiently.

We have also seen a unique phenomenon of Asian Tigers and Global Leaders from Singapore, like Funding Society, Validus, Nium, Matchmove, Thunes, Advance AI, Shopback and M-DAQ, acquiring Young Cubs in Singapore like Cardup, Klearcard, Socash, Shopmatic, Tookitaki, Jewel Paymenttech, Seedly and Wallex, respectively.

Funding Societies, a digital financing platform for SMEs in Southeast Asia, has announced its acquisition of CardUp, a regional payments solution. The purchase includes CardUp's payment capabilities, such as online acceptance, invoice automation tools, licences and integrations with third-party business software. These payment services will complement Funding Societies' lending products, providing a unified financial experience for SMEs across the region, allowing them to manage expenses, receive payments, and borrow funds on a platform. Venture capital firm Sequoia Capital backs both Funding Society and Cardup.[7]

Validus, a Singapore-based FinTech company, has acquired KlearCard's business payments and expense management platform to strengthen its upcoming SME business account offering. Validus will be able to enhance its digital banking capabilities and provide a more comprehensive solution for SMEs due to the acquisition. The combined company aims to integrate KlearCard's platform into Validus' existing platform and offer various financial services to SMEs.[8]

---

[7] https://fundingsocieties.com/press/2022/cardup

[8] https://validus.sg/2021/10/validus-acquires-klearcards-business-payments-and-expense-management-platform-to-bolster-its-upcoming-sme-business-account-offering/

Nium, a FinTech unicorn based in Singapore, has announced its acquisition of SoCash. This alternative payment platform lets customers use mobile devices to withdraw cash from retail shops. Transaction will provide Nium's customers access SoCash's network of retail shops, which can serve as cash pick-up points. Venture capital firm Vertex Ventures backs both Nium and SoCash.[9]

MatchMove, a Singapore-based FinTech company, has acquired Shopmatic, an Indian e-commerce platform. The acquisition will allow MatchMove to expand its suite of digital payment solutions to include e-commerce capabilities. MatchMove integrated Shopmatic's team and technology into its existing platform to offer an end-to-end solution for digital commerce and payments.[10]

Thunes is a financial technology company that offers a cross-border payments network to facilitate money transfers between individuals, businesses, and financial institutions. It has acquired a majority stake in Tookitaki, a regulatory technology firm, to enhance its anti-money laundering and counter-terrorism financing capabilities. This collaboration will enable Thunes to leverage Tookitaki's artificial intelligence (AI) and machine learning technology to improve its compliance processes and reduce the risk of financial crimes.[11]

Jewel Paymentech, a Singapore-based FinTech company specialising in fraud management and regulatory compliance solutions for banks and payment facilitators, has been acquired by Advance Intelligence Group. The acquisition aims to strengthen Advance Intelligence Group's risk

[9] https://www.businesstimes.com.sg/startups-tech/startups/fintech-unicorn-nium-acquire-alternative-payments-platform-socash

[10] https://matchmove.com/media/matchmove-acquires-shopmatic

[11] https://www.thunes.com/thunes-tookitaki/

management and compliance capabilities and expand its presence in Southeast Asia.[12]

ShopBack, a leading e-commerce cashback platform based in Singapore, has acquired Seedly, a personal finance management app, to expand its offerings in the financial services sector. The acquisition aims to bolster ShopBack's presence in Southeast Asia's FinTech market by leveraging Seedly's user base and innovative technology.[13]

M-DAQ, a Singapore-based FinTech firm, has acquired Wallex, a cross-border payments platform that enables businesses to send and receive payments in local currencies. The acquisition will allow M-DAQ to expand its cross-border ecosystem and offer its customers a more comprehensive suite of services. In addition, Wallex's technology and expertise in cross-border payments will be integrated into M-DAQ's existing platform, enabling businesses to make faster and cheaper cross-border payments in various currencies.[14]

Several Young Cubs have been acquired by overseas private companies, showcasing the diversity in the pool of acquirers for Singapore startups.

PayU, a Dutch FinTech company that provides online payment services to merchants, has announced its entry into the Southeast Asian market. The company aims to leverage its experience and technology to help regional merchants access a wider customer base and increase online sales. PayU has appointed a new CEO for its Southeast Asian operations and plans to launch several payment products tailored to the local market. This move is part of PayU's strategy to expand its global footprint and tap into the

---

[12] https://www.digitalnewsasia.com/startups/advance-intelligence-group-acquires-jewel-paymentech

[13] https://techcrunch.com/2018/05/07/shopback-seedly-acquisition/

[14] https://blog.wallex.asia/m-daq-acquires-wallex-to-expand-its-cross-border-ecosystem/

growing demand for online payments in Southeast Asia. The company aims to help accelerate the growth of digital commerce in the region and empower small and medium-sized businesses to take advantage of the digital economy's opportunities.[15]

Pine Labs, an Indian payment and merchant commerce platform, has acquired Fave, a Southeast Asian startup, for USD45M. The acquisition aims to expand Pine Labs' presence in Southeast Asia and provide Fave's merchant partners with access to Pine Labs' technology, including its integrated payments platform. The deal will also allow Pine Labs to offer its suite of merchant solutions to Fave's large regional customer base. This acquisition is part of Pine Labs' strategy to become a leading player in the Asian payment market and leverage Fave's expertise in mobile payments and loyalty programmes to provide innovative solutions to its customers.[16]

Gupshup, a conversational messaging platform, has acquired Active.ai, a conversational AI platform specialising in serving the banking and financial technology industry. The acquisition aims to enhance Gupshup's capabilities in providing cutting-edge conversational AI technology to its clients, particularly in the financial sector.[17]

The Australian financial comparison website Finderhas acquired the brand and assets of GoBear, a Singapore-based FinTech firm. The acquisition includes GoBear's proprietary technology and digital assets, which will help Finder expand its financial product offerings and enhance its user experience. The deal will also integrate GoBear's FinTech and financial services expertise with Finder's existing platform. This move is part of

[15] https://techcrunch.com/2019/07/04/payu-enters-southeast-asia/

[16] https://techcrunch.com/2021/04/13/pine-labs-acquires-southeast-asian-startup-fave-for-45-million/

[17] https://www.gupshup.io/resources/press-releases/gupshup-acquires-active-ai-the-leading-conversational-ai-platform-for-banks-and-fintech-companies

Finder's strategy to expand its presence in the Southeast Asian market and provide its customers with comprehensive financial services. The acquisition will enable Finder to offer a broader range of services, including credit cards, personal loans, and insurance. In addition, it will allow the company to tap into the rapidly growing FinTech market in the region.[18]

There have been some cases of global corporations, both Singapore-based and US-based acquiring Young Cubs in Singapore. For example, listed companies like Intuit, Grab Holdings, Latitude Payments and Vonage developed TradeGecko, Bento, Octifi and Jumper, respectively, over the years.

Intuit, a financial software company, has acquired TradeGecko for over USD80M. TradeGecko, a Singapore-based inventory and order management platform, will be integrated into Intuit's QuickBooks suite of products to provide small businesses with a comprehensive solution for managing their finances and inventory. The acquisition will help Intuit expand its Asia-Pacific presence and serve small businesses better.[19]

Latitude Financial has expanded into Asia by investing in Octifi, a Singapore-based FinTech company. The investment was made through a strategic partnership with Harvey Norman, a leading Australian retailer, and is aimed at providing financing solutions to customers in Southeast Asia. This move is part of Latitude's strategy to expand its regional presence and capitalise on the growing demand for digital financial services.[20]

Grab, a Singapore-based technology company has acquired Bento, a wealth technology startup. The acquisition will enable Grab to offer retail wealth

---

[18] https://www.finextra.com/pressarticle/87013/finder-acquires-gobear-brand-and-assets

[19] https://www.businesstimes.com.sg/startups-tech/startups/intuit-buy-tradegecko-over-us80m

[20] https://www.latitudefinancial.com.au/about-us/media-releases/latitude-expands-into-asia-with-harvey-norman.html

solutions to millions of customers in Southeast Asia, expanding its financial services offerings beyond payments and lending.

Overall, Singapore has been the focus of global VC and private equity interested in FinTech and financial services. Singapore has seen a good number of FinTech exits and there is an opportunity for Singapore to further develop the IPO route since in the first generation of FinTech startups, all the exits were from the trade sale route.

Trade sales can generate quicker though smaller in size than the global IPO. In the medium to long term, Singapore would need to diversify the exit route for its growth startups beyond the trade sales through innovative models like regional growth focused marketplaces.

Looking ahead, the venture capital landscape in Singapore's FinTech sector is poised for further growth and innovation. As technological advancements continue to shape the financial industry, Singapore is well-positioned to capitalise on emerging trends such as blockchain, AI, and decentralised finance. The government's commitment to fostering FinTech innovation through initiatives like the MAS FinTech Innovation Lab and regulatory sandboxes will continue to drive investment opportunities and fuel the growth of the venture capital ecosystem.

In conclusion, Singapore's venture capital landscape in the FinTech sector has undergone a significant transformation over the past decade. The impressive growth in investments, the emergence of successful FinTech startups, and the country's dominant position in the ASEAN region all point to a thriving ecosystem that offers abundant opportunities for venture capitalists and investors. With its supportive environment, Singapore is poised to remain at the forefront of FinTech innovation and attract further venture capital investments in the years to come.

Chapter 8

BUILDING LAUNCHPADS FOR FUTURE

Every organisation, irrespective of size, is already engaged in digital transformation, big or small, nascent or mature, and in some way, shape or form. Moreover, digital transformation, as we are witnessing today, directly touches the lives of every single individual, irrespective of the economic strata they belong to. Therefore, telling anyone in the C-suite that digital transformation is not just a growth but also a survival imperative is like preaching to the choir.

Let's look at this concept of **perceptual reality** and the power which gets us to where we are today.

Perceptual Reality

At the beginning of this journey, Singapore had already developed the infrastructure to support a growing FinTech ecosystem. However, it was still subjected to global scrutiny regarding its potential to establish itself as a FinTech hub. Singapore was tasked with establishing itself as a regional hub and proving its potential to be a global one. Before daring to do, one must first dare to dream; this philosophy has led Singapore down the path of progress. Singapore's belief in its potential allowed it to perceive and create its reality.

Perceptual reality is a tool with boundless potential, drawing upon one's imagination. The realisation of the Singaporean dream was no accident; it was dreamt into reality; its goals were clear, and in the process of building upon them, the country could not only realise the dream but transcend its expectations.

> *"The ones crazy enough to think that they can change the world are the ones who do."*
>
> *Steve Jobs*

Singapore FinTech Festival

The idea was born from a casual conversation in Copenhagen at a global FinTech event. The regulators saw that it would need to build its own international FinTech franchise to change the perceptions surrounding the reality of Singapore as a FinTech nation. One of the biggest pillars of Singapore in becoming a FinTech nation has been its Chief FinTech Officer of MAS, Sopnendu Mohanty. It was the first time globally a regulator created a position called Chief FinTech Officer to support and develop its FinTech industry. Sopnendu, lovingly addressed as "Chief" in the industry, joined the central bank after a long career at Citibank and brought new energy to give flight to Singapore's FinTech aspirations.

Chief defined new global standards of a central bank that would engage with the industry over the last five years. One of his biggest and boldest initiatives was the commitment he made in Copenhagen that Singapore would, in three years, host the world's largest FinTech event. So the world would come to Singapore and prove that every time the tiny red dot aspires to achieve something, it will overcome every obstacle and define new benchmarks of success.

If MAS is the brain behind Singapore FinTech, the Association of Banks in Singapore (ABS) is the heart. It has been the relentless execution machine behind achieving the perceptual reality. ABS is a non-profit industry association representing all the banks in Singapore.

ABS has long been the unified representation of the financial institutions here in Singapore. Its director, Ai Boon Ong, has been with them since the 1980s and has been instrumental in keeping the organisation nimble while being ready to address the industry's biggest issues. Back in 2015, this existential threat was that of FinTech.

At the onset of this decade, the bridge between financial services and technology was clearly forming, with technology ready to disrupt a change-resistant industry. The early days of FinTech revolved around replacing existing banking methods with new, more efficient modes, essentially replacing specific businesses or banks. This did not come to pass, which is not surprising considering the monumental task presented to these startups. Instead, the rampant digitisation of society forced the existing banking system to adopt new technologies. Meanwhile, FinTech startups realised it was easier to succeed as entrepreneurs when working with the existing system rather than replacing it. At this time, MAS approached ABS to support the first-ever Singapore FinTech Festival (SFF). It would be a premier event that would bring together all participants in the FinTech landscape, showcase new and innovative companies, and allow the existing major banks to support and get a firsthand look at new technologies. This event was a runaway success; originally billed with around 1,000 attendees, it blossomed into 10,000 attendees. In addition, the festival surprisingly netted a return of SGD1.4M, which was used to set up a fund that supports FinTech development in Singapore. Thus, began the journey of Singapore to becoming a true FinTech hub for Asia.

By Ai Boon's admission, much of this praise lies at the feet of MAS and its Chief FinTech Officer. The key development that allowed for a bridge to form between the incumbent financial institutions and new flourishing FinTech startups was the advent of the MAS Regulatory Sandbox. This entailed allowing financial institutions and FinTechs to collaborate on a different initiative within a regulatory safe zone. This allows for experimentation in innovations that would traditionally have been very hard to implement within the heavily regulated industry.

Another key point Ai Boon makes is that the development of FinTech is separate from Singapore, and many active FinTech companies are scattered around ASEAN. In her experience, the younger population in other ASEAN countries, such as Thailand and Vietnam, are far more willing to take risks and are hungry to succeed. Hence, with the leadership of MAS and the help of ABS, Singapore has been active in attracting and facilitating the growth of FinTech around ASEAN. For instance, the fund set up to support FinTech development also applies to those around ASEAN if they incorporate a local company and have a presence in Singapore. In addition, they help connect these startups to the ecosystem here in Singapore through ABS and showcase them worldwide.

The continued support for these efforts by ABS, and tangentially MAS, will be vital in growing the status of Singapore as a FinTech hub and maintaining its stature as a FinTech nation. According to Ai Boon, Singapore's key resource is human talent, which must be nurtured through the education system and supplemented through high-value outside talent. Only by doing this will Singapore maintain its competitive advantage in a highly competitive global FinTech marketplace.

The SFF is now the largest FinTech event, with more than 10 heads of state attending the event in the past few years. The SFF 2019 drew a record of more than 60,000 participants from 140 countries, featuring 569 speakers, close to 1,000 exhibitors and 41 pavilions comprising industry professionals, founders, investors, academics and government agencies. The final two days of the week focused on Innovation Lab Crawl, which featured more than 50 participating innovation labs, and 30 workshops and networking events. In 2022, the SFF brought more than 62,000 participants from over 115 countries. This is the largest gathering since the inaugural edition in 2016.

By providing a platform like the FinTech Festival and bringing together large numbers of FinTech startups, financial institutions, and venture capitalists, Singapore created an opportunity for networking, collaboration and matching money with ideas. One example is a startup using an artificial intelligence (AI) solution for compliance management. It was a finalist at the Festival's Global FinTech Hackcelerator competition in 2016. The team gained at the event, many financial institutions approached them to help them solve their compliance problems. As a result, the startup has expanded into regional markets and is doing well. The second is a FinTech startup that had an innovative way to offer banks competitive forex rates. As a result, it was able to use the FinTech Festival to gain recognition in the market.

> *"We didn't invest in these firms. We didn't relax any rules for them. But we provided a platform for them. We invited them, got them to network, and brought other parties to connect. These are things a facilitative regulator can do without compromising prudential standards."*
>
> *Ravi Menon, 2018*

Another key aspect of SFF was its ability to bring regulators from 20 countries under one roof with their booths, enabling FinTech startups to learn about entering multiple markets and companies from those regions to enter Asia. So while some Western analysts started referring to the SFF as the United Nations or Davos of FinTech, it has, over the years, become a category on its own in financial services.

From an event, SFF has emerged to become a platform to address the needs of society, startups and the business community. In 2020, as the world we knew changed, SFF stepped in to contribute to finding solutions for today's two pressing global challenges — COVID-19 and climate change. FinTech Awards and Hackcelerator pivoted in a startup manner with a new theme of "Building Resilience, Seizing Opportunities, Emerging Stronger".

As Singapore was building the FinTech nation, it understood that it needed to bring credible recognition to local Singapore FinTech companies and regional companies who are solving critical challenges for the region. The spirit of the awards was to bring international players to the area and get them to compete with local players. But, in the heart of **Singanomics**, the industry did not wish to live in a fool's paradise, assuming that local solutions were the best in every category. So global companies were invited to showcase solutions to local prospective customers and prove their mettle.

This was the first time globally that a regulator, especially with MAS's calibre, stepped up to create industry-facing awards. Local financial institutions were wary of procuring FinTech solutions and sought a stamp of credibility. The awards were set up to address that need. To ensure global best practices, the awards process was facilitated by an independent Big 4 auditor to manage the process.

Unlike some of the other awards, where only the finalists are known and talked about, the MAS FinTech awards became a platform and celebration of the achievements of the broader community. Every year, 40 startups are shortlisted from hundreds of nominations by an experienced pool of judges from over 20 industry leaders. In true Singapore *kampung* spirit, some of the judges from competing consulting firms help in the running of the awards process every year. Each of these 40 startups is showcased, given exhibition space during the festival and support to scale their business.

In the **Singanomics** principle of ensuring accountability for all the effort and resources invested, the awards have subsequently tracked the performance and outcomes of these companies. Shortlisting in the top 40 and getting the awards is the start of a life-long journey and association with the Singapore FinTech Nation, not the end.

Over the last five years, companies shortlisted for the FinTech awards have raised more than USD2B in funding with some of the leading beacons of innovation in Singapore like FOMO Pay, InstaReM, M-DAQ, Funding Societies, Spark Systems, and Cynopsis, which are featured in this book.

Haccelerator

FinTech and Innovation accelerators worldwide aspire to support startups, finetune their ideas and scale their businesses. FinTech startups' needs are complex since they need to comply with a host of regulations and align with the existing processes of financial institutions they want to work with to commercialise their solutions. Many startups with aspirations to enter ASEAN also need help acclimatising to local culture and being able to serve the needs of financial institutions in the region. Financial institutions were concerned about startups not being mature and customised enough for their needs and, more importantly, not solving their exact needs.

The ecosystem in Singapore saw that the traditional accelerator model was broken, and it needed to evolve to make it work for financial services. A top-down approach was taken, and MAS decided to be the first regulator globally to set up an accelerator programme, Hackcelerator. This was akin to Google producing the first Nexus phone as a role model setting the industry standard.

To resolve this "startups are from Mars and banks are from Venus" conundrum, MAS stepped in to resolve the deadlock and create the future path. In a classic example of **Garden Innovation**, it was identified that real innovation and acceleration to FinTech ventures could only happen by focusing on specific domain areas instead of working across the broad FinTech spectrum. From the first year of the Hackcelerator programme, MAS partnered with financial institutions to share problem statements for the areas where they were willing to collaborate with FinTech startups. The plan developed was to ensure that each FinTech startup received a sponsoring financial services partner to be able to join the programme. In addition, the financial institution would commit to supporting the startup during the programme and help them get enterprise-ready.

While a global hunt was underway for startups who managed to identify the world's best solutions, the startups were committed to pairing with the sponsor of their problem statement for the full duration of the Hackcelerator programme and were promised attractive funding. In the spirit of **Garden Innovation**, every year, the problem ideas for the Hackcelerator are focused on specific areas of innovation ranging from financial inclusion, InsurTech, RegTech, know your customer, payments, to trade finance. In addition, in the post-pandemic environment, the Hackcelerator has been called upon to identify COVID-19 and climate change solutions, with financial institutions ramping up support for solutions emerging from the platform.

One of the critical things for startups is finding the capital sources to scale up. In Singapore, there are diverse sources of capital across institutional investors, angel investors and corporate venture arms. All of these look for different things, with variations in deal size, risk appetite, exit horizon and geographical footprint of companies. Traditional venture capital (VC) firms with five- to seven-year funds tenure seek medium-term outlooks to be visible for the companies they back. Angel investors, several of whom are industry executives and, to some extent, former entrepreneurs, bring capital and connectivity to the market.

Private equity companies look for long-term returns beyond short-term market movements. Financial institutions such as banks and insurers invest for strategic reasons beyond the financial returns aspect of venture investments. For the longest time, investors believed there were not enough good-quality companies or that there was limited access to these companies. The startups faced the challenge of being unable to reach out to the right stakeholders, even if they knew the name of the investment firms. Startups needed help finding out whom to call and how to get to the right person in the firm. Investors' concern was that if they opened up more, they would receive a vast amount of companies seeking funding, and curating such a large quantity of inbounds would strain their limited capacity.

These challenges led to the birth of the world's first-ever curated FinTech dating platform to bring transparency, trust and ease of discoverability to startups and investors. The Chief FinTech Officer of MAS, Sopnendu Mohanty ("Chief") and one of the authors, Varun Mittal, were the architects of this dating concept. Over the years, the platform evolved significantly in its needs and target audiences.

At its birth, the moment they realised that they needed to get the investors in one room to address the needs and concerns of the capital provider side of the dating, another WhatsApp group was born as an offshoot of the FinTech *Choupal* group discussed earlier.

In a typical *kampung* spirit, within three hours, 80% of the VCs investing in FinTech in Singapore were in the new group. This was the advantage of being in a small community. After three hours, over 75 investors represented more than 80% of capital invested in the FinTech sector in the previous year. One week later, an open house session was hosted at MAS to get investors' feedback and identify data points they wanted to see from startups open to a dating concept. Several investors were proud of their proprietary deal flow and were nervous about being part of such an exercise lest it reduces their competitive advantage. However, in the **Singanomics** principle of focusing on the greater good, a message that the platform shall go ahead with or without the investors on edge helped convey the national commitment to bring about this exercise.

Similar smaller sessions were conducted with startups to understand their expectations and concerns about such a dating platform. For example, startups were conscious of their data not being visible to all investors since some investors could be working with their competition. Another unexpected issue which came up was a concern about signalling. If a startup looked too desperate to raise funding, it could impact its negotiation power and make its business-to-business customers nervous about the stability and longevity of the firm.

To address this, a double opt-in system was developed where startups and investors indicated their aspirational match qualities. Then, a team of volunteer experts would curate and seek approval from both sides before formally introducing them for the first virtual or physical meeting.

The Investor Summit 1.0 in 2017 saw the participation of more than 1,000 FinTech startups and 400 investors and resulted in 525 connections made among interested parties. Up to USD2B of capital was also made available for the startups.

As an extension of **Singanomics**, in 2018, the Investor Summit was expanded to include all other sectors of startups and SMEs to bring access to capital across all sections of the economy. The platform built and designed to address access to capital to FinTech was now called upon to get FinTech to serve the nation.

Over four months, roadshows were conducted all over Asia, from Indonesia to China, to showcase the opportunities in the region, seek their feedback, and bring personalised curation to thousands of connections made during the process. Another new addition, to the surprise of many people, was a physical "speed-dating" event, where investors and companies were "matchmade" to meet physically. Each company had 15 minutes to pitch their case to one investor before proceeding to the next investor. Throughout the event, investors were given opportunities to network with the participating startups directly.

With MATCH as the platform, MAS and EY helped startups reach out to relevant investors ranging from angel investors to VC and financial institutions, striving to connect stakeholders in the ecosystem better.

On top of the physical event, a digital MATCH platform was also launched to quickly connect investors and enterprises, further increasing the possibility of connecting face-to-face following a mutual match and enhancing the networking opportunities between investors and enterprises.

Three hundred and eighty participating investors enrolled for the SFF's deal-making platform, wherein they formally shared intentions to invest up to USD6.2B in ASEAN enterprises next year. An additional USD6B was earmarked for the subsequent two years.

Initiatives such as MATCH and FinTech Deal Day during the SFF 2018 were vital in powering the heartbeat of a flourishing FinTech era. These efforts to create an inclusive habitat for the global FinTech community bring about valuable opportunities for startups to flourish and grow. With improved initiatives and programmes in every subsequent edition of SFF, the returns are invaluable as they help to support the growth of startups and deliver untapped value to the world of financial services and businesses.

Every year, MAS organises Deal Fridays, virtual and physical meetups for startups and investors to meet, pitch and network with each other. In 2019 and 2020, over 100 investors and 500 startups have been part of these personalised, curated events to ensure vibrant access to capital.

Sustainability

Sustainable finance integrates environmental, social and governance (ESG) criteria into financial services to bring about sustainable development outcomes, including mitigating and adapting to the adverse effects of climate change.

As an island nation, global warming could impact us much sooner and more severely than it would affect other countries. Therefore, Singapore integrated its social conscience and business objectives to develop green finance. Interestingly, Singapore is one of the few countries that limits its car population and prices its usage. Today, the growth of the car population in Singapore remains at 0%.

Singapore's financial sector can be useful in catalysing sustainable and green finance in the region. Therefore, MAS is actively promoting sustainable financing in the financial industry. For example, MAS has engaged with financial institutions to consider the ESG criteria in decision-making processes and collaborated with local stakeholders and international counterparts to distil best practices. MAS has also supported adopting industry standards and guidelines and encouraged industry-led capacity-building efforts to develop the green bond market in Singapore.

> *"The pandemic provides a prime opportunity for countries to 'build back better'. More than ever, it is important that countries not only rebuild their economies and preserve jobs but also intentionally build a more sustainable new economy. As a result, there have been growing calls for governments to prioritise or accelerate green infrastructure development as part of recovery plans.*

"Infrastructure development is critical to driving economic growth and improving social outcomes, while climate change remains a significant threat to humanity. Therefore, a right balance between growth and sustainability must be achieved."

Jacqueline Loh[1]

Asset managers in Singapore have signed the UN Principles for Responsible Investment and developed the Singapore Stewardship Principles for Responsible Investors. In the spirit of **Right First, Fast Later**, Singapore started the process with policy initiatives by developing a mission to synergise smart finance and green finance and leverage technology and innovation to build resilience and expand markets. The industry has come together to support the vision in true *kampung* spirit. The three local banks ceased financing new coal power plants as they stepped up financing of renewable energy projects.

Another aspect of **Right First, Fast Later**, has been the development of common standards. Singapore worked with the rest of the ASEAN countries to develop and update the ASEAN Standards to align with the international green bond principle. For green bond markets to reach scale, common green bond standards must avoid fragmenting capital pools across borders and tackle greenwashing.

Singapore is now ASEAN's largest green finance market, accounting for nearly 50% of cumulative ASEAN green bond and loan issuances. Till June 2020, more than SGD8B of green, social and sustainability bonds

[1] "Keeping Green and Impact in Focus" — Keynote Speech by Ms Jacqueline Loh, Deputy Managing Director, Monetary Authority of Singapore, at Asian Venture Philanthropy Network (AVPN) Virtual Conference 2020 on 8 June 2020, https://www.mas.gov.sg/news/speeches/2020/keeping-green-and-impact-in-focus

have been issued in Singapore. In 2019, Singapore entities originated close to SGD5.5B worth of green loans and sustainability-linked loans (SLL), with Singapore originating over 35% of SLLs in the Asia-Pacific region.

Following **Singanomics**, MAS set up a USD2B green investments programme (GIP) in 2019 to invest in public market investment strategies with a strong green focus. It will help to support the Singapore financial centre in promoting environmentally sustainable projects and mitigating climate change risks in Singapore and the region. MAS's first investment under the GIP was a USD100M placement in the Bank for International Settlements' Green Bond Investment Pool. In addition, MAS introduced a Green Bond Grant scheme in 2018 to defray the costs of external review against green bond standards.

In the spirit of **Garden Innovation**, the rest of the platforms were marshalled to join the movement after addressing policy and access to capital perspective. As a result, sustainable finance is the general theme for the MAS Global FinTech Hackcelerator and the MAS FinTech Awards in 2020.

The theme for the Global FinTech Hackcelerator in SFF 2020 was "Building Resilience, Seizing Opportunities, Emerging Stronger". The Hackcelerator will identify solutions that enable financial institutions to respond to the pandemic and climate change. MAS has received a record 100 problem statements on pertinent areas, including:

- improving supply chain resilience amidst disruptions to manufacturing and the flow of goods and services during the pandemic;
- driving social impact by improving credit access for lower-income individuals and SMEs; and
- accelerating green finance flows to support low-carbon economic activities.

"The MAS is working on a comprehensive, long-term strategy to make sustainable finance a defining feature of Singapore's role as an international financial centre, just as wealth management and FinTech have become."

Ravi Menon[2]

Singapore has identified sustainable development and supporting green finance in all financial services. In the spirit of **Garden Innovation**, policymakers and government institutions have prioritised putting massive amounts of resources behind it. One such anchor projects is Greenprint, bringing together FinTech startups, regulators and traditional financial institutions and real economy players to tackle ESG data challenges and encourage ESG innovation to mobilise financing towards Asia's transition to a net zero economy.

Project Greenprint is a set of initiatives that aim to create a more transparent, trusted, and efficient ESG ecosystem to enable green and sustainable finance. Its key objectives are to grow a vibrant Green FinTech ecosystem in Singapore, drive partnerships between various stakeholders, and develop digital infrastructure to facilitate the flow of consistent, clear, and reliable ESG data. To achieve these objectives, the project team has developed a set of digital solutions, including the ESG Disclosure Portal, ESG Registry, Greenprint Marketplace and Data Orchestrator.

Living up to the model of **Singanomics**, Greenprint addresses the concerns that in the absence of market solutions offering reliable ways to collect, track and use the ESG data, financial institutions found it challenging to take credible financing decisions towards enabling a net zero economy.

---

[2] Managing Director, Monetary Authority of Singapore, SIAS 1st Master Series Investment Conference, https://www.mas.gov.sg/news/speeches/2019/the-wellness-of-investing

The ESG Disclosure Portal is an integrated disclosure portal that eases sustainability reporting and enhances access to ESG data. It allows reporting companies to upload corporate-level sustainability data onto the portal, which will map against various standards and frameworks. This initiative addresses corporates' current pain points where they must report in different systems, templates, and against multiple global standards and frameworks. In addition, these data can be shared with authorised recipients on a consent basis, facilitating consistent and comparable data access to stakeholders.

ESG Registry is a blockchain-powered data platform supporting a tamper-proof record of sustainability certifications and verified sustainability data across various sectors. This initiative provides financial institutions, corporates, and regulatory authorities with a common access point for these data, facilitating better tracking and analysis of corporates' sustainability commitments, measuring impact, alleviating greenwashing risks, and improving the management of ESG financial products.

The Greenprint Marketplace facilitates the growth of a vibrant green FinTech ecosystem by connecting green FinTech and green technology providers to investors, financial institutions, and corporates. The digital platform enables efficient discovery of solution providers, solution seekers, and investors, acceleration of partnerships, and channels investments towards green and sustainable solutions and initiatives.

The Data Orchestrator initiative aggregates sustainability data from numerous sources, including major ESG data providers, utility providers, the ESG Disclosure Portal, the ESG registry and sectoral platforms. It provides consent-based access to these sources and enables new data insights to be generated through data analytics to better support investment and financing decisions.

Project Greenprint's initiatives will create a more transparent, trusted, and efficient ESG ecosystem, enabling green and sustainable finance. It will foster a vibrant green FinTech ecosystem, enhance connections across various stakeholders, and develop digital infrastructure to facilitate the flow of consistent, clear, and reliable ESG data. The project will undoubtedly create new opportunities for stakeholders to participate in the green finance ecosystem and contribute to sustainable development.

Artificial Intelligence

Since 2015, there has been an exponential surge in the amount of data created and made available across all walks of life. It has led to an increasing need to manage, analyse and utilise this data to enable the growth of artificial intelligence and data analytics (AIDA).

AI has revolutionised the banking and finance sector worldwide, and Singapore, as a knowledge-based economy, has been at the forefront of leveraging this technology to enhance its global competitiveness. With a strong focus on technological advancements and innovation, Singapore has embraced the use of AIDA in various aspects of banking and finance.

One of the primary areas where AI is extensively used in banking is customer service and experience. Virtual assistants powered by AI, such as chatbots, are deployed by banks to provide 24/7 support, answer customer queries, and assist with basic banking transactions. These chatbots are trained to understand and respond to customer inquiries, providing quick and accurate solutions while reducing the need for human intervention. They can handle a wide range of tasks, including account inquiries, fund transfers, and loan applications, enhancing customer satisfaction and streamlining operations.

AI-powered algorithms are also employed in risk assessment and fraud detection within the banking industry. These algorithms analyse large volumes of financial data in real-time, flagging suspicious transactions or activities that may indicate fraudulent behaviour. By automating this process, banks can detect and prevent fraudulent activities promptly, protecting both customers and the financial institution itself.

In the lending and credit assessment process, AI algorithms are used to evaluate loan applications and determine creditworthiness. These algorithms consider a variety of factors, including credit history, income, and customer behavior, to make accurate lending decisions quickly. This helps banks streamline their loan approval process, reduce manual intervention, and offer personalised loan products to customers.

Furthermore, AI is utilised in portfolio management and investment advisory services. Machine learning algorithms analyse market trends, historical data, and other relevant factors to provide insights and recommendations for investment strategies. AI-powered robo-advisors have gained popularity, allowing customers to receive customised investment advice based on their risk tolerance, financial goals, and market conditions.

In Singapore, MAS has been proactive in promoting the adoption of AI and ensuring its responsible use in the banking and finance sector. MAS has established regulatory frameworks and guidelines to address the challenges associated with AI, including auditability and accountability. Financial institutions are required to maintain transparency and explainability in their AI systems to ensure compliance and prevent misuse.

To address concerns regarding fairness and ethical use of AI, MAS encourages financial institutions to conduct regular audits and assessments of their AI systems. This ensures that AI algorithms do not discriminate against vulnerable sections of society and adhere to ethical standards. MAS also emphasises the importance of robust data governance and protection to maintain data privacy and security in AI-driven processes.

> *"The adoption of advanced computing and data science in the financial sector will inevitably continue, and it will undoubtedly change how we work and transform the way financial institutions*

operate. There are many moving parts, necessary ingredients, and stakeholders; we will walk this journey as an ecosystem. Our collective responsibility is to seek out the opportunities in this revolution, not only ride the wave of disruption but facilitate the cultural transition."

Dr David Hardoon[3]

In the spirit of **Right First, Fast Later**, MAS brought together financial industry partners to create a framework for financial institutions to promote the responsible adoption of AIDA. Veritas framework enables financial institutions to evaluate their AIDA-driven solutions against the principles of fairness, ethics, accountability and transparency (FEAT). The framework ensures that AI solutions are designed and implemented fairly to all stakeholders, including customers, employees, and society.

In the uniquely Singapore model of working, instead of the regulators creating policies in isolation, MAS co-created with the industry to strengthen internal governance around AI applications and the management and use of data. Proper governance around the use of AIDA is critical to fostering trust and confidence in AIDA-driven decisions and financial services. As a result, the Veritas consortium was built with 17 members, comprising MAS, SGInnovate, EY and 14 financial institutions, with more members joining progressively.

To ensure processes and controls are future-proofed, MAS and Infocomm Media Development Authority, the technology and data regulators are to align on AI governance, Ethical Use of AI and Data, and an overall AI Governance Framework.

Another safeguard put in place ahead of the widespread adoption of AIDA is the insistence by MAS on "explainability" in the choice, development

[3] Former Chief Data Officer, Monetary Authority of Singapore.

and implementation of systems and models. A "black box" must be avoided to ensure technology serves the needs of humans instead of it being used to offload accountability by humans.

In the application of **Garden Innovation**, MAS and the financial sector created a collaborative project, **Veritas**, to test and deploy new use cases in AIDA domains. Its primary objective is to assist financial institutions in evaluating their AIDA solutions against the principles of FEAT jointly developed by MAS and the financial industry in late 2018.

Veritas prioritised specific areas instead of trying to address all possible scenarios of AIDA applications. Veritas comprises open-source tools with applications across different business lines, such as retail banking and corporate finance, and in different markets. It will also be available as a service on the APIX platform and has prioritised three focus areas: customer marketing, credit risk scoring and fraud detection.

MAS has led an industry consortium that has recently released assessment methodologies for financial institutions' responsible use of AI. The assessment frameworks aim to guide financial institutions in evaluating their AIDA solutions and ensuring their alignment with ethical and responsible AI practices. The consortium includes representatives from financial institutions, technology companies, academia, and civil society organisations. The release of the assessment methodologies is a significant step towards promoting AI's responsible and ethical use in the financial industry.[4]

In addition to the assessment methodologies mentioned earlier, the MAS consortium has developed the FEAT principles to guide financial institutions in the ethical use of AI. The FEAT principles stand for Fairness,

---

[4] https://www.mas.gov.sg/news/media-releases/2022/mas-led-industry-consortium-publishes-assessment-methodologies-for-responsible-use-of-ai-by-financial-institutions

Ethics, Accountability, and Transparency. By adopting the FEAT principles, financial institutions can provide the alignment of their AI solutions with ethical and responsible AI practices. In addition, these principles serve as a useful framework for evaluating the impact of AI solutions on various stakeholders and identifying potential biases or unintended consequences of AI decision-making. As a result, adopting the FEAT principles can promote trust and confidence in using AI in the financial industry.

Veritas, currently in its second phase, created a framework for the responsible use of AI during Phase 1, announced on 13 November 2019. During Phase 1, two core teams developed fairness metrics and assessment methodology for two banking use cases: credit risk scoring and customer marketing. UOB and Element AI focused on credit risk scoring, while HSBC, IAG Firemark Labs, and Gradient Institute focused on customer marketing.

During Phase 2 of the Veritas project, the focus was on four areas: credit risk scoring, customer marketing, predictive underwriting, and fraud detection. The Veritas consortium created three core teams to create plans to ensure that AI is used responsibly in each area. Swiss Re and Accenture's first team is developing a fairness assessment plan for insurance predictive underwriting. Second, UOB, AXA, and Accenture are developing an ethics and accountability plan for customer marketing and insurance fraud detection.

Finally, SCB, HSBC, and Truera are working on a transparency plan for credit risk scoring and customer marketing.

Credit risk scoring to assess the creditworthiness of borrowers is a critical function of the financial services industry and impacts most customers of financial institutions. To ensure AI-driven decisions do not systematically disadvantage any particular individuals or groups when determining credit risk scoring, UOB and Element AI are developing the metrics on credit risk scoring.

Customer marketing is another area with significant potential for AI adoption. As marketing processes become increasingly digitised and automated, there is increasing scope to use AI tools to analyse customer data and match products or services to customers. To ensure AI solutions recommend the right product to the right customer at the right time, HSBC, IAG Firemark Labs and Gradient Institute will develop the metrics on customer marketing.

Additionally, MAS has embraced AIDA technologies to enhance its supervision capabilities for the financial services sector. In the **Garden Innovation** spirit, they picked digital payment tokens as their focus. In addition, they committed resources to use "real-time" data gathering to enhance its assessment of money laundering and terrorist financing risks for licensed entities. MAS is experimenting with in-house and external technologies to draw insights from new data points, such as transactional information on public blockchains and other sources. Such data will provide useful early warning indicators alongside traditional sources of information such as suspicious transaction reports.

AI in finance is transforming the way we interact with money. AI is helping the financial industry to streamline and optimise processes ranging from credit decisions to quantitative trading and financial risk management. As customers are more informed, expectations of better, faster and cheaper financial services are heightened. Hence, financial institutions rely more than ever on call centre operations with conversational AI agents that can engage directly with customers for rapid and real-time banking transactions and resolutions. AI has given the world of banking and the financial industry a whole a way to meet the demands of customers who want smarter, more convenient, safer ways to access and use their money,

Financial markets increasingly turn to machine learning, a subset of AI, to create more exacting, nimble models. Data analytics and interpretation empower financial institutions to do data storytelling on trends, identify risks, conserve the workforce and ensure data-driven decision-making.

MAS plays a pivotal role in developing the FinTech industry. The roadmaps have provided support and strategic directions for the FinTech early adopters as they roll out.

In the spirit of **Garden Innovation**, AIDA is a special focus for Singapore. As a result, MAS has created a track of funding programmes related to AIDA, becoming the first vertical to have a dedicated sponsorship programme.

As part of the Financial Sector Technology and Innovation scheme under the Financial Sector Development Fund, MAS launched the AIDA Grant to strengthen the ecosystem and promote AIDA adoption. The grant focuses on AIDA adoption to improve decision-making or generate better insights. The AIDA Grant covers unique and non-unique use cases, including AIDA projects. Eligible projects can receive up to 50% of qualifying expenses, capped at SGD1.5M for unique use cases and SGD1M for Data Analytics projects. Non-unique use cases can receive up to 30% of qualifying expenses, capped at SGD750,000 for AI projects and SGD500,000 for data analytics projects. MAS has created a dedicated industry project to help financial institutions embrace new solutions and define guardrails around AI.

Under the Research Track, the AIDA Grant co-funded research institutions' AI or data analytics projects with precise applications for Singapore's financial sector. To balance accountability and efficiency, it provided up to 70% co-funding for eligible projects demonstrating local knowledge transfer and industry sharing.

In the spirit of **Singanomics**, MAS puts money where its mouth is by committing AIDA Grant to support the strengthening of the AIDA ecosystem in the Singapore financial sector for financial and research institutions.

Under the Financial Institution Track, the AIDA Grant co-funded up to 50% of project costs for Singapore-based financial institutions, leveraging

AI and data analytics techniques to generate insights, formulate strategy, and assist in decision-making. A key criterion of measuring success in the Singanomics spirit is the requirement for financial institutions to consider the impact of the AI or data analytics project on their workforce and develop appropriate training programmes, including upskilling and re-skilling staff.

AI has emerged as a dominant sector in the Singaporean FinTech landscape, driving global leadership and successful exits. Notably, four Singapore-based AI companies — Tookitaki, AiDA, Basis AI and Jewel Payment Tech — were acquired by Thunes, AIA, Aicadium, and Advance AI, respectively, to enhance their capabilities and expand their product offerings. It is worth highlighting that these companies specialised in distinct niche areas of RegTech, InsurTech, and lending, respectively. As a knowledge economy hosting headquarters of several global financial institutions, AI has been one of the shining stars of Singapore Fintech Nation.

Merkle Science, a blockchain analysis and cryptocurrency forensics company, has announced an extension of its Series A funding round to over USD24M. The company plans to use this funding to expand its presence globally, develop its technology and services, and accelerate growth. Merkle Science's platform provides anti-money laundering and compliance solutions to cryptocurrency exchanges, financial institutions, and law enforcement agencies. It aims to make blockchain technology safer and more accessible to mainstream users by preventing illegal activities such as money laundering and terrorism financing.[5]

Silent Eight, a Singapore-based FinTech company, has raised USD40M in a Series B funding round. SC Ventures, a subsidiary of Standard Chartered, led the investment and saw participation from existing investors like

[5] https://www.prnewswire.com/news-releases/merkle-science-announces-extension-of-series-a-to-over-24-million-301603048.html

Wavemaker Partners, OTB Ventures, and Koh Boon Hwee. Silent Eight provides AI-powered tools to help banks and financial institutions combat money laundering and terrorism financing.[6]

Insurance giant AIA's health tech arm, AIA Health Services, has acquired AI startup AIDA Technologies to bolster its data analytics capabilities. The acquisition will help AIA Health Services enhance its customer experience and develop personalised products and services based on customers' health and lifestyle data. AIDA Technologies, founded in 2016 and headquartered in Singapore, provides AI-driven predictive analytics solutions for the insurance, finance, and healthcare industries.[7]

Aicadium, founded by Temasek, acquired the Singaporean AI company, BasisAI. The acquisition is a strategic move aimed at strengthening Aicadium's AI capabilities and advancing its industry growth. Aicadium's acquisition of BasisAI will allow it to expand its product offerings and reach new markets. The deal is a significant milestone in Aicadium's growth trajectory and demonstrates its commitment to innovation and leadership in the AI industry.[8]

Conclusion

AI has revolutionised the banking and finance sector both in Singapore and on a global scale, ushering in significant transformations. Through the strategic utilisation of AI and data analytics, Singapore aims to augment customer experience, fortify risk management practices, and foster

[6] https://www.prnewswire.com/news-releases/silent-eight-raises-40m-in-series-b-round-301499126.html

[7] https://fintechnews.sg/68576/insurtech/aias-amplify-health-acquires-ai-startup-aida-technologies/

[8] https://www.prnewswire.com/news-releases/temasek-founded-aicadium-acquires-singapore-ai-firm-basisai-301365622.html

innovation within the financial industry. Nevertheless, it is imperative to confront the challenges associated with AI head-on, encompassing aspects such as auditability, accountability, and ethical considerations. Addressing these concerns is crucial to ensure the responsible and compliant implementation of AI technology, thereby fostering trust and benefitting all stakeholders.

Over the years, Singapore has honed its ability to conceive grand visions and effectively mobilise resources to translate them into reality. This remarkable feat is exemplified by various notable endeavors, including the establishment of the world's largest FinTech event, the initiation of a government-driven sustainability programme featuring industry utilities, and the pioneering creation of one of the world's foremost AI-focused regulatory and monetary support infrastructures. Singapore consistently sets benchmarks for excellence and provides a blueprint for policymakers on how to bolster the industry's ambitions while simultaneously considering the needs of society. By striking this delicate balance, Singapore showcases its unparalleled capacity to drive progress and shape the future of the financial landscape.

Chapter 9

TALENT — ONLY REAL MOAT

The FinTech industry has witnessed remarkable growth in recent years, disrupting traditional financial systems and introducing innovative solutions. As technology continues to evolve, the industry must prioritise upskilling and reskilling initiatives to equip professionals with the necessary competencies to navigate the future of FinTech. This chapter aims to provide an overview of talent development in FinTech today and shed light on specific actions that should be taken to address the emerging challenges.

This book aims to gain information and insights from the founders and early movers of FinTech in Singapore. Through the interviews, the key finding that arose with FinTech founders and others was the importance of talent. In FinTech, the importance of talent is second to none. An organisation must have the required talented workforce to attain its goal even if it possesses other factors such as proprietary technology, infrastructure and capital. The people take an organisation to its next level of success. Sustainability and scalability in FinTech are wholly dependent on human capital.

There are two things to look at within a startup: internal talent (i.e., founders and employees) and external support (i.e., government and societal support). This poses a chicken-and-egg problem. A startup must have an open-door policy and an entrepreneurial-friendly environment to lure founders. At the same time, successful founders need to push for more governmental and societal support. However, there is nuance to this in that government support must help companies succeed but not buoy companies with no viable business models.

Thus, there is a critical need to understand the current talent development practices to develop a contemporary paradigm that will support a radically different future. Talent, arguably Singapore's core resource and competitive advantage, is a key pillar in the development of the FinTech sector. Talent development is rapidly changing because of the accelerating integration of technology and information into the daily work environment. Unfortunately, there appears to be a dearth of talent development studies regarding organisations' strategies.

Developing human capital is challenging in every market, especially in a small localised market such as Singapore. Historically, Singapore depends on two sources of talent: importing skilled workers from abroad and developing the local population via education and up-skill training. While the first method continues to be a viable route, it is becoming a more tenuous proposition as there is a pushback against immigration on a global scale. Singapore can control the tool of developing local talent, from primary education to Institutes of Higher Learning (IHLs). Specifically, with the trend of micro-credentialing offered by IHLs, talent can continue to be cultivated locally.

Since the independence of Singapore in 1965, under the leadership of its founding father, Lee Kuan Yew, education has been key in the development of Singapore. Today, the education system is ranked as one of the world's best, especially when it comes to STEM (Science, Technology, Engineering and Math) subjects, as reported by *The Economist* pointing to the Organisation for Economic Co-operation and Development's Programme for International Student Assessment (PISA).[1] These developments have made the local talent pipeline very robust for STEM employers, leading to another reason for multinationals to base their Asian operations in Singapore. STEM subjects alone, however, do not guarantee futureproofing of new graduates as the world's technological applications develop at breakneck speed. This is nowhere more evident than in the FinTech space, where tried-and-tested pillars of financial services are being disrupted at their core.

Even traditional roles in accounting and finance are being transformed through the multitude of technological advancements. At IHLs, accounting and finance courses have begun incorporating FinTech to update curricula. Technological advancements such as data analytics, blockchain and cloud computing are changing the current educational position. Future accounting and finance professionals must think strategically, communicate effectively, and be tech-savvy to identify and capitalise on opportunities.

To give a holistic understanding of Singapore's talent development challenges, interviews were conducted, spanning from academia to industry. To do so, we have interviewed leaders at some of the major IHLs. Additionally, we approached those with private sector perspectives involved in developing higher education to address these talent challenges.

Talent Development Today and Challenges in the Future

Singapore's education system has been the cornerstone of development for the city-state since its independence. The result of these efforts is the formation of one of the highest-rated educational processes in the world,

[1] https://www.economist.com/leaders/2018/08/30/what-other-countries-can-learn-from-singapores-schools

having reached #1 in the PISA rankings in 2018.[2] Reaching the top spot in educational rankings does not mean we can rest on our laurels. The government has recently announced initiatives to revamp the system to incorporate lessons from other countries, such as focusing on children's development instead of test taking, and to futureproof students by incorporating technological skills such as coding from a young age.

When speaking with business leaders and those with a deep technological background in the private sector, talent development and access to quality talent are some of the biggest challenges that Singapore is facing today. This challenge is only expected to become more acute, especially in the FinTech sector. Recent surveys from the FinTech Employment report show that 94% of respondents believe the city-state is facing talent shortages.[3] Smart Nation Initiative report showed an expectation of 60,000 new jobs by 2023. With only 8,400 graduates focused on "Infocomm" or information communication studies during those years, a fall of 51,600 jobs will exist. To further drive home the point of FinTech playing an increasingly powerful role in the talent landscape of Singapore, in August 2020, the Monetary Authority of Singapore (MAS) said that FinTechs collectively employ nearly 10,000 people, which exceeds the employment numbers of major international banks such as HSBC and UBS.[4] Then there will be challenges for the private sector in securing key talent. The government will have the unenviable job of balancing economic growth and ensuring fair access to jobs for locals. Singapore's employers and professionals see the talent supply as critical in ensuring FinTech's ongoing success.

[2] https://www.economist.com/leaders/2018/08/30/what-other-countries-can-learn-from-singapores-schools

[3] https://www.michaelpage.com.sg/sites/michaelpage.com.sg/files/16785-sg_fintech_brochure_mp.v6_0.pdf

[4] https://news.efinancialcareers.com/hk-en/3004288/singapore-fintechs-employ-10000-people?utm_source=GLOBAL_ENG&utm_medium=SM_FB&utm_campaign=FANS

Private and Governmental Responses

Tan Chin Hwee and Dr. Yougesh Khatri were interviewed to better understand talent development challenges from private and government perspectives. Chin Hwee has a solid career in finance, currently holding the position of APAC CEO of Trafigura, and is a member of the Emerging Stronger Singapore task force and the MAS financial advisory panel. In addition, he runs his own family office that focuses on startups and FinTech space.

Singapore is no longer on the developmental curve but is on the frontier, indicating that growth will ultimately come from improvements in productivity or efficiency. This presents the unique challenge of balancing the needs of the local population by lifting them through acquiring advanced technological skills while maintaining an open economy to attract new immigrants with skillsets the country lacks.

When asked about the talent challenges facing Singapore, similar viewpoints on the world-class educational system and open access to global talent have been highlighted as key pillars to the success of Singapore. Chin Hwee comments that while Singapore remains one of the best systems in the world for imbuing technical skills in students, to become truly competitive in the increasingly global world, there needs to be an added focus on cross-disciplinary and soft skills development. Likewise, the World Economic Forum, as shown in the infographic titled "Top 10 skills of 2023", illustrated the increasing importance of soft skills such as critical thinking and creativity.

Continued access to global talent would be vital for the future. There needs to be a focus on facilitating high-value immigration, such as those with the talents and skills to address the shortfall in FinTech while maintaining fair access for the local population with the same opportunities. A key example of such high-value immigration was highlighted during the

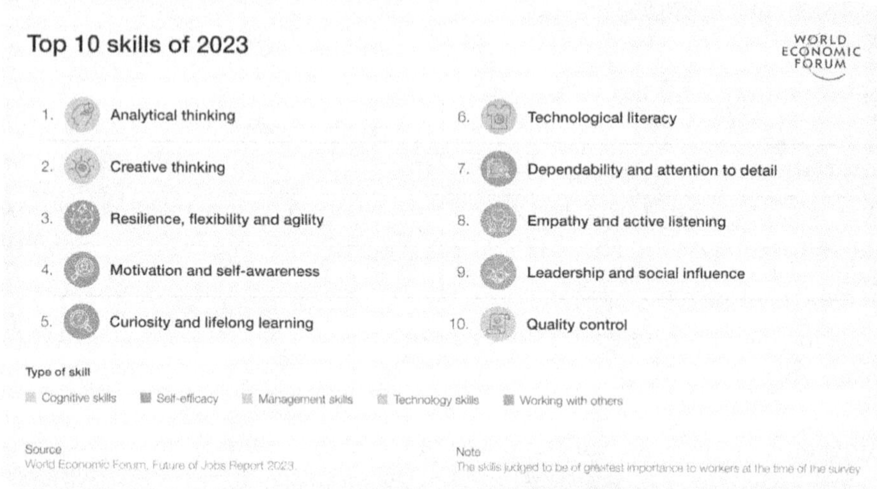

COVID-19 pandemic in the story of Sea Ltd, the owner of Shopee, and other technology companies based in Singapore. David Chen, Forrest Li and Gang Ye founded Sea Ltd in 2009 via Singapore's foreign talent schemes, and now a decade later, it is worth nearly USD51B.[5]

Being on the Emerging Stronger Taskforce, Chin Hwee has a first-hand look at the challenges for Singapore after the COVID-19 pandemic and the swift digitisation occurring across industries. A key industry that he believes will help alleviate the talent gap is EduTech or education technology. This refers to a digital disruption focusing on the education sector democratising access to educational resources. The task force is actively supporting such developments, and he believes that it will be a key piece in addressing the talent shortage by providing ease of access to retraining tools. Ultimately, by easing access to retraining, retrenched workers with strong, soft skills can learn the necessary technical skills to address the talent shortage. This is precisely what SkillsFuture is doing: providing support grants to Singaporeans

[5] https://amp-scmp-com.cdn.ampproject.org/c/s/amp.scmp.com/news/asia/southeast-asia/article/3096894/how-singapores-bid-lure-talent-paid-billionaire-founders

and permanent residents who are 40 years old and above, with a generous 90% funding of course fees when they complete training courses approved under the grant. The authors have been actively overseeing the FinTech Talent Programme (FTP), rolled out in 2017 under the Singapore FinTech Association (SFA) and the FinTech Academy.[6] The authors, together with a huge number of volunteers, carried out the planning and implementation as part of their "national service", dedicating time and energy towards ensuring the success of this initiative. This **Singanomics** model of development shows that the community understands that the nation cannot thrive unless the people get together to serve a larger, higher calling.

While addressing the development of talent in the medium- to long-term challenges for Singapore in the future, there remain the ever-present challenges today for talent in the city. As mentioned earlier, the FinTech space has a clear challenge in attracting and retaining relevant talent today and needs novel ways to address this. As the adage goes, necessity is the mother of invention, and that is exactly what has occurred across industries in Singapore when it comes to talent attraction, even more so in FinTech.

MAS has launched the Financial Sector Artificial Intelligence and Data Analytics (AIDA) Talent Development Programme. This initiative aims to address the shortage of AIDA talent in the financial sector by aggregating talent demands, collaborating with training providers and institutions, and creating tailored training programmes. The AIDA Talent Consortium, consisting of financial institutions, training providers, and educational institutions, will facilitate this process and contribute expertise in curriculum design.

AIDA Talent Consortium aims to increase the supply of AIDA talent to build deep capabilities in the financial sector. It focuses on improving the quality and quantity of trainers, channeling students with varying

[6] https://fintechacademy.net/

proficiency levels to the appropriate courses and improving the industry relevance of the curriculum. The consortium will facilitate the matching of financial institutions to training and education institutions, which can then curate and design programmes to meet the needs of the industry. Through the Consortium, MAS will aggregate financial institutions' talent demands across various AIDA roles based on their stage of AIDA adoption.

The consortium will design a skill progression pathway that will serve as a roadmap for the roles and skills the sector requires; case studies to provide examples of applying AIDA skills in local financial institutions and platforms to host hackathons that will allow students access to real-world industrial environments.

Graduates for a Digital World

The private and governmental sectors are key pillars in addressing talent challenges in Singapore, but with IHLs, it is possible to see the full picture. Singapore has many prerequisites for being a global hub in technology, seeing it already is one for finance. With proper branding and good governance, the aspiration to become a global education hub could materialise. This will be key to attracting the talent resource required to grow an economy at the frontier of the development curve. To further explore the challenges on one of the supply channels for talent, we reached out to four interviewees who were directly involved in FinTech and in preparing students to be future-ready:

- **Prof. Tjin Swee Chuan**, Associate Provost (Continuing Education) and **Prof. Soh Wai Lin Christina**, Dean of the Nanyang Technological University (NTU) business school, provided a good overview of the initiatives being taken at the university.
- **Dr. Douglas Rolph**, the Senior Lecturer of Finance from 2018 at the Singapore University of Technology and Design (SUTD), after being a

senior lecturer at NTU for seven years, gave his perspectives on the quality of talent capital that we have. His research focuses on FinTech ecosystems and the role of innovation in financial institutions, so he is an astute individual to answer the challenges of graduates entering the FinTech space.
- **Prof Lawrence Loh**, Director, Centre for Governance and Sustainability (CGS) at the NUS Business School, National University of Singapore (NUS).

IHLs are a crucial part of the ecosystem in ensuring the sustainability of local talent.

The IHLs in Singapore are all working towards futureproofing both their institutions and students in Singapore. However, how they go about this is all slightly different and nuanced. The deliberate differentiation amongst the major IHLs has blossomed into various talent pools to meet the varying demands of industries. NTU, for instance, has leveraged its strong scientific heritage to provide access to cross-disciplinary opportunities. Christina alludes to this by saying that at the undergraduate level, where most students reside, they have made it a common requirement for business students to learn computer coding skills. The Nanyang Business School and the School of Computer Science and Engineering offer a popular double degree in business and computing. She points out that this not only allows for proper teaching of crucial technical skills for the future, but the goal is for cross-collaboration between the two schools as students progress in their university journey. If a student in either school has a business idea, they will be empowered to work with the affiliated schools to obtain the input that they may lack. An example provided was a computer science student with an innovative idea needing to understand accountancy or finance. With this structure, the computer science student would already have interacted with students studying accountancy or finance, helping to form a strong team for a potential startup venture. Beyond the cross-collaboration,

NTU is attempting to instil an entrepreneurial spirit in its students by making Entrepreneurship a core course in the undergraduate programme. While some might sneer at entrepreneurship being taught in a classroom setting, it should provide frameworks and skillsets to navigate an entrepreneurial journey for startups. With further external stimulus in the form of founder visits, presentations by industry experts, and a general appetite for careers in emerging fields such as FinTech, it should further entrench the skills highly sought after by employers.

SUTD has an impressively progressive take on approaching the challenge of preparing talent for FinTech. SUTD, in general, as told by Douglas, tends to encourage risk-taking and entrepreneurship as a core tenet of the school. What sets it apart is the focus on students to build critical thinking and technical skills in unison. From Douglas' perspective, critical thinking will be a key requirement of success in not just FinTech but any industry in the future, a notion that has been highlighted frequently by the private sector.

Beyond the tangible skill sets being imparted at SUTD, the key ingredient institutions globally overlook in preparing students according to Douglas, is exposure to failure. Failure not in the sense that they fail classes but having the exposure to potential failure in practical project work in controlled settings while being able to glean lessons from them. To do this, SUTD worked with the Massachusetts Institute of Technology to develop an undergraduate programme that embraces risk-taking, inquisitiveness and inevitable failure in certain endeavours. This builds self-reliance, mental strength, and understanding that failure is part of learning. Within this framework, the students are placed in high adaptation environments in the form of real-life project work by completing a total of four projects. Of these four projects, two must be sourced independently, and each must result in real-world impact via the application of their coursework. Such projects give the students first-hand exposure to working with ambiguity and being able to apply creative solutions to nebulous problems. The outcomes of these projects and the creative use of technology to solve the presented problems help prepare the students for the challenges inherent in the working world.

Christina has also implemented such initiatives at NTU with granular private/institutional collaboration. These initiatives involve working directly with the industries to craft specific courses and then having industry practitioners do the teaching. The key difference between this initiative and others is that there is direct support by a key industry player that allows practitioners to teach as part of their working hours, removing the key obstacle of consistency in quality and reducing the reliance on alumni volunteerism. A great example is Deloitte, which has co-created a digital audit analytics course and has supported this at the corporate level.[7] For this course, Deloitte and Nanyang Business School worked in close unison to develop the curriculum, specifically for the challenges that Deloitte saw in practice while providing top practitioners from their offices to teach on the company's time. This allows for customised skills training for future hires and consistency in teaching quality. It is hoped that more such initiatives could occur over the next few years.

Talent Initiatives

One of the key initiatives in Singapore has been building talent clusters to support the growing needs of the FinTech industry, a multi-prong strategy.

As of June 2022, Singapore has a population comprising approximately 4 million citizens, permanent residents, and 1.56 million non-citizens. Nurturing local talent and attracting foreign talent are key priorities for the island nation. As technology adoption scales, Singapore faces a host of challenges. Incumbent financial institutions embracing digitisation possess

[7] https://www2.deloitte.com/sg/en/pages/careers/articles/deloitte-ntu-launch-new-course-audit-analytics.html

many operation staff who must be re-skilled and up-skilled to embrace the new jobs in the financial services and FinTech sectors. On the other hand, young graduates from local universities and polytechnics need specific deployable skills to satiate the ever-growing hunger for talent from FinTech companies in blockchain, data analytics, cybersecurity and other emerging solutions.

> *"To develop deep capabilities, we need to anchor Singapore's best international capabilities and grow our timber over time."*
>
> *Ong Ye Kung* [8]

As a community, everyone has come together to address these challenges. SFA brought together FinTech founders and professionals from the banks to run several training programmes where trainers contributed their time free of charge to up-skill the community. Public education is necessary to keep up with the challenges and nurture talent.

Speaking to **Deepak Khanna**, the Head of Wealth and Trading Revolut, Singapore, we gained valuable insights. The London-based digital banking app was launched in Singapore in 2018. As of April 2022, it obtained in-principle approval from MAS to operate a fully regulated cryptocurrency service and merchant acquiring services. Within the landscape of increasing regulations on cryptocurrencies in Singapore, Revolut has also managed to launch cryptocurrency services in August 2022.

Revolut has a grand vision: to build a global financial super app, allowing people to manage their money anywhere. This requires clients to trust the balance sheets and the platform to meet the needs of its users. With the trend of increasing adoption of cryptocurrencies, Revolut's role takes on a

---

[8] Minister for Education (Higher Education and Skills) and MAS Board Member, Launch of the Financial Services Industry Transformation Map.

crucial task: to be a responsible institution in educating the public. Particularly in Singapore, a three-pronged approach is required. First, clients gain access to learning tools, such as the "Learn and Earn" programme; second, to mitigate fraud risk for clients for crypto-related information; finally, to educate youths.

Deepak's journey started with a personal belief in the FinTech industry. He saw that FinTech was, and continues to be, the future of banking. It is also more agile and faster in terms of providing services. However, in Singapore, there are still challenges for the industry to overcome — specifically in the aspect of talent development and talent retention. With more jobs becoming automated and taken over by platforms, Singapore needs the workforce to understand the opportunities provided by this evolution. Furthermore, ensuring a productive and sustainable workforce will require services of skills mapping for individuals with career pathways and goals. His advice for people wanting to join the FinTech industry: think hard, consider your skills and culture, and decide whether you align with either side before joining them.

The Institute of Banking and Finance (IBF) has secured a commitment from 19 financial institutions to re-skill 4,000 existing finance professionals — to equip them with the skills necessary to take on new or expanded roles against the backdrop of transformed business activities. IBF has also provided career advisory and job-matching services to more than 600 finance professionals whose jobs have been affected by the change. It reviewed 121 distinct job roles in the financial industry, examining how data analytics and automation will likely change the individual tasks in these 121 job roles.

To illustrate an example of the *kampung* spirit, instead of competing, all the polytechnics set up a combined platform to engage industries to understand their needs, update their academic curriculum and partner with mentors to support these students. MAS saw this as a great bottom-up approach to building networks between companies and educational institutions. MAS supported the initiative by hosting some of the initial sessions.

The authors have been advocating this access to talent development opportunity by improving the accessibility and affordability of education to empower a generation of workforce to up-skill and re-skill when needed. Now, more than ever, with COVID-19 establishing the new normal, **Varun Mittal** sees that Singapore needs to move forward to facilitate greater adoption of FinTech in the region. **Dr Lillian Koh**, then teaching post-graduate courses at NTU, was invited to oversee FTP in SFA as the Talent Development Advisor to SFA.

SFA offers the FTP in partnership with the Fintech Academy (FTA). It comprises an eight-module course taught over 80 hours that culminates in a Capstone project where the participants will present on Demo Day. To qualify for SkillsFuture funding, where Singaporean citizens or permanent residents who are 40 years old and above receive a generous 90% funding of course fees plus further perks, the FTP course has to meet stringent criteria, fulfil competencies, and achieve standards required by the SkillsFuture.[9]

The authors were actively involved in the implementation of this programme. Dr Lillian Koh, the CEO and Founder of FTA, was physically there three times per week for the year to facilitate the 80-hour FTP, a course targeted at working adults with many years of industry experience. FTA is incorporated in Singapore to spearhead talent development programmes ranging from financial and FinTech literacy awareness to university deep dive courses. The academy maps the current curriculum to future skills needed and proposes new modules for weaving in FinTech for universities, including the PSB Academy. FTA also works hand in hand with professional

[9] https://www.ssg.gov.sg/skillsfuture.html

bodies like the Institution of Engineers Singapore, the Association of Chartered Certified Accountants and the Institute of Singapore Chartered Accountants to ensure that our professionals are kept abreast of the latest developments in FinTech through short courses and webinars. It will continue to curate innovative education programmes by integrating learning, industry and our growing community through collaborations with academia in research and development with industry practitioners.

Neelesh Bhatia, from Singapore Polytechnic, also taught FTP with Lillian and a team of trainers. Neelesh has 30 years of experience in entrepreneurship education, business innovation, media and technology. He is now the CEO and co-founder of his third startup, AKADASIA. He rallies for education accessibility and affordability for all.

These FTP cohorts, who benefitted from this programme, could choose the next deep dive course to pursue an alternative pathway. For others, it is acquiring awareness and acknowledging opportunities to apply the newfound knowledge to day-to-day work. A case in point is Vincent Tan, who graduated from the 2018 FTP batch.

Vincent's first exposure to FinTech was attending the Singapore FinTech Festival in 2017. Subsequently, he decided to join FTP to learn more about the FinTech world. After attending FTP and a few other modular courses in IHLs, he became more exposed to FinTech and technology. He began to be interested in the cybersecurity field. This has even led him to volunteer for the other portfolio and responsibility in his job to cover new cyber and technology risk initiatives from the business perspective in his company. One of the challenges he faced was gaining the technical knowledge he lacked, having spent most of his career in the business and operation areas within the banking industry. All the "why's and how's" led him to the path of exploration. In 2019, he decided to pursue a Master's programme in cybersecurity. He strongly believes that with Singapore focusing on growing FinTech on a large scale and digitalisation happening in many industries, security will play an important role in safeguarding the companies' assets and better fulfilling the requirements of his current work portfolio. With the government's support, he had a scholarship with the Infocomm Media Development Authority to pursue a two-year part-time Master of Science in Security by Design with SUTD. From his experience, he realised that most projects do not start with security in mind. The culture of security by design is still lacking in society. Conceptually, this should resemble locking his home or office door before leaving. This could be due to a false sense of security, lack of technical know-how, resources, or a combination of reasons. We should also expand the **Right First, Fast Later** and *Kiasu* spirits to security by design to ensure that we grow with a protection mindset. With the *kampung* spirit inculcated in Singapore, mutual help could potentially resolve this. With Singapore progressing into the digital age, we should incorporate cybersecurity as a core business objective, beginning with security in mind. This should be woven into an organisation's culture to build a long-term defence against major threats.

Talent Challenges or Opportunity?

In Singapore, the FinTech sector faces many challenges in talent availability. Companies and IHLs are rising to the challenge today, with innovations taking place to tackle the larger problems that are on the horizon. Singapore has always been pragmatic regarding managing its greatest resource, human capital, which will continue to be the case.

Prof. Tjin Swee Chuan, Associate Provost (Continuing Education) and Chief Executive of the Centre for Professional and Continuing Education (PaCE) from NTU, says, "Micro-credentialing has a significant role to play in talent development for the future of FinTech. Micro-credentials are short, focused credentials that validate specific skills or competencies. They provide individuals with a flexible and targeted way to upskill or reskill in specific areas. This allows them to quickly acquire relevant knowledge and demonstrate proficiency in specialised domains within FinTech.

Here are some reasons why micro-credentialing is relevant and valuable for talent development in the FinTech industry:

- **Agility and Relevance:** FinTech is a rapidly evolving field, with emerging technologies and industry trends constantly shaping the landscape. Micro-credentials enable professionals to stay agile and adapt to these changes by acquiring targeted skills in a shorter timeframe than traditional degree programmes.
- **Specialisation and Depth:** FinTech encompasses many domains, including blockchain, AI, data analytics, cybersecurity, and more. Micro-credentials allow professionals to specialise and develop in-depth knowledge in specific areas of interest or emerging technologies, enhancing their expertise and employability.
- **Industry Recognition:** Micro-credentials are often developed with industry experts, ensuring they align with industry standards and practices. Earning micro-credentials demonstrates to employers a commitment to continuous learning and staying up-to-date with the latest advancements in FinTech.
- **Flexibility and Accessibility:** Micro-credentials are typically offered online or hybrid and can be completed at one's own pace. This flexibility makes them accessible to working professionals, allowing them to balance their learning with their existing commitments. It also enables professionals to choose specific micro-credentials that align with their career goals or address specific skill gaps.
- **Lifelong Learning:** Continuous learning is essential in a rapidly evolving industry like FinTech. Micro-credentials support lifelong learning, as professionals can continuously acquire new micro-credentials throughout their careers, expanding their skill sets and staying relevant in the industry. It encourages professionals to embrace a growth mindset and

actively seek opportunities for skills enhancement. As the industry evolves, micro-credentials can be regularly updated to reflect emerging trends and technologies, ensuring that talent remains relevant and competitive.

- **Recognition of Prior Learning:** Micro-credentials allow professionals to showcase their skills and competencies, even if they gained them through practical experience or non-traditional learning paths. They can validate and acknowledge the skills professionals have acquired outside formal education, enabling individuals to leverage their existing knowledge and experience.

To fully harness the transformative power of micro-credentialing in talent development, the FinTech industry must forge strong collaborations with educational institutions, industry associations, and certification bodies. By working together, these stakeholders can design and deliver impactful micro-credential programmes that align with the evolving needs of the industry. Employers must also acknowledge the value of micro-credentials and integrate them into their hiring and promotion processes, recognising them as reliable indicators of specialised expertise and commitment to professional growth.

A shining example of such collaboration is the partnership between FTA and NTU. This strategic alliance allows industry professionals and academia to create a dynamic learning environment, empowering participants to gain comprehensive knowledge of FinTech and its practical applications. By leveraging the collective wisdom and experience of industry experts and academic scholars, this initiative equips learners with the cutting-edge skills and insights necessary to thrive in the fast-paced FinTech landscape. By incorporating micro-credentials into talent development strategies, the FinTech industry can foster a culture of continuous learning, address specific skill gaps, and ensure a workforce that is adaptable, skilled, and prepared for future challenges and opportunities in FinTech.

By fostering robust partnerships between educational institutions, industry associations, and certification bodies and recognising micro-credentials' significance, the FinTech industry can build a talent development ecosystem that propels innovation, bolsters competitiveness, and ensures a sustainable future for FinTech professionals.

Micro-credentialing has a significant place in talent development for the future of FinTech. It provides a targeted, flexible, and industry-relevant approach to upskilling and reskilling, allowing professionals to acquire specific competencies and demonstrate their expertise. By embracing micro-credentials as part of their talent development strategies, FinTech companies can nurture a skilled workforce well-equipped to tackle emerging challenges and drive continued innovation in the industry.

In an interview with Prof. Lawrence Loh the following points were discussed.

As FinTech refers to the use of technology in the financial sector to provide innovative solutions and improve efficiency, FinTech has a significant role in advancing green finance in both the banking and finance sectors and the corporate world. Here are some use cases that demonstrate the relationship between green finance and FinTech:

Sustainable Investment Platforms: FinTech platforms can provide digital solutions for investors to access and invest in green financial products such as green bonds, renewable energy funds, and sustainable portfolios. These platforms offer transparency, accessibility, and tools to track the environmental impact of investments.

Green Payment Solutions: FinTech companies can develop payment systems that incentivise and promote eco-friendly behaviours. For example, they can offer rewards or discounts for sustainable transportation or purchasing from environmentally responsible merchants.

Smart Energy Management: FinTech solutions can integrate with smart energy systems to enable efficient energy usage and monitoring. This includes smart meters, energy analytics, and demand response systems that help individuals and businesses optimise their energy consumption and reduce their carbon footprint.

Carbon Footprint Tracking: FinTech applications can provide individuals and organisations with tools to measure and track their carbon emissions. This data can be used to calculate carbon footprints, set reduction targets, and incentivise sustainable practices through rewards or lower interest rates on loans.

Green Lending and Crowdfunding: FinTech platforms can facilitate green lending by connecting borrowers with lenders interested in financing environmentally friendly projects. Additionally, crowdfunding platforms can help raise funds for renewable energy projects or other sustainable initiatives.

Sustainable Supply Chain Finance: FinTech solutions can enable transparent and efficient supply chain financing, specifically targeting sustainable and ethical suppliers. Blockchain technology, for example, can ensure traceability and accountability throughout the supply chain, promoting fair trade and sustainable sourcing practices.

These use cases highlight how FinTech can support and enhance green finance initiatives in the banking and finance sectors and the corporate world, fostering sustainability and driving positive environmental impact. Therefore, professional development in ESG (Environmental, Social, and Governance) is crucial in today's rapidly evolving landscape. Use cases showcasing the role of FinTech in supporting green finance initiatives across banking, finance, and corporate sectors highlight the potential to foster sustainability and drive positive environmental impact. To effectively contribute to this transformative shift, professionals need to prioritise continuous skill upgrading and stay abreast of the latest trends and innovations. With the world constantly changing, staying knowledgeable and informed is essential in order to seize opportunities and make a meaningful difference in advancing ESG goals. By investing in professional development, individuals can equip themselves with the necessary expertise to navigate the complexities of ESG, effectively contribute to green finance initiatives, and shape a more sustainable future. These are courses offered by NUS in partnership with Fintech Academy.

In conclusion, the FinTech industry's growth trajectory relies heavily on the availability of a skilled workforce. Talent development today encompasses various initiatives promoting cross-disciplinary expertise, collaboration, and continuous learning. However, challenges such as talent shortage, evolving technological landscape, and regulatory complexities pose significant obstacles for the future. FinTech companies must proactively address these challenges through strategic partnerships, innovative recruitment practices, and ongoing talent development programmes to foster a sustainable and inclusive FinTech ecosystem.

Chapter 10

MORPHING DIGITAL BANKING

One of the key facets of Singapore's growth has been the strong top-down development of a roadmap while encouraging private enterprises to charter their paths as long as they are aligned with the roadmap. Financial services have been a critical component of this dual-path strategy adopted by Singapore.

Most financial centres worldwide have multiple authorities for functions like regulatory supervision for banking, insurance and capital markets, currency issuance and monetary policy. For example, in Hong Kong, regulation is split between the Hong Kong Monetary Authority, the Insurance Authority, and the Securities and Futures Commission. In the UK, the law is divided between authorities like Prudential Regulation Authority, Payment Systems Regulator, Financial Conduct Authority, and Financial Reporting Council.

In Singapore, the Monetary Authority of Singapore (MAS) is the single, all-powerful watchdog responsible for monetary policy, issuing currency, and regulatory supervision of banking, insurance and securities. In addition, MAS is also responsible for market development and trade promotion for the financial services sector. The acronym for its name resembles *mas*, the word for "gold" in Malay. This ingenious one-stop solution of putting everything under one roof ensures speed, agility and coordination. It can be traced back to the country's founding father, Lee Kuan Yew, "**Singapore Works**". As a result, MAS can have a consolidated approach to the regulatory sandbox and FinTech promotion, create support programmes across sub-sectors, and remove the challenge of inter-agency delays and conflicts from the equations.

FinTech, as we know it now, got its formal recognition in August 2015 when MAS formed a FinTech and Innovation Group (FTIG) within MAS to drive the Smart Financial Centre initiatives. Led by its Chief FinTech Officer, Sopnendu Mohanty, now known as "Chief" in community circuits, it was entrusted to lead the charge to build on the foundations of the previous generation and set the stage for the future.

In 2016, a FinTech Office was formed by MAS and five other prominent government agencies: Singapore Economic Development Board, SGInnovate, Infocomm Development Authority of Singapore, National Research Foundation Singapore, and Standards, Productivity and Innovation Board (SPRING Singapore), to serve as a one-stop virtual entity for all FinTech-related matters.

The FTIG is what we call in national service parades, the "Flag Bearer" of change and innovation for the ecosystem. Just like there would be no Israel Startup Nation without the talent pool of the Israel Military, there would be no Singapore FinTech Nation without FTIG. The FTIG instilled a *garang* (a Singlish word for the meaning of "fierce") enthusiasm in everyone to bring rapid scaling up initiatives to support FinTech across pillars of policy, capital, talent, demand, and develop a credible brand.

Such is the obsession and commitment to FinTech by the Singapore government that it has the highest number of posts and mentions amongst any category on the MAS website and is more than the second and third-highest categories combined. The tone is set up from the top, and that is what makes Singapore click.

Digital Banks

1997 was a turning point in the history of financial services in Asia since most countries were hit by the Asian financial crisis, and it caused financial systems in multiple countries to collapse. As a port city with a strong contribution of financial services to GDP, Singapore realised it needed to make radical changes to its financial services sector to remain competitive and ensure its survival. Just like how Asian mothers are famously known as *tiger moms* due to their aspiration to accept nothing except the best from their kids, Singapore Inc also pushes its constituents outside of their comfort zones to face and conquer their worst fears.

Singaporean banks understood they must become regional and global to be viable and relevant. The government wants to ensure that domestic priorities are addressed and that local banks are there to support the country in times of need, but they can only expect protection for a while. Leaders forecast that the internet would democratise financial services. Even if customer acquisition branches could be helpful, most of the servicing and the rest of the financial service lifecycle would move online.

In the post-2008 financial crisis era, neo banks, or challenger banks, have gained traction, with multiple European markets having over 30 digital banks. These markets faced many changes during the financial crisis, wherein financial institutions were deemed too big to fail and had to be bailed out with public money. The general sentiment was against using public funds, and the regulators responded by making changes. New licences for new financial service players were offered for digital banks, and various laws were passed for consumer transparency.

Singapore FinTech startups and many Western observers joked about Singapore not having digital banks even though it is the FinTech Nation of the world. While that may be the case, it should be noted that as of the end of 2022, MAS has issued five digital bank licences. Singapore understood the value of the internet in financial services before most countries. Tharman Shanmugaratnam, served as the Senior Minister of Singapore from 2019 to 2023, has been the birthfather of FinTech in Singapore. "**Senior Minister**", like many other terms, is a role defined only within Singapore. The position is traditionally held by a political veteran, who advises the Prime Minister and the rest of the cabinet.

Along with his responsibilities, he was the Chairman of the Board of Directors in MAS, Singapore's central bank and financial regulator. In addition to his duties in the government, he was Deputy Chairman of the GIC (formerly known as the Government of Singapore Investment Corporation) and chaired its Investment Strategies Committee.

In 2000, Singapore was the first country to announce a clear framework for internet-only banks, embracing that future consumers will interact with financial services over the internet. But, take a breath; this was when there was only a dial-up connection, no smartphone, basic 2G internet, no touch screen, and the tiny red dot announcing, "Let's prepare for internet banking".

Singapore learnt from history that laws alone would not make digital banks successful. Many building blocks in the ecosystem are needed. Digital banks in some neighbouring jurisdictions have yet to be able to launch their services even after 15–18 months of licence award due to the absence of these underlying infrastructures. Singapore identified these building blocks as the ability to identify and onboard digitally (MyInfo/CorpPass), move money seamlessly (PayNow), and citizen/business consented verified data exchange. Singapore chose to wait to introduce its digital bank licensing regime until these things were addressed, thus sticking to the **Right First, Fast Later** ideology.

As per **Singanomics**, Singapore's digital bank licensing regime was unique in enabling innovation with a level playing field to address society's unmet and unserved needs while preventing any value-destructive competition.

As a proud owner of some of the strongest banks in the world that have withstood multiple regional and global crises, financial stability and confidence in the financial sector are non-negotiable pillars of progress.

Singapore kept the capital requirement for digital banks to be the same as the traditional ones, not to subsidise competition while conveying to existing banks that they must prepare themselves to be globally competitive. Singapore's capital requirements for a retail digital banking licence are among the highest globally, thus prioritising safety over theatrics to appease armchair commentators.

New Entry — A Digital Bank

Regulators across ASEAN have embarked on the journey to issue new digital banking licences for new financial services entities, and incumbent banks have launched new platforms to compete with challenger banks. In addition, consortiums and joint ventures between startups, internet businesses like ride-hailing, gaming, e-commerce and traditional industries like telecom, insurance and real estate required a new approach, capabilities and operating model.

Challenger banks are small, recently created retail banks that compete directly with the established banks in the country, sometimes by specialising in areas underserved by the large traditional banks. In addition, most challenger banks aspire to harness modern financial technology practices, such as online-only operations, that avoid the costs and complexities of conventional banking.

Singapore has been another milestone across Asia for those new to financial players, big techs and FinTechs to seek digital and virtual banking licences. Singapore received many applications for the limited number of available slots for new digital banks. Hong Kong and Singapore received 29 and 21 applications for approval from eight and five digital banks, respectively. While the number of applicants is not the sole metric we should look at, it is a good indicator that diverse applicants are keen to address unmet and unserved customer needs. Even if unsuccessful in the eventual application, the process helps them embark on a journey to support customers using their existing regulatory status and collaborate with other banks to offer services they aspire to bring to market. After MAS's new licence application announcement in June 2019, various players in Singapore from the financial and non-FI sectors have come together to apply for digital bank licences. The underlying principle of Singapore awarding digital banks licences is to focus on consumers' "unmet and unserved" needs by bringing inclusive financial services.

In the Asian landscape, Korea Financial Services Commission accepted applications in 2015, and by 2017, the first batch of new digital banks in Korea was available to consumers. Hong Kong Monetary Authority started accepting applications in 2018, issued eight licences, and by December 2019, the first new digital bank in Hong Kong, "ZA", was launched. Taiwan Financial Supervisory Commission granted three digital banking licences in 2019, and digital banks were established in 2020. Bank Negara Malaysia released the Expectation Draft in December 2019 and later awarded five new digital bank licences, three universal and two Islamic. Bangko Sentral ng Pilipinas, the central bank for the Philippines, has granted six digital bank licences. Otoritas Jasa Keuangan (OJK), the central bank for Indonesia, has supported several e-commerce and FinTech companies to acquire traditional banks to transform them into Digital Banks. Finally, MAS, the central bank for Singapore, had the most diverse mix of new digital banks with five new banks — two universal, two wholesale and one internet-only bank.

Historically, every decade had its unique propositions for financial services and lifestyle. 2000 was the year for dot com, 2010 was the year for mobile apps, and 2020 was the year for digital banks. We see an emerging trend of FinLife, combining financial services and lifestyle to enable seamless customer experience and innovative financial products.

One key thing to note is new digital banks' long-term sustainability and viability since many of them have yet to become profitable globally. In an economic downturn, new digital banks could face operational challenges. The overall winner of this exercise shall be the end consumers and small and medium-sized enterprises (SMEs), who will end up with a larger pool of solutions and service providers.

One of the critical motivations for seeking a Singapore digital bank licence is that it is easier to demonstrate a proven track record and regional connectivity to other regulators in ASEAN, where digital banks will be available in the future. In addition, ASEAN countries have strong cultural, social and economic ties and can showcase a badge of trust from one of the most progressive regulators in ASEAN, MAS. It also helps consolidate investor and ecosystem partner trust, which is crucial for addressing capital requirements and customer acquisition challenges.

Digital bank consortiums primarily focus on developing a combination of capabilities across the four pillars of distribution, technology and operation experience, financial products, and capital. A digital bank consortium's strength and success will depend on capabilities represented by members, trust and connectivity with the daily lives of the average consumer, and the long-term sustainability of business models.

As the digital banks will not have physical branches and access to ATM networks, the defining proposition will be daily life touchpoints through transport cards, retail shops and SME service providers. Another critical aspect of the long-term sustainability of digital bank consortiums is the profitability and cash generation capability of the core business of consortium partners. Building and scaling a digital bank is a long journey. Funding digital banks through the initial years of operation is essential until banks generate a positive contribution margin. The next few years will open a world of opportunities for consumers and SMEs in Singapore as they can experience new service providers who will focus on reimagining financial services.

The new digital banks will target the underserved retail and wholesale sub-segments through the effective use of technologies. Over time, they will broaden their scope towards the "high-value pool" segments reasonably well served by the incumbent banks.

Singapore has a fast-growing gig economy with over 680,000 individuals taking up short-term or event-based work. However, these customers have traditionally been ineligible for credit and need personalised insurance coverage. Another emerging customer segment is digital natives, with over 700,000 young millennials heavily influenced by lifestyle platforms. They are receptive to a truly differentiated experience at the level offered by consumer internet companies like ride-hailing and e-commerce.

Most banks traditionally served small and micro enterprises through branches for basic transactional needs. As more SMEs digitise their business, they expect an experience akin to retail customers regarding technology and product offerings. Historically, the SME segment is underserved due to the high cost of onboarding and servicing smaller players. Singapore has potentially a hundred thousand businesses that need more financial history and track record requiring digital management tools due to a need for more resources. In addition, about 120,000 firms may not possess assets for collateral to get traditional loans from the banks.

Digital banking is neither a fancy mobile app nor providing existing brick-and-mortar bank branches online. The onset of competition from digital banks requires incumbent banks to think beyond digitising current operations. They need to realign it to meet consumer needs and the competitive landscape that has evolved rapidly. The new banks will aim to become a one-stop shop for their target segments' lifestyle or business needs. Therefore, the new digital banks' products must be more innovative and differentiated than just a copy of incumbent solutions.

Incumbent banks in Singapore and elsewhere compete with new players on various fronts, like distribution, data access and brand awareness. Challengers will likely access a large customer base with multiple touchpoints daily through their core business lines like e-commerce, ride-hailing, food delivery, gaming and social media messaging. Hyper personalisation and the ability to offer contextual services to customers leveraging data will be critical tactics challenger digital banks use.

Newer players with strong marketing brands and digital-first DNA are able to achieve strong brand awareness in the market, with a base of loyal customers open to trying the new digital banking products.

The new-age customers expect transparency and frictionless experience from their banks. The incumbent banks have an opportunity to leverage and strengthen the trust and relationship building with their customers. In the post-COVID world, they can re-evaluate their strategy and invest in understanding evolved customer needs. In addition, customers expect a digital experience at par with leading technology platforms which are part of their daily lives.

Regional Giants — Next Generation Leaders

The first generation of regional banks in Southeast Asia is the outcome of challenges endured by the region, namely the Asian financial crisis (1997–1998) and the SARS outbreak (2002–2004). As a result, several banks went through cycles of expansion, contraction and, finally, stabilisation. There are only two banking groups across ASEAN with retail banking presence in all 10 significant markets in ASEAN, namely UOB and CIMB. Due to the ASEAN markets' diverse, fragmented nature, there will likely be only two regional digital bank players in the next generation of new financial services. Singapore, the first in ASEAN to issue digital bank licences, requires the retail bank applicant to be Singapore's headquartered and controlled. One of the long-term implications of that requirement is that those who won the permit in Singapore be most suited to build a Pan-ASEAN digital banking franchise. Grab Holdings and SEA Group led a consortium that awarded the two Singapore retail banks licences. Both are the two largest and most valuable technology companies from ASEAN listed in the US. With a few hundred million users using their platforms every week, they are in the best place to build such a regional franchise to bring ASEAN financial services to the next phase of evolution.

Such ambitions do not exist in isolation, and through their growth and evolution, both have established partnerships and collaborations with incumbent financial institutions.

▸ *Grab*

Grab Holdings Inc., commonly known as Grab, was founded in 2012 and is a Singaporean multinational company headquartered in Singapore. In addition to transportation, the company offers food delivery and digital payment services via a mobile app. With its presence in over eight countries and over 200 million application downloads, Grab is the biggest ride-hailing company in Southeast Asia. With almost more than 30% of the Southeast Asian population with the Grab app downloaded on their phones, these statistics show Grab's dominance in Southeast Asia.

Grab started with only one service — Grab rides. However, with the founder Anthony Tan's mission to build a company with a dual bottom line in financial outcomes and social influence, Grab started slowly introducing more FinTech products, such as GrabPay.

When entering the Southeast Asian market, Grab adopted a hyperlocal approach where they gave massive importance to the culture and the value system of the various Southeast Asian countries. As a result, Grab is specially designed and offers a locally friendly and customised service to its users, allowing it to stand out better from competitors.

One of the challenges in digitising the driver and rider ecosystem was ensuring access to formal financial services ecosystems. As a result, drivers got access to wallets and bank accounts for the first time through partnerships with Grab Financial Group (GFG).

Grab's products are built based on a simple thesis: accessible, convenient, and seamlessly embedded into a customer's everyday life. It explains why GFG fractionises and creates "micro-everything" products like micro insurance and microloans.

Grab has successfully raised funding to grow its payment and financial services. In 2021, Grab Financial's funding accounted for 63% of Singapore's Fintech fundraising in Q1. GFG is the FinTech arm of Grab, which launched a new brand called GrabFin in 2022. It aims to promote greater access to its financial service products, with Earn+ as an investment product.[1]

Grab announced a debt financing deal of USD700M to finance the growth of its vehicle fleet. In addition, Grab managed to secure a SGD500M facility from HSBC Singapore to finance its Grab Car business. The debt financing deal was oversubscribed by 250%, evidencing a strong appetite for debt

[1] https://www.grab.com/sg/press/tech-product/grab-financial-group-launches-new-brand-grabfin-and-introduces-earn/

facilities for non-traditional companies and the market's belief in Grab as Southeast Asia's leading FinTech platform.

In addition to banks investing in Grab, non-traditional investors such as Hyundai, Microsoft and Booking Holdings invested almost USD3B into Grab. Since Series H, Grab has raised more than USD6B from investors, a record-breaking figure for a Southeast Asian startup.

Grab started developing its GrabPay system by acquiring iKaaz and Kudo in Bangalore in 2018. It also used iKaaz's product knowledge in point of sale and mobile payment experience and Kudo's partner network to boost its offline network.

Kudo is a leading online-to-offline (O2O) e-commerce platform in Indonesia. Kudo has a unique O2O platform that enables Indonesia's unbanked consumers to shop online by connecting them with online merchants and service providers through its vast existing network of agents and merchants across Indonesia. With the acquisition, Grab accelerated Kudo's agent network expansion while leveraging its reach to attract more Grab users.

In 2018, Grab announced a partnership with Maybank, promoting GrabPay in Malaysia.[2] Additionally, Grab announced its strategic alliance with Maybank in 2018, promoting GrabPay in Malaysia as the underlying financial system to GPay Malaysian Network's payment ecosystem and business vertical. This led to products launched, such as the Maybank Grab Mastercard Platinum, in 2020.[3]

---

[2] https://www.straitstimes.com/business/companies-markets/grab-partners-maybank-to-promote-grabpay-in-malaysia

[3] https://www.mastercard.com/news/ap/en/newsroom/press-releases/en/2020/august/maybank-grab-and-mastercard-jointly-launch-the-brand-new-maybank-grab-mastercard-platinum/

Due to Indonesia's low banking penetration rate, where 90 million people are unbanked (in 2022)[4], regional financial companies are expanding quickly to capture a slice of the lucrative digital banking share. Furthermore, Grab's recent purchase of Emtek in 2021 and the merger of OVO in 2021, a mobile wallet associated with Indonesia's Lippo Group and Taralite, show its expansion into the Indonesian market.[5] OVO is the third-party wallet integrated with Grab, occupying a far lead of 37% in terms of the market share for the e-wallet market. Furthermore, by adding Taralite's online lending features, Grab can accelerate its growth by extending loans and credits to consumers using a "Pay-Later" option to OVO's existing network. Grab also invested USD100M into Indonesia's state-backed e-wallet LinkAja to accelerate its goal of improving financial inclusion in Indonesia.

Grab has also entered the wealth management market by acquiring Bento, a Singapore-based robo-advisory startup. Bento rebranded into GrabInvest, democratising access to retail wealth management products to its existing customer base through this acquisition. GrabInvest aims to make wealth management services accessible by adopting an easy-to-understand model, transparency in fee structure and a reliable form of financial product backed by an MAS licence.

A consortium between Grab–Singtel was among the five of several firms awarded a full digital-banking licence by MAS in December 2020.

While other industries are suffering a decrease in demand due to the COVID-19 pandemic, Grab was a massive accelerator. As a result, Grab recorded positive growth in 2020. With Grab's merchants' count increasing

---

[4] https://www.businesstimes.com.sg/international/asean/indonesias-large-unbanked-population-offers-opportunities-singapore-fintech#:~:text=Serving%20the%20unbanked%20in%20Indonesia,not%20have%20a%20bank%20account.

[5] https://asia.nikkei.com/Business/Business-deals/Grab-takes-90-share-in-Indonesian-digital-wallet-OVO

by 500,000, coupled with an increase in take-up on insurance and wealth products through AutoInvest, digital payment adoption increased exponentially.

In addition to its aggressive expansion plans in Indonesia, Grab also formed a strategic partnership with MOCA Technology and Service Joint Stock Company to promote cashless payment in Vietnam. Both platforms will leverage each other's technology expertise and partner networks to improve payment services to the Vietnamese market.

Mitsubishi UFJ Financial Group, Inc. (MUFG) is Japan's largest financial group and the world's second-largest bank holding company. Since 2012, MUFG has invested more than USD14B in four strategic regional banks in ASEAN. MUFG owns a 19.7% stake in Vietnam Joint Stock Commercial Bank for Industry and Trade (VietinBank) in Vietnam, 76.8% in Bank of Ayudhya (Krungsri) in Thailand, 20% in Security Bank Corporation (Philippines) and 94.1% in Bank Danamon (Indonesia). Together with its partner banks, MUFG has a network of more than 3,000 offices and branches in Asia, offering a full suite of banking services catering to the entire client spectrum, from retail customers to SMEs and large corporations. Over the last few years, MUFG has been expanding its focus to collaborate with FinTech startups to grow its customer base and further capture business opportunities in the ASEAN region.[6]

As part of this, MUFG undertook a strategic alliance with Grab. As a result, MUFG invested USD706M in acquiring a nearly 5% stake in Grab. In addition, the two companies worked jointly to develop digitised forms of financial services, including payment systems, joint lending models, and insurance and rewards systems.[7]

---

[6] https://www.straitstimes.com/business/banking/mufgs-976m-investment-in-grab-shows-japanese-banks-growing-interest-in-region-fitch

[7] https://www.focusfinance.org/post/mufg-s-investment-in-grab

From this investment, MUFG will become the largest stakeholder in Grab among financial institutions and become the "First Choice Bank" to Grab. It enables MUFG to tap into Grab's vast ASEAN user network to deepen synergies in its ASEAN network and benefit from Grab's established reputation, brand, dedicated user base and vital data collection abilities throughout the region. Southeast Asia's 98 million-strong population is more likely to be underbanked and need access to sophisticated financial services, so this alliance presents an attractive business opportunity for MUFG.

Thailand's leading financial conglomerate, KBank, in collaboration with Southeast Asia's leading O2O platform, Grab, introduces a co-branded mobile wallet in Thailand in 2018.[8] As 68% of all transactions in Thailand are done using cash, this strategic partnership will benefit users and retailers across Thailand by adopting cashless transactions. In addition, this partnership provided seamless services across the features of KBank's "K PLUS" and the Grab apps. Furthermore, it facilitated the two parties to grow their business together by introducing a wider variety of joint-financial services on their platforms.[9]

▶ *SEA Group*

SeaMoney is a part of Sea Group, a leading global consumer internet company. SeaMoney's mission is to better the lives of individuals and businesses in our region with financial services through technology. SeaMoney's offerings include mobile wallet services, payment processing, credit offerings, and related digital financial services and products. These

[8] https://www.businesstimes.com.sg/garage/news/grab-partners-thailands-kbank-to-launch-e-wallet-in-2019-gets-us50m-investment-from-bank

[9] https://www.grab.com/sg/press/others/kasikornbank-partners-with-grab-to-join-the-largest-fintech-ecosystem-in-southeast-asia/

are available in seven markets across Southeast Asia and Taiwan under various brands, including AirPay, ShopeePay, and SPayLater.

While preparing for a digital bank infrastructure in Singapore, Shopee's parent group, Sea Group, acquired local Indonesian lender Bank Kesajakteraan Ekonmi (Bank BKE).[10] Following its success in obtaining a fully digital bank licence in Singapore in 2020, this acquisition also aims to develop a fully digital bank in Indonesia.

UOB and Shopee signed a memorandum of understanding in 2020 for an exclusive collaboration between the e-commerce platform and UOB Mighty. This collaboration allowed both platforms to explore data analytics and application programming interfaces to personalise the customer's online shopping experience through a reward points system and a wider variety of digital payment options. It was a mutually beneficial relationship whereby spending on online retail purchases made by UOB cardmembers using UOB's flagship cash-back credit card on Shopee has grown by 50%.[11]

Lending

Lending FinTechs are targeting commercial banks' revenue pools by offering greater transparency and faster credit decisions compared to the traditional black-box lending products offered by the incumbents. FinTech business models have seen the greatest success in areas whereby the effects can be standardised and technological advantages leveraged to provide efficiency gains. In addition, the underserved segment is a key area of focus as lending FinTechs aim to extend credit options to customers who would not have access to it otherwise.

---

[10] https://www.businesstimes.com.sg/startups-tech/startups/indonesian-banking-regulator-says-shopee-acquires-bank-bke

[11] https://sbr.com.sg/financial-services/more-news/uob-shopee-sign-mou-offer-exclusive-perks-customers

▸ *Global Trends*

Lending is the second largest product group within FinTech, comprising about 3,700 companies and over USD56B in equity funding. There has been increasing investment activity within the space until 2018 when a plateau was reached at USD11B.

Although funding remained relatively steady in 2019, there was a notable shift between business lines. Funding for retail lenders saw a significant slowdown as investors' focus shifted towards the SME space. As a result, financing for SME lenders reached new highs due to the successes of players within supply chain finance and working capital, line of credit and invoice factoring, and generally secured lending-focused digital banks. Global funding had slowed down in the first half of 2022, with FinTech companies raising USD108 billion.

▸ *Singapore Trends*

Despite the global funding slowdown, investors remain confident in Singapore's FinTechs. In the second quarter of 2022, Singapore's global market share in deal value for FinTech had more than doubled compared to 2021, rising from 3.1% last year to 6.4% the past quarter. The total funds raised also increased from SGD340M in the first half of 2021 to SGD570M in the first half of 2022.

▸ *Funding Society*

Funding Societies (Modalku) is one of Southeast Asia's largest SME digital finance platforms, co-founded by Kelvin Teo and Reynold Wijaya in 2015. The company gives SME owners control over their cash flow, starting with various fast and flexible short-term financings such as business term loans, trade finance and corporate cards. In 2022, aided by the acquisition of payments platform CardUp, investment into Bank Index in Indonesia and investment from SoftBank Vision Fund, Funding Societies has since rolled out new offerings such as business accounts, receivables and payables products, providing a full suite of payments, financing and cash flow management solutions for SMEs.

The company is licensed in four countries notably Singapore, Indonesia, Malaysia, and Thailand and also operates in Vietnam and Hong Kong. It addresses a problem faced by over 80% of small businesses today — difficulty managing cash flow and accessing capital. Many small businesses operate on tight 45–60 day cash cycles, with late receivables being the most common cause of cash flow issues, limiting their growth. Funding Societies solves this, by leveraging on its tried-and-tested credit underwriting models in the last eight years or so, to recommend solutions that alleviate cash flow pressures. The company has disbursed more loans by combining Fin and Tech while maintaining default rates.

Funding Societies focuses on SMEs unserved or underserved by banks, specialising in smaller, shorter-term unsecured financing. Hence it is invested by banks such as BRI and SMBC. As SMEs in Southeast Asia slowly but steadily shift from O2O, the company takes an omnichannel approach to serve SMEs. The company establishes direct channels while working with partners in e-commerce, supply chain and business adjacents.

At the core of the business is risk management and diversification. Not only has Funding Societies actively diversified its borrowers across segments, sectors and six countries, but it has also diversified its funding. Whilst it originally started as a peer-to-business lender — connecting SMEs to retail investors who are looking for a form of liquid, short-term, fixed income — Funding Societies has now evolved to include large institutional investors on the balance sheet too. An example of this is the USD50M debt financing line from HSBC in 2022 and loan channelling from BRI, BCA and DBS Indonesia.

Financial inclusion makes up the genesis of why Funding Societies was started: to create a virtuous cycle of funding to uplift SMEs, who are the underdogs but bedrock of the economy. The founders share the vision of creating a more bottom-up economy powered by small and medium businesses, possible in today's context. The company's results prove that they are delivering on this vision — at the time of writing more than USD3B in business financing has been disbursed to nearly 100,000 SMEs across the region, amounting to over 5 million transactions.

In fact, since 2019, Funding Societies has operated on two key areas: driving growth and profitability. Reflecting on the sustainability of growth, Kelvin mentions that Funding Societies aspires to continue doing so. Moreover, as part of its commitment to contribute positively to societies, Kelvin highlights the importance of prioritising productive loans for SMEs. Funding Societies has also been focusing on providing a larger range of financial services for SMEs, further fulfilling its core purpose of improving financial inclusion in Singapore and Southeast Asia.

Speaking to Kelvin, he noted that the FinTech industry has matured under stress testing from 2020 onwards. FinTech players have had to prove their resilience by responding appropriately to challenges such as changing regulations and constraints, rising interest rates, geopolitical instability, and supply chain disruption. The larger FinTech players have increasingly taken on the role of consolidators in the market, which he believes has led to "an increase in the number of quality players".

Funding Societies is fearless in taking a hands-on approach and adapting when necessary. For example, in Indonesia, the company served the *warungs*[12] directly. However, once it realised the unit economics was not viable for its operation, it changed the strategy to help them through partnerships. One example is its financing partnership with Bukalapak to serve the *warungs* through an O2O approach. The company is also the biggest e-commerce merchant financing company in Indonesia, and it holds

[12] https://sbr.com.sg/financial-services/more-news/uob-shopee-sign-mou-offer-exclusive-perks-customers

partnerships with big names such as Tokopedia, Bukalapak, Lazada and Shopee.

Funding Societies is backed by SoftBank Vision Fund 2, SoftBank Ventures Asia, Sequoia Capital India, Alpha JWC Ventures, SMBC Bank, BRI Ventures, VNG Corporation, Rapyd Ventures, Endeavor, EBDI, SGInnovate and Qualgro, among others. It holds several awards and accolades to its name, including the MAS FinTech Award in 2016, the Global SME Excellence Award at the United Nations' ITU Telecom World in 2017, KPMG Fintech100 in 2018, Brands for Good in 2019, and ASEAN Startup of the Year by Global Startup Awards in 2020. In 2021, it received the Platinum award for Responsible Digital Innovator of the Year at the 2022 Global SME Finance Awards organised by IFC (under the World Bank Group).

▸ *Validus*

Founded in 2015 to address the unmet financing needs of SMEs, Validus is headquartered in Singapore and is growing rapidly across its four markets — Indonesia, Singapore, Thailand and Vietnam. To date, Validus has disbursed more than SGD3.5B in loans to small businesses across Southeast Asia and is the leading all-in-one SME financing platform in Southeast Asia.

Validus drives financial inclusion and prosperity for small businesses by leveraging data and artificial intelligence (AI) to drive growth financing to the underserved SME sector — resulting in faster and effortless one-stop digital finance solutions that increase the business customers' productivity and cost savings.

Across ASEAN, the processes for SMEs to access credit continue to be time-consuming, tedious and inefficient. Where available, the digital finance offering from existing financial institutions still needs to be impeded by credit underwriting requirements that have yet to evolve, and existing players have struggled to balance the needs and credit characteristics of SMEs with the stringent criteria set out by local regulators.

Validus' core value proposition for SMEs is based on Accessibility, Convenience, and Affordability. The business model is centred around leveraging technology, data, AI and strategic partnerships to provide accessible, faster and more affordable financial services to SMEs. Validus has developed a suite of digital financial products and services that are designed to meet small business owners — from loans to business accounts, corporate cards, cross-border international payments, and expense management.

As a FinTech, Validus has the advantage of being agile and flexible without being hampered by outdated processes and clunky core legacy banking systems. This has enabled it to launch innovative alternative financing solutions for SMEs — including partnership-led supply chain finance solutions and using non-traditional data sources coupled with AI-driven automation to expand credit access and supplement the underwriting of underserved segments.

Recognising this pain point faced by SMEs, Validus is the first in the industry to innovate and develop a proprietary AI-powered credit underwriting algorithm that leverages alternative data and predictive models to automate the underwriting and credit risk decisions for small-ticket working capital loans (of up to SGD150,000) in just one minute. SMEs need only submit two documents for credit assessment, 67% fewer than banks and other financial institutions.

One of the major highlights in 2022 was Validus becoming the first FinTech in Southeast Asia to acquire an incumbent lending portfolio and received a USD100M securitisation facility. Validus acquired Citibank Singapore's CitiBusiness portfolio. For innovation in automating credit underwriting and decisions for small-ticket working capital loans, Validus also won the first runner-up award (Singapore FinTech category) at the prestigious Singapore FinTech Festival (SFF) Global FinTech Awards 2022, supported by MAS. The company has formal alliances with ST Engineering, SMRT, and Keppel Shipyard.

Validus is founded by Vikas Nahata (Top 10 FinTech Leaders in 2021, SFF Global Fintech Awards) and Nikhilesh Goel (Top 10 FinTech Leaders in 2019 and 2020, Singapore Fintech Association Awards).

It is backed by leading Financial Institutions and Venture Capital firms including Norinchukin Bank, NongHyup Financial Group, Vertex Ventures SEA & India, Vertex Growth Fund, FMO and VinaCapital Ventures.

Banks such as OCBC and DBS only provide SMEs secured loans against hard collaterals. Banks do not consider soft collaterals such as receivables and inventory. On the other hand, Validus lends against no collateral whatsoever. Due to the nature of whom it lends to, it is very appealing to service-oriented companies.

▸ AIG

Headquartered in Singapore and operating across Asia, Advance Intelligence Group is on its way to becoming Asia's leading AI-powered digital financial services company. Founded in 2016, the Group has built an ecosystem of AI-powered, credit-enabled products and services, including leading buy now pay later platform Atome, Indonesia's top digital lending platform Kredit Pintar, leading software-as-a-service provider of enterprise digital identity, compliance and risk management solutions ADVANCE.AI, and omnichannel e-commerce merchant services platform Ginee. Today, the Group serves over 500 enterprise clients, 235,000 merchants and 40 million individual consumers. Year to date, it has also disbursed over USD4B in loans. Atome continues to consolidate its regional leadership in the consumer space by offering its consumers greater financial flexibility and providing value-added services to its vast network of merchants. ADVANCE.AI is evolving into a world-class end-to-end risk management platform in the enterprise space, providing know your customer, know your business, compliance, and alternative credit scoring solutions. The Group raised a Series D round of over USD400M in 2021, making it one of Singapore's most valuable FinTech startups. The Group, which also counts Standard Chartered Bank as a regional strategic partner underpinned by strong regional product and funding collaborations, is backed by top-tier investors SoftBank Vision Fund 2, Warburg Pincus, Northstar, Vision Plus Capital, Gaorong Capital and Singapore-based global investor EDBI. Its early investors include GSR, Pavilion Capital, eGarden Ventures, Unicorn Capital Partners, and Provident Growth. The Group is co-founded and led by former hedge fund manager Jefferson Chen, a former Farallon Capital Management executive who led private investing in Greater China. Before that, he worked at Goldman Sachs, where he was involved in initial public offerings and mergers and acquisitions of Asian companies, including Baidu Inc. Born in China, he became a Singapore citizen and had an MBA from Stanford University. In 2021, the Group was named Fintech Employer of the Year at the MAS Global Fintech Awards. Since its inception, the Group's headquarters has been at 80RR Fintech Hub SG in the heart of Singapore's CBD.

▸ *Tyme*

Tyme is a Singapore digital bank headquatered in South Africa and the Philippines. It was founded based on a passion for financial inclusion, with a vision for a multi-country bank that can democratise access to financial services. The name also embodies this vision and passion, where Tyme means 'Take your money everywhere'. In August 2022, GoTyme Bank managed to receive clearance from the Philippines' central bank to operate as one of the digital banks in the country. Having been deployed in South Africa to much success, it was especially intentional in selecting Singapore as its headquarters, with the Philippines as the first market. There are two reasons for choosing Singapore as the home base: the first one is that Singapore provides access to talent, and the second reason is due to the optimal regulatory environment. Trust, the backbone of banking and financial services, can be built with a good regulatory environment.

Trust has been a key principle that guides how Tyme structures its services for emerging markets. For instance, in South Africa, brand representatives in the physical environment must be from the community being served. This allows customers to learn about the products and services offered by someone they know. Hence, it is evident that trust is an ongoing relationship between customers and service providers through such intermediaries. To strengthen this relationship, Tyme has also taken up the responsibility of mitigating the risks of easy access to financial services. Citing GoalSave, TymeBank's savings product, as an example in the context of 'Buy Now Pay Later', Coen Jonker points out how customers can be guided to make more sound financial decisions through its design interface. These design features appear in the form of confirmation prompts for users when they submit a request to withdraw money from their savings account. When clients are tempted to withdraw money for certain expenditures, the prompts encourage them to reconsider their financial decisions. Customers are also given incentives to keep their money in their savings accounts with certain bonuses. Such measures help shape customers' behaviour in making responsible financial decisions. Ultimately, customers can be assured that these products can both provide financial inclusion while incorporating valuable lessons on making responsible financial decisions.

> *"I think it's very important that we recognise up front that access to financial services is a double-edged sword."*
>
> *Coenraad Jonker, co-founder of Tyme*

Coen acknowledges the realities of running a startup — the initial stages are motivated by the need for survival, which can spur teams to action. However, the sustainable motivator is purpose. When like-minded individuals join a startup to fulfil a vision that contributes positively to society, they know that what they do matters. This helps to ensure high morale in the face of teething pains, which are common challenges for startups. At the same time, businesses must adapt to changing environments, especially in the context of digital banks. Coen likens digital banks to building cities: Continuous improvements are made as the city evolves, and the products offered must be constantly upgraded. The key to success is continuously rebuilding and rethinking how business is done while responding to customer needs.

Conclusion

As a FinTech nation, Singapore has been working to build regional digital banking and digital lending leaders with operations across ASEAN. The development and scaling of such leaders in Singapore create a ripple effort in terms of developing of the ecosystem, talent and support services. Singapore can become a global talent magnet on the back of regional leaders who need to build best-in-class technology, business and operations capabilities. The next phase of Singapore Fintech Nation would see the mature players access the global scale by either accessing the public market through initial public offerings or merger and acquisition through larger global players.

Chapter 11

INSURTECH — RISING ASPIRATIONS

Insurance

Singapore started its journey as a trading hub, thus insuring that commerce activities became one of the foundational use cases for the insurance industry to blossom in the country. Great Eastern Life Assurance, Singapore's oldest locally licensed insurance company, was established on 26 August 1908. The company was founded with a capital of $250,000 and offered life insurance and annuity services. As the first local insurance company, Great Eastern provided an alternative to those who wanted to use something other than the services of foreign insurance companies. Under the leadership of its first managing director, A. H. Fair (a Canadian), a significant portion of the premium income was invested in high-quality industrial shares in Canada.

The insurance sector remains one of the formidable market segments for startups to crack into, despite the lack of penetration in the insurance space. There was a need to increase awareness and education to reduce mis-selling and costs in the sector. The Monetary Authority of Singapore (MAS) had to figure out how digital sales in insurance would work. Today, video conferences and digital signatures are commonplace. Singapore focused on how to bring value to consumers through digitisation. As a result, PolicyPal became the first company to enter the Sandbox. After that, two more companies focused on the insurance domain and graduated from the MAS FinTech Sandbox.

InsurTech, a blend of insurance and technology, has emerged as a disruptive force in the insurance industry. By leveraging advancements in data analysis, blockchain, and artificial intelligence (AI), InsurTech is transforming the traditional insurance business model, making it more efficient, customer-centric, and technologically-driven. Contrary to popular belief, InsurTech and FinTech are closely intertwined, with InsurTech playing a crucial role in reshaping the landscape of financial technology.

The integration of technology in the insurance sector has opened up new possibilities for streamlining processes and delivering enhanced services to policyholders. Data analysis, one of the key components of InsurTech, enables insurance companies to extract valuable insights from vast amounts of data. By leveraging advanced analytics tools, insurers can analyse customer data, claims history, and risk profiles to make more accurate underwriting decisions. This not only speeds up the policy issuance process but also allows insurers to offer personalised products tailored to individual needs.

Furthermore, the implementation of blockchain technology has revolutionised the way insurance contracts and claims are handled. Blockchain, a decentralised and transparent digital ledger, ensures the immutability and security of data, reducing the risk of fraud and improving trust in the insurance ecosystem. Smart contracts powered by blockchain can automate claims processing, eliminating the need for intermediaries and expediting the settlement process. This seamless automation reduces administrative costs, enhances operational efficiency, and ultimately benefits policyholders by enabling faster claims resolution.

AI is another vital component of InsurTech that is revolutionising the insurance industry. AI algorithms can analyse massive amounts of data, identify patterns, and make accurate predictions, allowing insurers to better assess risk and price policies accordingly. Chatbots equipped with natural language processing capabilities are being employed to provide instant customer support, answer queries, and guide customers through the insurance purchasing process. These AI-powered virtual assistants enhance customer experiences and ensure round-the-clock availability of support.

InsurTech's integration with FinTech is a natural progression, as both sectors seek to leverage technology to enhance financial services. By incorporating InsurTech into the broader FinTech ecosystem, insurers can leverage advanced data analytics and AI capabilities to better understand customer behaviour, create personalised offerings, and streamline the entire insurance value chain.

The benefits of InsurTech extend beyond operational efficiency and improved customer experiences. It also fosters innovation by encouraging the development of new insurance products and services. InsurTech startups are constantly pushing boundaries and exploring new areas such as parametric insurance, peer-to-peer insurance, and usage-based insurance. These innovative approaches leverage technology to offer more flexible coverage, reduce costs, and cater to emerging customer needs.

However, as with any technological advancement, InsurTech also presents its own set of challenges. Data security and privacy concerns arise as vast amounts of sensitive customer information are collected and analysed. Ensuring regulatory compliance, protecting customer data, and establishing robust cybersecurity measures become paramount in this digital age.

▸ *Global in Digitalisation of Insurance*

When digital banks become institutionalised, governments will more likely be open and focus on this area. Unlike other jurisdictions that immediately awarded multiple virtual insurer licences, MAS decided to wait and work on the core infrastructure first. Instead, it focused on creating infrastructure surrounding a secure digital know your customer (KYC), digital identity and digital data. Today, these are available through MyInfo, as a great equaliser to all service providers.

Insurance is a key pillar of any financial services in any financial services ecosystem. Together with InsurTech, both play a vital role in the world of FinTech, bringing innovation, efficiency, and improved customer experiences to the insurance industry. InsurTech refers to the use of technology, data analytics, and digital platforms to transform and disrupt traditional insurance processes and products.

The integration of InsurTech within the broader FinTech landscape has brought significant advancements and opportunities. One key aspect is the digitisation of insurance processes, enabling seamless transactions, streamlined claims management, and improved customer interactions. InsurTech solutions leverage technologies such as AI, machine learning, blockchain, and data analytics to automate underwriting, risk assessment, and claims processing. This automation leads to faster and more accurate decision-making, reducing administrative costs and enhancing operational efficiency.

Insurers are often less talked about than their other financial services peers like banking, payments and lending but with an equal, if not bigger, impact on long-term lives, well-being and upliftment of all ecosystem participants like consumers, providers, advisors, brokers and facilitation agents.

With a changing lifestyle compared to counterparts of the previous generation, their perception of risk for the current generation has changed, along with how they handle this risk, whether with InsurTech or not even getting insured, by embracing instant gratification across all walks of life.

With remote and gig economy work, the job market has changed the landscape of employee benefits, retirement coverage, and income protection. In addition, the younger generation aspires to undertake multiple careers and jobs in parallel. The older generations often viewed it as moonlighting in the past, but it is evolving now with regulators and employers looking at providing support to their contractors and employees.

Incumbents and challengers have acknowledged and accepted the coexistence of advisors and digital solutions to offer an omnichannel offering to customers, focusing on the right proposition, place, product, time and price. In addition, regulators are increasingly adopting flexibility to enable providers to undertake risk-based governance and compliance to ensure cost does not hinder bringing financial inclusion to marginal sections of society.

The incentives to start saving and contributing to pensions for marginal and vulnerable sections of society will never be higher than now since the trident of inflation, longer expected living age, and increasing cost of healthcare make it critical to start compounding savings at the earliest. The foundations of such a solution will be the trusted store value facility, guarantee of safe investment availability, competition among providers and visibility to regulatory authorities to ensure compliance. Moreover, the growth and prevalence of technology solutions combined with decreasing cost of bringing that to an ever-growing number of customers trigger a network effect, bringing about a permanent shift in the industry's operating model.

As the role of technology grows across verticals, the role of AI is one of the risks the industry needs to manage and proactively prepare. While AI can create unique experiences for customers reducing costs and bringing efficiency, it is also vulnerable to propagating and perpetuating the biases held by humans. Therefore, responsible uses of AI with safeguards and regulatory supervision are critical for ensuring widespread adoption across industry verticals and product segments.

AI in insurance must be responsible for taking AI models to live, scale and impact. AI developers need strong explainability and alignment with the insurers, reinsurers, and regulators. Improvements in data quality can bring us closer to real improvements in customer experience, engagement, and risk management. With the regulatory environment still early, industry and startups can build and test emerging AI models without compromising risk.

COVID-19 has brought millions of first-time investors to the investing world through zero brokerage, fractional ownerships and crypto platforms aided by social trends like Reddit forums and meme stocks. While media saw an unprecedented surge during COVID-19, now such usage has normalised due to the tempering down of stock markets, increasing inflation and the overall macroeconomics situation. The overall expansion in addressable user base sets the industry for solid foundations to create solutions to help consumers.

COVID-19 also got customers to understand the importance of financial planning, life and health insurance and preparing for a rainy day. Several industries and job roles were impacted during the crisis, thus making the importance of emergency funds and bringing financial literacy to consumers. Incumbents and challengers have undertaken digital content and offline engagement to obtain access and information for consumers during and after the COVID-19 crisis.

3D Disruption — Demand, Democratisation and Distribution

Insurance, Pensions and WealthTech are undergoing generational shifts and transformations in how customers and providers engage by evolving models of discovery and consumption.

- Demand for new products and segments — New segments, like the gig economy and remote workers, need specialised solutions unavailable on existing provider shelves. In addition, the evolution in employment models has created a need to rethink business models, pricing and cost to meet such segments' unmet and unserved needs with innovative products and delivery models.
- Democratisation of access and manufacturing — The advent of scalable technology solutions to manufacturing and service financial services solutions like cloud, AI agents and digital onboarding have enabled large-scale access to non-traditional customer segments and products through owned and non-owned channels and social media platforms.
- Distribution by digital channels and embedded finance — The presence of more mobile phones than toilets has opened up opportunities for financial institutions to access these customers through digital KYC, collection and servicing capabilities. Additionally, digital commerce players have increasingly embedded themselves as distributors of lightweight financial services.

These generational shift and transformation are creating new opportunities for insurance and pension providers to meet the needs of a changing customer base. By embracing new technologies and business models, providers can position themselves to succeed in the future.

The insurance landscape is going through a generational transformation primarily driven by two actors, marketplace operators and regulated manufacturers. Marketplaces focus on bringing access to customers by getting the most comprehensive range of options, while manufacturers focus on enabling, embedding and co-creating products with distribution channels.

Digitisation is gaining traction as a long-term solution for the insurance sector's problems. Insurance providers have relied on hard selling techniques to sell unsuitable products. Insurance aggregators' value proposition to customers is to offer convenience and choice. This comes in the form of immediate price discovery.

In Singapore, the government has been making a conscious effort to help its citizens to manage their money well and make sound financial decisions independently. It also started its national financial education programme, MoneySense, in 2003. MAS also owns and operates an insurance aggregator, compareFIRST. Singapore trade cooperative National Trades Union Congress (NTUC), which holds an insure, additionally uses MoneyOwl, a joint venture between it and Providend Holding Pte Ltd, a fee-only financial advisory firm.

Insurance traditionally has always been considered a product sold and not bought. However, multiple digital comparison platforms have focused on promoting the DIY purchase journey in the last few years. Rising customer awareness has enabled customers to undertake price comparisons actively, and there is a strong reason for them to do that — price variation across platforms for the same and similar products. However, for insurance distribution platforms to establish trust and long-term success, they must work with insurance partners to establish price predictability and develop broader service offerings to justify price differentiation.

Insurers have realised that industry connections allow each ecosystem participant to focus on its core competencies. A shift to an ecosystem-led insurance landscape means that all participants will be deeply connected to every other ecosystem player and can leverage the expertise of others to improve their products or services.

Compared to the current traditional insurance landscape, the fundamental change is the large-scale data sharing on a centralised platform. As a result, one of the insurer's most significant competitive advantages is the data ownership acquired through year-long relationships, claims handling and research. However, the new age of insurance suggests that this exclusivity of owning data may be temporary, and the ones affected by this change must seek new forms of value creation.

From insurer-centric enclosed systems focusing on traditional distribution channels with proprietary interfaces, the industry is evolving to platform-centric open systems based on collaboration between industry and non-industry actors. Ecosystem rollout involves enabling simple onboarding of various distribution channels and business-to-business solution providers (including other participating insurers or re-insurers supplying white-label products and services) to foster the design of new and innovative products.

Insurance is not the most discussed topic, given how traditional it is and how youths may understand the importance but not bother with it. InsurTech startups have repackaged insurance attractively to appeal to children. However, many of them need to be more insured, with only 52% of millennials holding life insurance, according to findings from LIMRA. The rationale is that 80% of millennials have bigger financial priorities than insurance, including living expenses, student loan debt, and their focus on experience over settling in a permanent residency. With a changing lifestyle compared to counterparts of the previous generation, their perception of risk has changed, along with how they handle this risk, be it with InsurTech or not even getting insured.

Younger consumers have contemporary lifestyles and preferences, including an even greater need for speed and digital self-serve with COVID-19, which many traditional insurers need to catch up in the products and services they provide, while agile InsurTech could provide tailored and real-time services and seamless customer experience. More than half of insurance customers (nearly 52%) interviewed in the World Insurance Report (WIR) 2018 placed high importance on mobile, internet, or website channels for conducting insurance transactions. Such change in consumer behaviour is visible across industries and functions, where shopping, education, information exchange and more have seen a push in digitalisation. The challenge here is not only the tech integration, which can be done by tech hires or acquisition but the people and culture within insurance companies that may need help to adapt at the same pace.

Insurance agents are the cornerstone of financial planning. By leveraging the constantly improving AI, machine learning and the Internet of Things, rising InsurTechs offer more personalisation and greater speed and efficiency of financial planning services to fit into the new generation of customers' digital way of life.

Although these tools are handy, it is debatable whether robo-advisors and InsurTech startups can completely replace financial advisers and their human touch. More than 60% of InsurTech companies offer non-life insurance, as life insurance can be more complex but is also the most profitable for insurers. What is important now is creating a seamless omnichannel experience, with a tad of physical interaction when it comes to personalised financial planning or filing claims for life insurance where empathy cannot be replaced. At the same time, InsurTech would be the go-to for general insurance.

Government Nudges

The Singapore government is committed to keeping healthcare costs low and ensuring that no one is denied medical treatment because they cannot afford it.

The government has two financial programmes to ensure mandatory saving: MediSave and need-based relief through an endowment named MediFund. In addition, there are three government-administered insurance programmes: compulsory health insurance and a hospitalisation programme called MediShield, and two long-term and disability care programmes, mandatory CareShield and optional ElderShield.

Long-term care financing in Singapore is based on the principle of collective responsibility, with multiple tiers of support via (i) targeted government subsidies and financial assistance or community support for those with less financial means; (ii) insurance to pool risks across the population, and (iii) personal/family savings for individuals and families to take responsibility for their care.

MediSave, MediLife, MediFund, CareShield, and ElderShield are all programmes in Singapore that provide financial assistance for medical expenses. MediSave is a national medical savings account for inpatient and outpatient medical expenses. It is funded through mandatory contributions from employees and employers. It can be used for a wide range of medical costs, including hospital stays, surgeries, and certain types of outpatient treatment. MediLife is a voluntary insurance plan that provides financial protection for medical expenses. It covers a wide range of medical costs, including hospital stays, surgeries, and certain types of outpatient treatment. MediFund is a national fund that provides financial assistance to individuals and families who cannot pay for their medical expenses. It is intended for those who cannot pay medical costs even after using their MediSave accounts and other financial assistance. CareShield is a long-term care insurance plan that provides financial assistance for those who require long-term care due to disability or severe illness. It covers many expenses, including nursing home care, home care, and rehabilitation. ElderShield is a long-term care insurance plan that provides financial assistance for those who require long-term care due to disability or severe illness. It covers many expenses, including nursing home care, home care, and rehabilitation.

These programmes provide financial assistance for medical expenses in Singapore, including hospital stays, surgeries, and long-term care. They are funded through a combination of mandatory contributions and voluntary insurance premiums and are designed to help individuals and families cover the costs of medical treatment.

Bancassurance

Bancassurance is no exception from other financial services players, who must also master the omnichannel battle. As fewer customers visit physical bank locations, being unable to continue with the application on different devices will significantly limit the chance of sales conversion. Bancassurance players must understand this when integrating channels and platforms into their customer journey.

From "channel providers" to "holistic financial advisors", banks and insurers must work together, utilising data, AI, etc., to drive insurance conversion among savers. This can be done by offering personalised advice. For example, some leading players have utilised AI to develop the "someone-like-you" feature, providing personalised insight and financial planning and introducing the best insurance solution based on customer profiles. Some also use data to build a "true risk score" to enhance underwriting capability, saving costs and time for approval. Lastly, embedded insurance will play a big role in certain lines of products in reshaping distribution channels and improving customer acquisition and conversion. Customers increasingly trust digital platforms as the potential provider of their insurance.

Singapore has been witness to some of the largest bancassurance transactions locally, showcasing the prowess of bank insurance relationships. In 2020,

DBS Bank announced a partnership with Manulife to offer insurance products to its customers in Singapore. Under the partnership, DBS Bank will distribute Manulife's insurance products through its branches and digital channels worth over SGD1B. OCBC Bank, as the largest shareholder of Great Eastern Insurance, provides its customers with a range of insurance products through its branches and digital channels, including life, health, and general insurance products. In 2018, United Overseas Bank (UOB) announced a partnership with AIA to offer insurance products to its customers. Under the partnership, UOB will distribute AIA's insurance products through its branches and digital channels.

Incumbents Regionalisation

Singapore is home to one of the highest saturated insurance markets globally — measured by gross written premiums (GWP) as a percentage of per-capita gross domestic product. A report by Bain showed incumbents accounted for more than 45% of GWP, and annual growth was at 1% for the general insurance market. Furthermore, traditional distribution channels through agents and financial advisors remain the preferred avenue for local consumers to purchase their policies. Given the Republic's high insurance penetration rate, the value proposition of InsurTechs does not lie in reaching new customer segments. Instead, it is working with incumbents to improve insurance services and offerings. Therefore, the bulk of services offered by InsurTechs is intended to assist incumbent providers in being more customer- and data-driven. This means that startups and incumbents must work together, with the incumbents' providing customers and the startups providing innovation. The recent mergers and acquisitions within the InsurTech industry represent a step in the right direction and could be a glimpse into the future of how incumbents and startups can work together. An example of this is the Aviva–Singlife and HSBC–AXA mergers. As a small market, Singapore has always looked at developing and supporting regional champions in every space, whether banking or insurance. As a result, over the last few years, multiple international insurers merged their Singapore operations with local and regional players, giving them scale and opportunity to be leaders in ASEAN.

Singlife

In 2020, Singaporean digital life insurance company Singlife merged with Aviva Singapore in the largest transaction on record in the Singapore insurance sector at SGD3.2B. It also created a mobile-first insurance savings account, which rapidly gained popularity. Then CEO and founder Walter de Oude said the company will build upon its new ties with Aviva to build "a homegrown, Southeast Asian, technology-enabled and customer-centric financial services company." The merger with Aviva will provide Singlife with a customer base, and in return, Singlife will bring its technology-driven and mobile-first strategy.[1]

Singlife was founded in 2014 to provide digital life insurance services, initially targeting private banking customers and high-net-worth individuals. In 2018 it acquired Zurich Life Singapore, and in 2019 it acquired Yolopay's payment service.

Singlife established a vibrant and holistic ecosystem to digitise Singapore's SMEs, bringing together regional leaders like Grab, Shopback and Razer to launch Odyssey. Singlife also partnered with several InsurTech and digital commerce startups to create one of the region's first InsurTech accelerators, Connect. In the Philippines, Singlife gained over 100,000 customers and partnered with the largest digital platform and wallet, Gcash,

[1] https://www.businessinsider.com/singlife-largest-insurer-singapore-after-23b-merger-2020-12

to create digital products enabling the highest level of affordability and flexibility.[2]

NTUC

NTUC Income, one of the largest insurers in Singapore, was historically owned by a cooperative society. It announced in early 2021 that it would convert itself into a corporate entity, citing the need to be more competitive amid "intensifying headwinds" in the insurance sector. It cited the objective of "achieving operational flexibility and gaining access to strategic growth options to compete on an equal footing with other insurers locally and regionally".[3] Income has partnered with various ecosystem players like telecom and ride-hailing companies to utilise their lifestyle products to push microinsurance and investments onto existing customers and employees.

NTUC Income developed SNACK, a lifestyle-based microinsurance proposition acting as an insurance underwriter and platform owner, embedding insurance in a person's lifestyle through commuting on public transport, dining out or clocking 5,000 steps. As a result, SNACK partnered with lifestyle brands that have never been typical partners of insurers, aiming to change consumers' conventional perception of insurance. Additionally, business partners who viewed insurance conventionally can view it as a novel point of differentiation to engage and reward loyal customers.[4]

[2] https://iotbusiness-platform.com/insights/singlife-philippines-officially-launched-its-partnership-with-gcash-to-offer-no-fuss-protection-to-filipinos-manila-bulletin/

[3] https://www.channelnewsasia.com/singapore/ntuc-income-corporatisation-company-co-op-existing-policies-coverage-benefits-2418561

[4] https://www.income.com.sg/about-us/corporate-information/press-releases/ntuc-income-and-zhongan-enter-strategic-partnershi

Across the region, Income also works with ecosystem partners via our Insurance-as-a-Service platform, HIVE, in embedding insurance protection into the day-to-day lives of underserved segments and has seen how gig workers such as domestic helpers, rider-hailing drivers and food delivery riders have benefitted from it.[5,6]

▸ *HSBC–AXA*

In August 2021, HSBC announced a merger with Singaporean AXA Insurance. AXA Singapore is the eighth largest life insurer in Singapore by annualised new premiums, the fifth largest property and casualty (P&C) insurer, and a leading group health player. The proposed acquisition, which is subject to regulatory approval, is a key step in achieving HSBC's stated ambition of becoming a top wealth manager in Asia by expanding its insurance and wealth franchise in Singapore, a strategically important scale market for HSBC, and a major hub for its ASEAN wealth business. Both businesses have complementary products across insurance solutions and distribution channels. At the same time, AXA Singapore provides access to a sizeable tied-agency sales force, several leading independent financial advisory firms, and a large pool of insurance policyholders and corporate relationships. This combined business will materially scale up HSBC's presence in the regional insurance market and provide an excellent platform for future growth.[7]

---

[5] https://www.coverager.com/ntuc-income-offers-insurance-as-a-service/

[6] https://www.insurancebusinessmag.com/asia/news/breaking-news/income-expands-into-japanese-market-426176.aspx

[7] https://www.hsbc.com/news-and-media/media-releases/2021/hsbc-to-acquire-axa-singapore

InsurTech Innovation

InsurTech has been rapidly evolving and gaining traction worldwide. It has transformed the insurance industry by leveraging technological innovations such as data analytics, blockchain, and AI. Some key trends and developments in the field of InsurTech include:

- **Digital Transformation:** InsurTech has driven the digital transformation of the insurance industry, encouraging traditional insurance companies to adopt digital platforms and tools. This shift towards digitisation has improved customer experiences, streamlined processes, and increased operational efficiency.
- **Personalisation and Customisation:** InsurTech has enabled insurers to offer more personalised and customised insurance products and services. By leveraging data analytics and AI algorithms, insurers can assess risks more accurately, tailor coverage to individual needs, and offer personalised pricing options.
- **Innovative Insurance Models:** InsurTech has facilitated the emergence of innovative insurance models such as peer-to-peer insurance, on-demand insurance, and usage-based insurance. These models leverage technology to provide flexible coverage, real-time risk assessment, and pay-per-use options, catering to the evolving needs of customers.
- **Improved Claims Processing:** InsurTech has streamlined the claims processing and settlement procedures, reducing paperwork and manual intervention. By utilising technologies such as AI, blockchain, and image recognition, insurers can automate claims assessment, verification, and settlement, leading to faster and more efficient claim resolutions.
- **Partnership and Collaboration:** InsurTech startups and traditional insurers are increasingly forming partnerships and collaborations to leverage each other's strengths. Traditional insurers gain access to innovative technologies and ideas, while InsurTech startups benefit from the industry expertise and customer base of established insurance companies.

- **Data Analytics and Risk Management:** InsurTech leverages data analytics to gain insights into customer behaviour, risk profiles, and market trends. This enables insurers to make data-driven decisions, improve risk management strategies, and enhance underwriting processes.
- **Regulatory and Compliance Challenges:** InsurTech operates in a highly regulated industry, and compliance with insurance regulations and data protection laws is crucial. InsurTech companies need to navigate complex regulatory landscapes to ensure compliance and build trust with customers.

Overall, the state of InsurTech is characterised by continuous innovation, digital transformation, and a focus on customer-centric solutions. InsurTech has the potential to revolutionise the insurance industry by improving efficiency, enhancing customer experiences, and introducing new business models.

Singapore-based bolttech achieved unicorn status after the largest ever InsurTech Series A funding of USD247M led by Activant. Following through, Tokio Marine invested USD50M as part of the deal, which will bump up the InsurTech firm's valuation to USD1.5B. The InsurTech firm currently processes USD50B worth of annualised premiums. In addition, it has connected more than 800 distribution partners with over 200 insurance providers.[8]

Igloo, a Singapore-based InsurTech focused on underserved communities in Southeast Asia, announced it had raised a Series B extension of USD27M, bringing the round's total to USD46M. The first tranche of USD19M was led by Cathay Innovation, with participation from ACA and OpenSpace.

---

[8] https://www.techinasia.com/tokio-marine-bolttech-series-b

Igloo develops its insurance products and then partners with insurers who underwrite their policies. Igloo currently works with 20 global, regional and local insurers across Southeast Asia. In addition, it distributes its insurance products through partnerships with over 55 companies in seven countries. It now offers 15 products, including policies for gig workers, gamers, cars and farmers in Vietnam, and announces it has facilitated more than 300 million policies.[9]

Doctor Anywhere, a regional tech-led healthcare company headquartered in Singapore, has raised nearly USD140M from investors like Asia Partners, Kamet Capital, Square Peg, IHH Healthcare, EDBI and OSK-SBI Venture Partners. Since its launch in 2017, DA has grown exponentially to serve more than 1.5 million users across Southeast Asia through 2,800 doctors and medical professionals within its network in the region. The COVID-19 pandemic has also catalysed to fast-track the adoption of telehealth services in the area, an innovation which enabled the healthcare industry to continue providing high-quality, affordable care to families through the crisis.[10]

Singapore-based digital health app Speedoc has raised SGD34.7M in funding through two rounds. The latest round, a Series A funding round led by Vertex Ventures, raised SGD6.7M to expand Speedoc's services across Southeast Asia and develop new products. The second round raised SGD28M and was led by SoftBank Ventures Asia, with participation from other investors. The additional funding will enhance Speedoc's platform and expand its operations in Singapore and other Southeast Asian markets.[11]

---

[9] https://techcrunch.com/2022/11/28/igloo-series-b-extension/

[10] https://doctoranywhere.com/blog/2021/08/31/doctor-anywhere-series-c-release/

[11] https://techcrunch.com/2022/11/08/southeast-asia-health-tech-platform-speedoc-raises-28m/

Ecosystem Innovation

Embedded insurance is all about bundling coverage or protections within purchasing a product or service, offered in real-time or at the point of sale. It provides new ways of looking at insurance products by putting them in the context of day-to-day life. It offers unconventional ways to forge relationships with new customers who may not have engaged with insurance.

Another fundamental aspect of successful ecosystem partnerships is access to data. Instead of wrestling over ownership of customer data, what is more important is working with ecosystem partners to collectively derive insights that can translate into better customer propositions and value and co-create personalised offerings. Embedded insurance permeates the offline human advisory space where providers are looking at carving a comprehensive suite of solutions for customers, including those from their peers and competitors, to bring the best option to the consumers.

We have seen leading insurers make significant progress in this area. For example, in Southeast Asia, Grab's insurance launched a partnership with Chubb to offer travel, accident, hospitalisation and other critical insurance as part of integrated solutions providing embedded in the ride-hailing customer journey. Another player in the insurance industry, Ping An, has launched Ping An Good Doctor, China's leading online healthcare service, which charges a monthly subscription fee that embraces an insurance fee.

Grab, the Singaporean rideshare company, has expanded into insurance with ambitions to become a major insurer throughout Southeast Asia. In 2019, it partnered with Chinese internet-based insurer ZhongAn Online P&C Insurance Co to create a digital platform to distribute insurance products in Southeast Asia.[12] It also tied up with NTUC Income to launch a

[12] https://www.businesstimes.com.sg/garage/news/grab-in-jv-with-chinas-zhongan-to-distribute-insurance-products-in-south-east-asia

microinsurance product for critical illness.[13] This product is designed to protect Grab drivers from essential disease costs. Grab drivers decide how much money per trip they want to add to their premium and accumulate the corresponding coverage for each trip they complete. Grab also partnered with Chubb, a causality insurance company, to provide a travel insurance product for their passengers. This product lets customers add insurance before departure to their bill so that they are insured against accidents as they ride.[14]

Singtel Dash, a mobile wallet programme run by a Singaporean telecommunication company, and Etiqa Insurance, an insurance firm, collaborated to create the Dash PET. Dash PET is an insurance savings plan which helps users get high-return savings in a low-interest environment. The selected policyholders also get complimentary coverage of up to SGD50,000 for Death & Total and Permanent Disability in the users' first Dash PET policy year. This particularly benefits young people with a Dash account, as many lack coverage. By adding complementary coverage to their membership, they are now insured. In addition, Singtel also provides insurance for migrant workers based on buying data plans.[15,16]

Conclusion

At its foundation, Singapore has focused on mandatory state-led insurance and protection benefits to the population to ensure that none is left behind because of the inability to afford basic insurance. The private sector has taken the opportunity to leverage national digital identity and payment

[13] https://fintechnews.sg/32780/insurtech/grab-ntuc-grabinsure/

[14] https://www.techinasia.com/grab-chubb-launches-apppurchasing-travel-insurance

[15] https://www.straitstimes.com/business/singtel-enters-insurance-market-with-cover-for-migrant-workers-other-products-to-come

[16] https://fintechnews.sg/55413/insurtech/singtel-dash-etiqa-offer-free-insurance-coverage-with-dash-pet/

infrastructure to create more inclusive insurance for residents. As one of the highest-value per-customer markets in Singapore, there is an unparalleled opportunity for homegrown insurance and InsurTech players to become not just ASEAN but even global leaders using Singapore as the testing ground for innovation.

On innovation in the insurance industry, InsurTech has disrupted the insurance industry by harnessing the power of technology. By leveraging data analysis, blockchain, and AI, InsurTech has made insurance processes faster, more efficient, and customer-centric. Its close association with FinTech has further accelerated innovation in the sector, driving the development of new insurance products and services. As the insurance industry continues to embrace technological advancements, it must also address the challenges of data security and privacy to maintain customer trust and regulatory compliance. InsurTech is set to shape the future of insurance, bringing about a more connected, efficient, and personalised insurance experience for individuals and businesses alike.

Chapter 12

STRENGTHENING CAPITAL MARKETS

Entry of Robo-advisors in Singapore

Wealth and capital markets are closely interrelated yet are distinct components in the world of FinTech. Wealth commonly refers to the assets or net worth of individual investors. At the same time, capital markets are financial markets that facilitate buyers and sellers trading financial assets such as stocks, bonds and currencies. The major players are typically larger corporations. Wealth inequality is a common phenomenon in Singapore and beyond. Reasons contributing to the current state span across the individual's lack of basic financial knowledge and, possibly, procrastination. The lack of transparency in financial information and pricing can become the stumbling block for the initiated who likes to self-serve digitally. As a country with an ageing population, there must be sufficient retirement planning. The need for planning is further compounded by the emergence of more than 300,000 individuals in the gig economy, i.e., freelance workers, who do not have the safety net of Central Provident Fund (CPF) savings for retirement. If not addressed promptly and appropriately, it is a problem that will inevitably blow up in 15 years.

Singapore became the first country in Southeast Asia to open the pension funds market to private players. CPF funds are well-known to be extremely sticky. Endowus is an example of a FinTech in Singapore where consumers can invest their CPF savings. Syfe came in to focus on real-estate investment trusts. StashAway allows individuals to invest their Supplementary Retirement Scheme funds from their CPF savings. Kristal.ai participated in the Sandbox to go directly to consumers to provide them with customisable investment products, primarily focusing on accredited investors

With the appearance of robo-advisors, banks started to feel a strong fear of missing out. So DBS launched a product in collaboration with Quantifeed, and OCBC launched RoboInvest by working with WeInvest.

Incorporated in Singapore in September 2016, StashAway is the first robo-advisor that obtained a full capital markets services licence from the Monetary Authority of Singapore (MAS). Michele Ferrario co-founded StashAway together with Freddy Lim and Nino Ulsamer. Before StashAway, Michele was Group CEO at Zalora and worked in the financial services industry.

One of the pioneers in Southeast Asia's digital wealth management space, StashAway currently operates in Singapore, Malaysia, the Middle East and North Africa, Hong Kong, and Thailand. StashAway aims to make intelligent investing simple, transparent, and cost-effective. The company offers investment portfolios and cash management solutions to both retail investors and high-net-worth individuals, to empower more people to build wealth for the long term.

StashAway delivers institutional-level asset allocation sophistication to clients through its proprietary investment strategy, ERAA® (Economic Regime-based Asset Allocation). ERAA® uses macroeconomic data to minimise risk and maximise returns for every portfolio throughout economic cycles. In addition, the company has partnered with one of the world's largest asset managers, Blackrock®, to offer clients access to a suite of globally diversified multi-asset model portfolios.

To address the needs of its growing high-net-worth clientele, StashAway launched an offering designed exclusively for accredited investors, StashAway Reserve, which enables access to private equity, venture capital, angel investing and crypto, on top of dedicated wealth advisory. In addition, with a minimum investment amount of just SGD250,000, StashAway Reserve lowers the barriers to entry to private market investing, allowing clients to invest in funds from some of the world's leading fund managers including KKR, SilverLake, CD&R, Lexington Partners, and Khosla Ventures.

In collaboration with XA Network, StashAway Reserve also brings clients access to promising early-stage startups in Southeast Asia. With this, accredited investors can gain diverse exposure to 10 to 20 startups with a single amount, starting from as low as USD20,000.

Apart from its investment portfolios, StashAway has continuously led innovation in cash management solutions. Its suite of cash management portfolios aims to empower clients to earn higher returns on their cash through all economic cycles. StashAway Simple™ and StashAway Simple™ Plus have no lock-ins or minimum balances. At the same time, its latest offering, StashAway Simple™ Guaranteed, offers guaranteed returns on any investment amount over a lock-in period of six months.

To Michele, the main competitor is cash sitting in the bank. There is an estimated SGD1.1T of household financial wealth in Singapore, and 36% of this sits in bank savings accounts. This is extraordinarily large, considering only 14% of wealth is in savings accounts in the US.

Today, StashAway is the region's largest digital wealth management platform and operates in Singapore and Malaysia. As of 2021, it worked in five economies: Singapore, Malaysia, the United Arab Emirates, Hong Kong, and Thailand. The company aims to empower people to build wealth in the long term. StashAway is a business-to-consumer (B2C) company whose value proposition has three pillars: making investing simple, cost-effective, and intelligent. By managing fractional shares in the backend, which allows it to do away with minimum deposit requirements, the company has made investing accessible to everyone. In June 2020, StashAway raised USD16M in its Series C funding round led by Square Peg Capital, a venture capital firm based in Australia.

In 2023, StashAway was ranked in the top 20 high-growth companies in Asia-Pacific (APAC) by *The Financial Times*. StashAway took first place in the category for Singapore Financial Institution at the Singapore FinTech Festival (SFF) Global FinTech Awards 2021 presented by MAS and the Singapore FinTech Association. The company was also awarded a spot in FinTech Global's 2021 WealthTech 100 list.

Endowus is Asia's leading digital wealth platform and an industry pioneer of the fee-only model. Licensed by MAS, and the Securities & Futures Commission of Hong Kong, Endowus is the first and largest digital advisor in the region to span both private wealth (cash) and public pension savings (CPF and SRS in Singapore), helping investors grow their total assets with expert advice, access to institutional-class solutions at low and fair fees, through a personalised digital wealth experience.

Endowus has raised SGD67M in funding from UBS, EDBI, Prosus Ventures, Z Venture Capital, Samsung Ventures, Singtel Innov8, and leading global venture capital firms Lightspeed Venture Partners and SoftBank Ventures Asia.

In one of the unique moves of challengers acquiring the incumbents, Endowus Group acquired a majority stake in Hong Kong-based multi-family office Carret Private, serving tens of thousands of clients with assets over USD4B and becoming one of the largest independent wealth managers in Asia.

Endowus is an independent and strictly fee-only wealth service that is holistic and aligned with the client's best interests. As the first wealth platform to return all trailer fees to clients as cashback, Endowus is leading the industry by introducing greater transparency so investors can keep more of their returns and compound their wealth.

Building trust with clients is a core tenet of Endowus' business. With its open platform architecture, it partners with more than 50 of the world's leading global and local fund managers to offer individual investors the best of institutional share-class funds. Where alternatives have been traditionally marketed exclusively to institutional and ultra-high net worth investors, Endowus Private Wealth clients can also gain access to sophisticated private and illiquid assets that broaden the diversification of their portfolios across private equity, private credit, and multi-strategy hedge funds — at a cost that is only a fraction of the industry average. Its proprietary Wealth Implementation Plan, exclusive to private wealth clients, formulates an investment strategy uniquely tailored to each client and can be implemented in part or in whole — depending on their unique circumstances.

The company adopts an evidence-based approach for the highest probability of success in its investment portfolios. At a low cost, it combines strategic passive assets allocation with global diversification, expressed through best-in-class funds. This approach is designed to help investors stay disciplined amid market volatility and track towards their long-term goals across cash, CPF and SRS.

The portfolio of choice for most Endowus' clients, the Endowus' core Flagship portfolios are globally diversified and have a strategic passive asset allocation to take advantage of broad market opportunities for long-term compounding returns, at the lowest possible cost. Endowus Satellite portfolios allow the ease of selecting key sectors or themes that may complement their overall investment portfolios such as Technology, Megatrends, Real Estate and more.

Savvier investors who prefer to create their portfolios or buy single funds use Endowus Fund Smart platform, an open fund platform with over 200 curated best-in-class funds from top-tier global fund managers. At a low cost of 0.3% per annum, the platform can save clients up to 50% or more per year on their all-in investment costs for all unit trusts. Many funds available to retail clients have previously only been available to institutional and ultra-high-net-worth investors, or the top 0.1% of society.

Endowus has consistently been the top-rated robo-advisor on Seedly and on both iOS and Google Play stores. Besides winning Startup of the Year and WealthTech of the Year at 2022's Asia Fintech Awards, Endowus was also featured on LinkedIn's list of Top Start-ups in 2022, Forbes' 100 To Watch list, and most recently won Singapore's Best Digital Wealth Management at The Asset's Triple A Digital Awards and Asia Asset Management's Best of the Best Awards 2023.

Its CIO, founding partner and Chairman, Samuel Rhee, feels that due to a misalignment of interests between providers and consumers, what is currently in the market for consumers is a fragmented and broken experience. The clients are owned by distributors such as banks, which is problematic as incumbents have no desire to change this structure. In the wealth space, Samuel believes that what is critical is allowing individuals access to good products and acquire the advice to help them get there and make informed decisions. In addition, a lack of knowledge among consumers means there needs to be more direction and a sense of purpose in saving up for retirement. This is what pushed the founders to set up Endowus to fill this gap in the market.

Endowus' main aim is to provide a platform that allows people to invest their money for the future and rest easy for today. It is the first and only robot-advisory platform in Singapore that enables individuals to invest their CPF funds seamlessly, allowing them to earn an average return of 3–8% p.a. on CPF savings which has a baseline of 2.5% p.a. Endowus accomplishes this in a tri-faceted manner: investment advice, providing access to products, and minimising cost. It has partnered with major incumbents, such as UOB Kay Hian, to allow customers to invest seamlessly on the platform. In addition, by asking PIMCO for access to the institutional share class, it has drastically lowered the costs passed on to investors by two-thirds. Reducing costs allows it to align directly with clients and act in their best interests in an agnostic manner. It is important to partner with these asset managers and brokers who have been in the industry for a long time to cut through the noise in the industry and provide simple solutions.

Samuel also sees the importance of better educating people to manage their wealth and elevating financial literacy. He also feels that the human touch continues to be important in the robo-advisory area. While algorithms are involved in rebalancing and creating portfolios, algorithms are still "junk in, junk out". Human expertise is needed in making these algorithms work when providing robo-advisory services.

Syfe is an all-in-one digital wealth management platform on a mission to empower people to build their wealth for a better future. Built on the pillars of access, advice and innovation, Syfe caters to the full spectrum of an individual's wealth needs across discretionarily-managed portfolios, cash management solutions and a full-fledged stock brokerage.

With customer centricity at its core, Syfe focuses heavily on customer education and personalised insights so that individuals can make optimal decisions towards their financial goals.

Syfe was founded in 2019 in Singapore, its headquarters, and is now also present in Hong Kong and Australia. To date, Syfe has more than 100,000 customers in Singapore who trust Syfe with their money. The company has introduced several firsts in the digital wealth management industry — including Asia's first customisable exchange-traded fund portfolio builder and a unique partnership with the Singapore Exchange to launch a REIT+ portfolio. Most recently, Syfe partnered with PIMCO, a global leader in active fixed income, to launch income portfolios powered by PIMCO's forward-looking views and time-tested investment approach. The company is backed by leading global investors, including Peter Thiel's Valar, Unbound and DST Global partners and has raised USD52M since its inception in 2019.

It remains the only digital wealth manager with a brokerage offering, enabling investors to build wealth their way through fractional trading and an easy-to-use platform to access the US and local markets in Singapore and Australia, for Singapore Exchange (SGX) and Australian Securities Exchange respectively.

Syfe has won multiple industry awards including Best Digital Wealth Advisory Solution by the DigFin Group Innovation Awards, Top Startups 2022 by LinkedIn Singapore, Future of Digital Infrastructure by the IDC Future Enterprise Awards 2022, and Wealth Management FinTech by the Asian Banking and Finance Awards 2022. In 2021, Syfe's CEO and founder were also awarded Top 10 FinTech Leaders by SFF.

While Stashaway, Endowus and Syfe focused on retail and affluent clients, Kristal took a different focus to primarily focus on customers traditionally served by private banks.

The company's background and achievements can be summarised as follows. Firstly, the company began as a business-to-consumer (B2C) entity in Singapore in 2016, and subsequently established B2B2C channels in 2020. Secondly, Kristal became the first asset manager to emerge successfully from the MAS sandbox. Thirdly, the company has established a presence in over 20 countries, such as Singapore, the UAE, and India. Fourthly, the company has an impressive asset under management of USD1.35B. Fifthly, the company offers access to a diverse product portfolio consisting of more than 20 asset classes, including Structured Products, Alternatives, Private Assets and Bonds, which can be fractionalised for as low as USD10,000 per cheque. Lastly, Kristal has forged partnerships with several renowned banks as well as more than 150 boutique wealth managers.

Kristal is a B2B2C enterprise wealth platform that connects wealth managers in emerging markets to global financial products. Their investment infrastructure covers the gamut of product discovery, intelligence, compliance and execution — making them indispensable to wealth managers.

While wealth managers excel at distribution, they need access to various global products at affordable ticket sizes to ensure they can service the more than 30 million affluents and high-net-worth individuals (USD0.1–5M net worth) in emerging markets. This underserved population leads the way in incremental wealth creation and digital wealth adoption, making it a more than USD5T opportunity.

With a comprehensive set of proprietary pipes to a diverse range of financial products, Kristal has successfully democratised access to more than 600 global financial products for more than 150 wealth managers, thereby creating the ability for wealth managers to serve the needs of a significantly larger customer base at affordable ticket sizes.

The Exchange at Every Interchange

Singapore has historically been the centre of capital and wealth management. However, as more traditional assets started digitising, the focus evolved towards decentralising these assets. As a result, Singapore saw hundreds of blockchain companies set up in the past few years and the emergence of several global leaders in the domain. For example, Ethereum founder, Vitalik Buterin, calls Singapore home and is an active member of the Singapore blockchain community.

Singapore is emerging as a digital securities trading hub whereby exchanges to trade these innovative securities are being set up by local and external players, hoping to attract issuers and investors to their platforms.

Exchange — Singaponomics Style

Singapore Exchange (SGX) is a listed investment holding company that manages Singapore's leading stock exchange and offers additional securities and derivatives trading services.

In an authentic Singanomics manner, SGX is a Self-Regulatory Organisation with a dual nature of commercial and regulatory obligations. It has for-profit commercial objectives as a listed company, regulatory responsibilities, and a public interest duty as a market regulator.

A natural tension may arise within SGX from being both a listed company and a market regulator. This conflict of interest is known as a "Regulatory Conflict", and efficient management gives SGX its unique character. To achieve this, the Singapore Exchange Regulation (RegCo) is responsible for formulating and maintaining arrangements and processes within the SGX Group for managing regulatory conflicts and is accountable to SGX.[1]

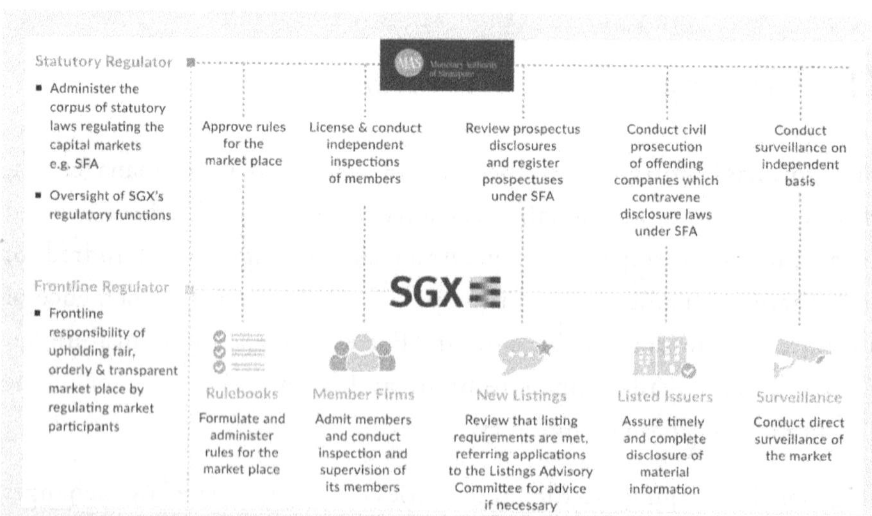

[1] https://www.sgx.com/regulation/about-sgx-regco

In a bold series of events, Singapore's largest bank DBS announced a digital asset exchange in December 2020, collaborating with SGX, which took a 10% stake in the venture. The project aspired to provide an ecosystem for fundraising through asset tokenisation and secondary trading of digital assets.

As an example of the Singanomics model, the largest bank of Singapore and the local exchange of dual commercial and regulatory characters come together to launch a regulated platform for issuing and trading digital tokens. Such tokens represent financial assets, such as shares in unlisted companies, bonds, and private equity funds.

In the spirit of **Right First, Fast Later**, in the first phase, digital currency exchange will aim only to offer exchange between four cryptocurrencies and four fiat currency pairs, thus building solid foundations before embracing scale. The chosen four fiat currencies were SGD, USD, HKD and JPY, while the four selected cryptocurrencies were Bitcoin, Ether, Bitcoin Cash and XRP.

As a testament to **Garden Innovation**, only accredited and institutional investors initially access the solution until the suitability and scalability of solutions mature to serve all users.

> *"That interest is quite high, given the amount of interest in all four cryptos we trade now. And therefore, it will pick up. But whether it picks up to tens of millions or hundreds of millions of income over the next few years, it's hard to say. So let us get in there, figure it out and grow and then get a better sense of how big this could be in time."*
>
> *Piyush Gupta, DBS CEO*[2]

[2] https://vulcanpost.com/745061/dbs-ceo-cryptocurrency-blockchain/

Till March 2021, the DBS trading desk, open only to professional investors and wealth managers in Singapore, hit a daily trading volume between SGD30–40M with 120 investors onboarded.[3]

Additionally, DBS partnered with JP Morgan and Temasek to create a new blockchain platform, Partior, for payments, trade and foreign exchange settlements. Partior is a digitised M1 commercial money that can offer a credible alternative to the traditional cross-border payments "hub and spoke" model, allowing for more efficient payment clearance and settlement. In 2022, Standard Chartered Bank joined the partnership to enhance the interbank network. Its multi-currency payment is based on the US and Singapore dollar, with six currencies onboarding as of 2022.[4]

▸ *SGX Invested in Two Digital Asset Platforms, ISTOX and Capbridge*

To advance Singapore's position as a world-class financial hub, SGX collaborated with Heliconia Capital Management to develop a capital market platform called iSTOX. It is a platform that will offer the ability to trade and issue security tokens. It is also a future-ready platform for alternative capital fundraising, offering substantial benefits to complement Singapore's existing capital market mechanisms.[5]

Istox has aimed to incorporate blockchain and smart contract technology to provide fast time-to-issuance and high user transparency.

[3] https://blockworks.co/dbs-digital-assets-business-building-steadily/

[4] https://www.ledgerinsights.com/partior-jp-morgan-dbs-blockchain-payments/

[5] https://www.straitstimes.com/business/invest/sgx-temasek-unit-invest-in-capital-market-platform-istox

In May 2021, the company rebranded from iSTOX to ADDX as it entered a new growth phase. ADDX unveiled plans for more issuance deals — at least 20 in 2021, with more than double the sales completed in 2020. The rebranding followed several blue-chip issuances listed on ADDX in the first half of 2021, including the Mapletree Europe Income Trust, the Astrea VI private equity bonds, and a fully digital commercial paper by CGS-CIMB.

Furthermore, SGX has partnered with CapBridge to develop a licensed private stock exchange, 1exchange(1X), which aims to increase the efficiency of private deals by improving mutual access for investors and companies on a single platform. As a result, a formal private deals marketplace can increase audience reach exponentially, aggregating collective demand and increasing the efficiency of the price discovery mechanism.

▸ ***SmartKarma***

Additionally, SGX collaborated with Smartkarma in 2019, a Singapore-based FinTech that facilitates alternative data and wisdom sourcing in investment research. This global research network can provide the market community with an added source of research data and analysis, providing listed companies with a direct touchpoint with investors.

This partnership is aligned with RegCo's aim to improve the readiness of the local capital market community to handle any associated risks involved in the innovation process. RegCo restructured its regulatory framework, tightened listing rules on accounting and property valuation and loosened regulations on specific areas such as the minimum trading price. It aims to build a more mature marketplace where the market and participants are effectively self-governing.[6]

[6] https://www.sgx.com/media-centre/20190709-sgx-invests-fintech-smartkarma-advances-investment-research

MAS–SGX

In 2018, SGX, in collaboration with MAS, developed delivery versus payment (DvP) capabilities to settle tokenisation assets across different blockchain platforms to help simplify post-trade processes. The DvP allows large financial institutions and corporate investors to exchange and settle digital currencies and securities across other platforms.[7]

SGX–Trumid XT Platform

SGX partnered with Trumid and Hillhouse Capital to enhance liquidity and execution of the Asian bond market for global clients through XinTru. Xintru will operate Trumid XT, an electrical bond trading infrastructure powered by advanced technology and rich analytics. With Trumid XT facilitating international access to Asian bond markets and Asian investors, participants globally will enhance the vibrancy of Asia's fixed-income market and thus increase corporate bond issuance and inflows to Asia-focused funds.

SGX has Invested in and Acquired Multiple FinTech Companies All over the World

SGX — BidFX

As part of SGX's multi-asset strategy to strengthen Singapore's position as a global FX over-the-counter (OTC) market, SGX acquired BidFX in 2020, intending to integrate the OTC and futures FX markets in a single venue with an integrated workflow management system.[8]

The union of SGX and BidFX's expertise, distribution and client networks will accelerate SGX's ambitions to offer end-to-end FX platforms and

---

[7] https://www.sgx.com/media-centre/20181111-mas-and-sgx-successfully-leverage-blockchain-technology-settlement-tokenised

[8] https://www.sgx.com/media-centre/20200629-sgx-fully-acquire-bidfx-advancing-its-global-ambitions-offer-end-end-fx

solutions, placing Singapore on the global map as the one-stop venue for international FX OTC and futures participants.

SGX's Involvement in Climate Action

SGX, DBS Bank, Standard Chartered and Temasek partnered to establish Climate Impact X (CIX) in 2021, a global exchange and marketplace for high-quality carbon credits.

This platform allows corporations to meet their carbon emissions requirements while supporting the development of new carbon credit projects globally. In addition, CIX will leverage SGX's internationally recognised financial, legal and commodities hub infrastructure to strengthen CIX in becoming a global carbon service and trading hub.[9]

SGX Index Edge — CryptoCompare

SGX also collaborated with CryptoCompare in 2020 to launch crypto indices under the SGX iEdge index suite. This collaboration can bring greater transparency to cryptocurrency trading by providing high-quality data and indices to facilitate digital currency trading in Singapore.[10]

▸ ***Marketnode***

Marketnode, an SGX Group and Temasek joint venture is transforming capital markets by building end-to-end digital markets infrastructure. The company's vision is to be APAC's trusted, neutral infrastructure for tokenised traditional finance assets via providing issuers and asset managers with a one-stop infrastructure encompassing data, workflow, and tokenisation

[9] https://www.sgx.com/media-centre/20210520-dbs-sgx-standard-chartered-and-temasek-take-climate-action-through-global

[10] https://www.sgx.com/media-centre/20200901-sgx-index-edge-launch-crypto-indices-collaboration-cryptocompare

capabilities across select asset classes such as fixed income, funds, and structured products.

Built by and for the ecosystem, Marketnode partners with financial market participants, such as global financial institutions, intermediaries, and regulators, in identifying infrastructure inefficiencies and co-creating solutions using technologies such as blockchain and smart contracts. These solutions aim to improve the speed and security of financial market transactions, reduce errors and lower costs throughout the lifecycle of an asset — from origination, transaction, and settlement to the registry.

Marketnode is proud to be part of the MAS-led initiative Project Guardian since its inception, which seeks to explore the economic potential and value-adding use cases of tokenisation. Under Project Guardian, Marketnode is developing a common market infrastructure in collaboration with HSBC and UOB to create an asset and wealth management token factory enabling seamless creation, distribution, and servicing of such assets, leading to a more democratised wealth management ecosystem.

In August 2022, the Singapore Funds Industry Group announced the initial phase of Fundnode, Singapore's national investment funds utility built using distributed ledger technology operated by Marketnode, which will begin by streamlining fund processes, facilitating simplified subscription, redemption, and record-keeping workflows for funds offered to retail investors in Singapore. Set to be operational in Q3 2023, Fundnode will provide fund distributors, fund managers, transfer agents and service providers with a single platform for transaction management, funds processing, and record-keeping.

SGX's First Digital Bond Issuance on Marketnode

Singapore Exchange worked with HSBC Singapore and Temasek, successfully replicating a SGD400M 5.5-year bond issue and a SGD100M tap of the same issue by Olam International in 2020. SGX's digital asset issuance, depository and servicing platform, Marketnode, utilised DAML (smart contract language created by Digital Asset) to model the bond and its distributed workflows for issuance and asset servicing over the bond's lifecycle. Until May 2021, Marketnode's platform had the highest volume of digital bonds issued on an exchange-operated network in Asia, at SGD2B.[11] Critical efficiencies of the project are seamless settlement in multiple currencies to facilitate the transfer of proceeds between the issuer, arranger and investor custodian, timely ISIN (identifier) generation, elimination of settlement risk, reduction in primary issuance settlement (from five to two days), and automation of coupon and redemption payments.

Following the success of the issuance, SGX and Temasek entered into a joint venture (JV) in the same year. As a result, they became Asia-Pacific's first exchange-led digital asset venture focusing on capital markets workflows through blockchain, ledger, and tokenisation technologies.[12] In addition, this JV is looking to partner with FX issuance platforms to connect its post-trade and asset servicing infrastructure, providing a more comprehensive issuance-to-settlement network for Asia's bonds.

FinTech and Incumbents Tango

As digital assets become mainstream in different shapes and forms, Singapore has seen an exciting trend unique to Singapore. Globally, the largest exchanges for trading and distribution of these digital assets are new FinTech players.

[11] https://www.sgx.com/media-centre/20200901-sgx-collaboration-hsbc-and-temasek-completes-pilot-digital-bond-olam

[12] https://www.sgxgroup.com/media-centre/20210122-sgx-and-temasek-partner-advance-digital-asset-infrastructure-capital-markets

Singapore has been unique in that direction, with some of the most traditional incumbent security brokers seeing this as an opportunity to reinvent themselves. Singapore has been a global centre of wealth and hosts several assets through its banking system.

For any asset class to become mainstream, it must have regulated, trusted, and widely accepted platforms for creating, distributing and servicing the products. The more evolved and sophisticated the product mix becomes, the need for trusted providers increases proportionally. The onset of digital assets has created a demand for digital asset exchanges to become part of the mainstream economy.

For any exchange to succeed, it must build a vibrant ecosystem. The exchanges must offer low bid-ask spreads on trade, on-exchange and off-exchange liquidity and governance mechanisms to protect investor interests. Additionally, advanced products like derivatives, multi-currency support and data solutions are vital to bringing digital asset exchanges to the same level as traditional exchanges.

While the new FinTech firms paced to build the technology solutions and bring digital assets to the market, banks have identified that they would need to make significant investments to build consumer trust and distribution. The traditional brokers and exchanges already have a large setup of consumers, bringing confidence and distribution to the table.

▸ *Cryptocurrency Custodian for Institutional Investors: Zodia*

SC Ventures by Standard Chartered and Northern Trust launched Zodia Custody, an institutional-grade custody solution for cryptocurrencies. Zodia aims to enable institutional investors to invest in emerging cryptocurrency assets such as transaction and settlement activities.

The fundamental value proposition of Zodia is to combine traditional custody principles, the regulatory expertise of a bank and the operational agility of a FinTech company to provide an infrastructure that meets the changing expectations of institutional investors.

▶ *CGS-CIMB*

CGS-CIMB (jointly owned by China Galaxy Securities and Malaysia's CIMB Group) is a financial service provider with over 2,600 institutional and 400,000 retail clients. iSTOX enabled CGS-CIMB Securities to issue blockchain-based tokens for commercial paper.

The commercial paper market in Asia is an attractive underserved market as Asian companies have historically been more accustomed to raising funds through bank loans, bonds or equity issuance.

CGS-CIMB collaborated with iSTOX, a Singapore-based security token platform, to issue blockchain-based tokens for commercial paper up to SGD150M. As a result, CGS-CIMB published a SGD150M multi-tranche Commercial Paper as digital securities on iSTOX. Accredited individual and corporate investors oversubscribed the first tranche of SGD10M on the iSTOX platform. iSTOX provides a 364-day commercial paper programme that offers multiple tranches over the next few quarters, up to a maximum amount of SGD150M. The paper matures three months from issuance, and investors can decide whether to subscribe for a new three-month term.[13]

▶ *SIX Digital Exchange & SBI Digital Asset Holding Joint Venture*

Six Digital Exchange (SDX) is a regulated market infrastructure providing end-to-end trading, settlement and custody service for digital assets. SBI Digital Asset Holding (SBI) is a digital assets umbrella of SBI Holdings,

[13] https://fintechnews.sg/50845/blockchain/cgs-cimb-issued-s150-million-commercial-paper-in-digital-securities-on-istox/

which has inroads into banking and securities infrastructure across Asia with businesses in Thailand, South Korea, Hong Kong and Malaysia.

Regulated digital securities markets have been growing exponentially with the increasing volume of cryptocurrency transactions adopted by institutional money. As a result, a rising number of newly introduced assets in the market, such as digital bonds, digital equities, and digital securitised loans, are all forms of on-ledger tokenised securities.

With the growing demand for public and private institutional digital assets, the joint venture platform provides institutional-grade services, including issuing, listing, trading, central securities depository, infrastructure and custody of digital assets and cryptocurrencies. The joint venture aimed to go live by 2022, subject to regulatory approvals from MAS.

ARA Asset Management's Acquisition of Minterest

ARA Group is one of the premier real estate and asset management providers. ARA Asset Management was acquired by the ESR Group in 2022.[14] Before this, it received a controlling stake in wealth management and lending platform Minterest to bring liquidity, distribution and trust to the segment.

In early 2021, blockchain platform Digiassets Exchange (Singapore) (SDAX) and FinTech company Minterest Holdings merged to build a global digital asset exchange ecosystem. The ecosystem will offer fully integrated solutions across deal origination, fundraising, digital securities offering and secondary trading.

Singapore-based Minterest Holdings connects borrowers with global investors and had raised over SGD190M by 2021. Minterest provides

[14] https://www.mingtiandi.com/real-estate/finance/esr-completes-takeover-of-ara-asset-management/

corporations with access to private capital markets. Investors can access alternative investment opportunities across various asset classes, including institutional-grade real estate and private corporate and consumer debt. The company also owns a consumer financing platform, Minterest Money.

SDAX is a blockchain-powered digital asset trading platform with full trading functionalities and on-chain settlement. It traced its origins from RHT Fintech Holdings and was leveraging the RHT network of legal and professional services.

Minterest holds a capital markets service licence, and Minterest Money holds the licence to provide personal loans. In addition, SDAX has received in-principle approval from MAS to operate a digital asset exchange.

John Lim, the co-founder of ARA Asset Management, says, "We are able to deliver a winning global digital asset ecosystem through the merger by bringing together SDAX's comprehensive and robust exchange technology capabilities with our well-established distribution network and deep expertise in deal origination."[15]

> *"Through our work and close interaction with the many stakeholders in the traditional capital markets, we realised a gap and a need for better efficiency and wider inclusion. We wanted to build a platform to help businesses raise funds faster and cost-effectively within a strong and trusted regulatory framework. Blockchain technology was a natural choice as the building blocks for such a platform, and we built the Digiassets Exchange (Singapore), also known as SDAX, over two years."*
>
> *"It's always exciting to be ahead of the curve, where few can claim to own a cutting-edge exchange. We are thrilled by the many*

[15] https://www.businesstimes.com.sg/banking-finance/fintech-companies-sdax-and-mintere st-to-merge-build-digital-asset-exchange-ecosystem#Amendment%20note

new possibilities and innovative digital solutions across different asset classes such a platform will bring."

Mr Tan Chong Huat, Non-Executive Chairman of the RHT Group of Companies

SDAX's institutional-grade digital asset exchange enables asset owners and institutional and accredited investors to access a new world of fundraising and investment opportunities by listing and trading asset-backed digital securities. Through SDAX, global asset owners can unlock the value of their assets by tokenising and listing their assets on the exchange to raise funds from a pool of qualified investors efficiently.

This vision to democratise financial access and create new aspirations in the new world of financial markets saw SDAX joining forces with ARA Minterest to leverage their combined strength towards building a global digital assets exchange. Their mission is to harness the capabilities of blockchain technology to enhance efficiency and raise accessibility for market participants. "We believe SDAX will bridge the gap in traditional systems to enable equal opportunities to capital markets and alternative investments," Chong Huat adds.

▸ *UOB Kay Hian and ECXX*

Backed by the UOB Group, UOB Kay Hian (UOBKH) is one of Asia's largest brokerage firms. Headquartered in Singapore, it has over 80 branches worldwide, including a growing network of offices across Southeast Asia, Greater China, the United Kingdom and North America.

UOBKH expanded its exposure to digital assets by embracing securitised token offerings (STOs) offered by technology company ECXX Global. Under the new offering, both sides will facilitate tokenisation projects and market and distribute tokens to potential investors under UOBKH. According to UOBKH and ECXX, the STOs will comply with regulations for token issuance while providing investor education and analysis on tokenisation and token investment.[16]

According to Esmond Choo, senior executive director of UOBKH: "The ECXX platform is designed to be very versatile and will serve the fast-growing digital asset space ... We believe this collaboration will allow us to leverage our respective strengths to grow our presence in the fintech sector."[17]

ECXX raised SGD6M by selling its 20% stake in its company to Hatten Land, another real estate group like the ARA Group, which invested in another digital asset exchange.[18]

Singapore FinTech BondEvalue launched BondbloX Bond Exchange (BBX)[19], a blockchain-based exchange enabling fractional bond ownership by trading in smaller denominations. It paves the way for many more investors to buy and sell bonds, making bond trading much faster, highly transparent, and cheaper.

Wilhem Lee, Senior Executive Director of UOB Kay Hian, says: "As the largest brokerage in Singapore, we are proud to be the initial launch partner of BondbloX. Asian bonds remain attractive to local and regional investors despite the global uncertainty and market downturn. We are confident that this partnership will provide our customers access to new sources of returns and opportunities to build a more diversified portfolio."[20]

---

[16] https://www.businesstimes.com.sg/banking-finance/uob-kay-hian-ecxx-jointly-offer-securitised-token-offerings

[17] https://finance.yahoo.com/news/ecxx-uob-kay-hian-collaborate-034800942.html

[18] https://www.businesstimes.com.sg/companies-markets/hatten-land-to-acquire-20-stake-in-digital-asset-exchange-ecxx-global-for-us6m

[19] https://bondevalue.com/news/the-bondblox-bond-exchange-goes-live/

[20] https://bondevalue.com/news/the-bondblox-bond-exchange-goes-live/

Phillip Capital and HGX

Since 1975, the Phillip Capital network has grown into an integrated Asian financial house with a global presence that offers a full range of quality and innovative services to retail and high-net-worth individuals, family offices, and corporate and institutional customers. With over 3,500 employees and over 1 million clients worldwide, Phillip Capital has assets under custody/management of more than USD30B, with shareholders' funds over USD1B.

Globally as companies start to remain private longer and delay their initial public offerings, opportunities have become abound in the private capital markets. HGX's newly appointed chairman Richard Teng observes that the private capital markets are steadily gaining momentum in deal volume, with their "vibrancy in activities" surpassing public counterparts.

The finance veteran says, "We are harnessing our strength to further transform the ecosystem by offering the market greater liquidity options."

HGX is leveraging the network of brokers and customers of its three founding members, Phillip Capital, PrimePartners and Fundnel, to link 500,000 investors online automatically. Besides securities in the traditional non-digital format, HGX is also allowed to offer digitised assets using blockchain technology. It allows buying and selling off smaller lots at a fraction of the charges associated with a public listing. It will benefit issuers who seek partial liquidity or own a limited share, such as employees of private companies with equity gained via employee share options or ownership plans.

Conclusion

Capital and capital markets are fluid, operating across borders and regulatory jurisdictions based on liquidity, taxation, ease of doing business and availability of qualified talent. Singapore has been blessed with a flight to quality and haven perception in the light of geopolitical issues in North Asian hubs like Hong Kong and financial instability in European hubs like Switzerland in the aftermath of the Credit Suisse crisis. Over the long term, Singapore would need to capitalise on the short-term impetus it has received to make them permanent long-term propositions.

Chapter 13

NEW FRONTIER

This book has been an illustrative journey of Singapore's development into The FinTech Nation. From the start, the three pillars of Singapore as The FinTech Nation have been **the ecosystem, the regulators, and the relentless individuals** who delivered a playbook to achieve the dreams and aspirations of the Tiny Red Dot.

As the non-profit platform serving Singapore Fintech Community, Fintech Nation has chronicled and published the journey of Singapore becoming a global FinTech hub using the Fintech Nation Book series.

As Singapore set itself to become a FinTech nation in 2015, it identified some key areas and priorities to build the foundations for innovation. Singapore achieved significant success during the first phase of this journey from 2015 to 2023 as Fintech Nation 1.0 (FN1). As we aspire to create a Fintech Vision for Singapore and opportunities for the next phase from 2023 to 2030, Fintech Nation proposes to define it as Vision 2030. We look at critical achievements and future opportunities where industry and regulators can collaborate during the next phase of 2023–2030 as Fintech Nation 2.0 (FN2).

During FN1, Singapore created one of the most comprehensive payment regulations in the world wherein one licence covered consumer and merchant payment, wallets, remittance, digital tokens and account issuance.

Singapore also created the national infrastructure for digital know your customer (KYC) for consumers and corporates, enabling low-cost KYC, authentication and digital signature under the aegis of GovTech. As a result, MyInfo has become the foundation for FinTech, incumbents and digital banks to build and scale their solutions rapidly.

FN1 also saw Singapore build experimentation and infrastructure for enterprise usage of blockchain through Project Ubin, enabling incumbents and FinTech to collaborate to create next-generation solutions. FN1 witnessed awarding five new digital bank licences opening up the market for competition after decades of overall consolidation in the banking space. One of the first digital banks to launch managed to get over 10% of the population as customers within the first year. Singapore also created comprehensive regulatory and support infrastructure to make ESG and sustainability a priority for financial institutions. FN1 successfully established Singapore as a global FinTech leader, and we look forward to the future. Therefore, it is essential to look at the next frontiers.

Over the past few years, Singapore has established itself as a FinTech hub for capital, talent, regional infrastructure and policy initiatives. It has attracted founders and investors worldwide to build a digital business in financial services. Moreover, it has inspired hundreds of founders to build their ventures in Singapore, making it the centre of global growth.

FinTech firms are not a threat to banks but "enablers" whose success will lie in partnering with and enabling them to succeed. The initial fear that FinTech firms will steal their lunch has gone away. Hence, it is no longer perceived as a disruption, but rather, it is a transformation. Sopnendu Mohanty, Chief FinTech Officer of the Monetary Authority of Singapore

(MAS), set the tone for the FinTech industry in March 2016 at the start of Singapore's FinTech journey.

> *"They are working very hard with the banks to co-create, co-participate — which is the right thing."*
>
> *Sopnendu Mohanty*[1]

Innovation brought Singapore to where it is today, but the immediate concern is how it can continue to innovate in the post-pandemic world. The key ingredients are the long-term thinking of the government, the conviction to build infrastructure and institutions for the future, develop its model of Singanomics and its commitment to excellence. However, there are challenges on the horizon like the potential US–China decoupling, limited depth on ASEAN stock exchanges for high-growth companies, which will be the driver of the next generation of growth, the war for talent, and lastly, the acceptance of business being done remotely will impact high-cost locations like Singapore in striving to stay competitive.

Singaporeans need to adapt and innovate. The key factors that established Singapore as The FinTech Nation have been its relentless obsession with excellence and meticulous execution of the three principles of **Right First, Fast Later (RFFL)**, **Singanomics** and **Garden Innovation**.

The Singapore DNA of being **RFFL** is more crucial than ever as we prepare for the future. As more and more services become digitised, we must ensure that the vulnerable sections of society are not left behind by building hybrid solutions to ensure that "digital empathy" is at the core of the future. In addition, data privacy and security standards need to ensure that new solutions do not lose sight of ensuring safety and stability in the rush for launch.

---

[1] https://www.straitstimes.com/business/banking/fintech-firms-will-help-banks-succeed-not-eat-their-lunch-mas

In the spirit of **RFFL**, firstly, MAS spent over two years developing its comprehensive payment law (Payment Service Act) in multiple consultations with industry players. As a result, Singapore is the only country in the world to have legislation to govern e-money wallets, merchant acquisition, online and offline payment, remittance, loyalty programmes and digital tokens. The industry must ensure that these systems are accessible widely and affordable to all residents and businesses as digital business transactions move faster.

Secondly, Singapore implemented policy initiatives by developing a Synergise Smart Finance and Green Finance mission. The Green Finance Action Plan comprises four key thrusts:

- strengthen the financial sector's resilience to environmental risks;
- develop green financial solutions and markets for a sustainable economy;
- harness technology to enable trusted and efficient sustainable finance flows; and
- build knowledge and capabilities in sustainable finance.

The three local banks ceased financing new coal power plants as they began financing renewable energy projects. In addition, asset managers in Singapore have signed the UN Principles for Responsible Investment and developed the Singapore Stewardship Principles for Responsible Investors.

Thirdly, MAS brought together financial industry partners to create a framework for financial institutions to promote the responsible adoption of Artificial Intelligence and Data Analytics (AIDA). Veritas framework[2] enables financial institutions to evaluate their AIDA-driven solutions against the principles of fairness, ethics, accountability and transparency. As more parts of our lives embrace AIDA, it is imperative to ensure that technology

[2] https://www.mas.gov.sg/news/media-releases/2019/mas-partners-financial-industry-to-create-framework-for-responsible-use-of-ai

does not hurt the vulnerable sections of society with bias and that none gets left behind.

As people start to relook at their financial health post-pandemic, initiatives like the Financial Planning Digital Services initiative supported by MAS aim at giving consumers greater access and control over their financial data. In a unique **RFFL** focus on implementing API Banking, considerable time was spent to ensure that all banks adopt common standards and create sustainable implementation roadmaps.

In times of economic uncertainty, it is imperative to use Singapore's model of **Garden Innovation** to utilise resources to focus on the most urgent needs of the medium-term and long-term development of The FinTech Nation. During the first phase of the journey, Singapore picked vital focus areas of innovation like payments, blockchain, artificial intelligence, retirement solutions and green finance. It then provided all possible resources to nurture them like a compassionate gardener. The digitisation of the two most prevalent aspects of Singapore residents' daily lives — hawker centres for affordable food and public transport — results from the focus on **Garden Innovation**.

As a small country with a population of 5 million, it was imperative to channel limited resources to maximise social impact. This move towards maximising social impact led to the design of the new digital bank licensing regime. In line with **Garden Innovation**, sections of society were identified to achieve social equality and financial inclusion. New digital banks are expected to help gig-economy workers and small and medium-sized enterprises (SMEs). In the spirit of **Garden Innovation**, the rest of the platforms were marshalled to join the movement after addressing policy and access to capital perspective. Sustainable finance was the theme for the MAS Global FinTech Hackcelerator and MAS FinTech Awards in 2020.

As the world becomes more protectionist, for instance, the trade tension between the US and China, and with economies worldwide facing contractions, **Singanomics**, long practised by Singapore, is its biggest hope for the path ahead. As a system of economics which orchestrates a balance between state-driven development and efficient private enterprise, the financial services sector will be the backbone of any economic recovery.

In the past, **Singanomics** ensured the building of critical national infrastructures like identity (SingPass and MyInfo), which was one of the most powerful defences that were utilised for contact tracing against COVID-19, and payments rails (Paynow and FAST), which ensured a smooth transition to digital and contactless commerce.

As per **Singanomics**, Singapore's digital bank licensing regime is unique in enabling innovation for a level playing field to address unmet and underserved needs of society while preventing any value-destructive competition. Singapore will have five new digital banks in the coming years. They are expected to play an important role in supporting vulnerable sections of society in collaboration with existing banks and financial institutions. Several of these digital banks also have ambitions to build a regional digital bank franchise, ushering in a new era of development and growth for financial services in Singapore.

The role of **Singanomics** in addressing climate change and sustainable development is crucial for the global future. MAS and financial institutions have taken significant measures for these initiatives and shall continue to be the driver for a better future for the planet.

MAS has been driving greater financial inclusion, and the steps to do so include organisation domestic infrastructure, leading to better solutions for consumers. Financial inclusion is not just about access to various financial products but also about making those products affordable and accessible to the end customer. We interviewed **Pradyumna Agrawal**, Director, Blockchain@Temasek, a global investment company headquartered in Singapore. Temasek sees emerging technologies like blockchain as key enablers to accelerating the journey to building commercially viable financial infrastructure and driving corporate innovation and financial inclusion. Temasek supports organisation's efforts emerging from projects like Ubin and Libra to advance these objectives globally. Other sectors in the financial sphere that they are keen to track are FinTech and InsurTech, as they believe that more cost-effective and inclusive solutions can broaden credit and insurance access and improve financial planning.

Temasek strongly aligns with the UN Sustainable Development Goals, focusing on climate change and mainstreaming sustainability. This aligns with the organisation's stated aim of achieving carbon neutrality by 2020, tracking and reporting its consumption of water, paper, electricity and air miles, and working with its portfolio companies to halve the greenhouse gas emissions of its entire portfolio by 2030. It will be exciting to see how Singapore is proactively doing new projects towards this cause through leveraging emerging technologies.

Concentration Risk

One of the biggest pillars of Singapore's development and success as The FinTech Nation has been the role played by MAS and Financial Technology Innovation Group (FTIG). The challenge that the future poses are the level of dependence on the MAS and FTIG to carry out some of the initiatives. This dependence must be reduced over time, with the industry taking responsibility for more initiatives and activities.

MAS balances strict regulation with forward-looking regulatory clarity to achieve the best for FinTech companies. Institutional support in Singapore's ecosystem is also very strong, providing great comfort to companies operating here. In addition, MAS has a consolidated approach to the regulatory sandbox through FinTech promotion, the creation of support programmes across sub-sectors and the removal of the challenge of inter-agency delays and conflicts from the equations.

In the future, Singapore is working to create a pathway for such platforms to become independent and sustainable. However, the needs of the next phase are different; how Singapore evolves to meet those needs will define the future of The FinTech Nation.

Talent

Another key contributor to the success of Singapore's journey has been its ability to attract global talents from founders to contributors who make Singapore its home. Many global companies chose Singapore as their Asia and global headquarters due to Singapore's ability to find and attract the best talents to Singapore. In the post-pandemic world facing increasing protectionism and travel controls, Singapore must urgently defend this strength. On the one hand, there is the need to strengthen the local talent pool and ensure reskilling of existing talents at a rapid pace. On the other hand, Singaporeans have to understand that international talents bring different viewpoints and experiences. Imported talent combined with existing local capabilities create a winning combination. Maintaining this balance between the different sources of talents while forging ahead in the new global order will be the real test of The FinTech Nation.

The pandemic has been helpful for the growing talents across the industry. There were many assumptions around the on-premise roles, and it is incredible to see how people have found ways to work through them remotely. Suddenly, many roles for which employers would want the employee onshore were now done offshore, so the captive pool you can hire has grown tenfold. In addition to the remote hiring, it also created alternate career paths for a fresh talent pool in the absence of campus placements. The context of people working for multiple companies simultaneously through many platforms has created many opportunities. The emergence of a contingent workforce is also an area of growth across the industry. Sometimes, companies are not looking at onboarding full-time employees depending on the nature and work requirements. Considering all these factors, it is fair to say that the industry is moving forward.

The two most important skills that employees need to learn are handling ambiguity and hybrid working because some parts of the team will be onshore while others will be offshore, and they need to create a balance to build the right business model. Of course, every model is flawed. However, every company has to develop a model that works best for them. For instance, if you have remote teams, you will have to accept both synchronous and asynchronous forms of communication since everyone will not be available at the same time. So, you need to acknowledge, recognise and thrive in an environment where we can balance both types of communication. Regarding soft skills, EQ learning is believed to be more important than IQ learning since the past two years or so have been about people locked up in their houses and working remotely.

▸ *Regional Leaders Programme*

For Singapore to develop more of its local talents into regional and global leaders, it needs a structured programme along the lines of management associate programmes operated by large corporates. One of the key missing pieces for Singapore talent is regional experience and exposure.

The Economic Development Board could create a structured programme with participation from local corporates wherein young and emerging leaders serve two to five years in their respective regional offices to expose them to markets and leadership training.

▸ *Long-Term Visas*

Singapore competes with global centres like the UK, the US and the UAE for talent. Several of these countries offer long-term residency for talent influencing families' decision to choose Singapore as their preferred choice of residence. Singapore can improve its visa and residency programmes to cater to this constituent of family and emotional needs.

Capital

Capital markets work across traditional country borders, and Singapore has leveraged its neutrality and strong legal system to be a hub in that space. Globally, the West has seen a strong trend for special purpose acquisition companies and private investment in public equity for growth startups to tap into public markets by listing without the traditional initial public offering (IPO) process. On the other hand, Hong Kong and its connected exchanges in China have been the platform of choice for IPO. As a result, Singapore needs to evolve fast to reform its public markets to ensure global and Asian companies consider it a viable avenue for listings.

Historically, Singapore's public markets are small due to the small local population and the mandate for sovereign wealth funds to diversify globally. Singapore investors have also been more risk-averse than some from other countries. As a result, they have mainly embraced more traditional asset-based Real Estate Exchange Traded Funds (REITs), making it one of the largest markets globally for REITS.

Capital transcends borders and finds its flow where it is more attractive. Singapore has been a global leader in attractiveness to family offices to set up bases in Singapore. Even though Singapore handles large capital inflows, a significant part is invested outside of Singapore.

▸ *Exchange*

One area which could catapult global finance service centres is expanding the depth and access of its public markets. Singapore has one exchange for public markets and a few for private markets. From a liquidity perspective, Singapore is heavily dominated by dividend stocks and REITs.

One way to address this limitation is by enabling global exchanges to have Singapore operations or take a stake in existing Singapore exchanges by bringing Singapore into global liquidity pools.

▶ *Fixed Income*

Singapore leapt to the forefront of trading and FX order booking by starting offshore dollar trading in the 1970s. Singapore can replicate the same in the fixed-income domain by leveraging its time zone, open currency infrastructure and trust in the regulatory system.

Enabling trading and liquidity in Asian and global bonds in other regions beyond Europe and the USA will bring a unique value to the market.

Policies

▶ *Trust*

As a developed market with an ageing economy, one of the challenges Singapore will face will be the development of retirement solutions complementing the existing Central Provident Fund offerings.

Singapore currently has a regulatory regime for trust licences, foundational for creating private pensions and benefits platforms. Existing regulations must expand to allow FinTech and incumbents to develop and offer such solutions. Currently, the solution providers have to use licences from Brunei or BVI, thus increasing the cost and complexity of such platforms. Such offshore solutions could be more cost-efficient for consumers and enable employers to get tax credits for supporting their employees' retirement planning.

Micro VC

Globally, micro VC and emerging fund managers have created a vibrant ecosystem. However, compared to other global jurisdictions like Delaware, BVI, and the UK, the cost of setting up and operating a micro VC fund in Singapore for a sub-10 M fund is quite prohibitive. Therefore, for Singapore to let a hundred flowers bloom, it must develop a regulatory policy regime balancing risk management and innovation.

The National Research Foundation (NRF) fostered the development of 11 venture funds and four corporate ventures in three batches from 2008 to 2016 by becoming a source of capital and anchor limited partners for such funds. As a result,[3] Singapore could become a beacon of innovation with a two-pronged strategy of lowering the regulatory cost of operations and enabling the NRF to support Limited Partners (LP) for micro-VC funds.

The Fintech Nation aspires for Singapore to have more than 100 micro VC funds registered and headquartered in the city-state to serve non-ASEAN and global venture markets.

Markets

Singapore has successfully created regional giants in the banking domain. Singapore's next phase could create regional leaders in digital banking, neo-banking and insurance domains. Supporting such players must include developing public market access for them to list in Singapore or globally.

Digital Banks

The two digital banks in Singapore, GXS (backed by Grab and Singtel) and Maribank (SEA Group), already have licences in Singapore, Malaysia and Indonesia, setting up foundations for regional footprint. Over the next

[3] https://www.nrf.gov.sg/funding-grants/early-stage-venture-fund

few years, they will be able to enter the Philippines, allowing foreign banks to set up 100% subsidiaries and potentially secure the Thailand licence once it is available in the coming years.

▸ *Regional Insurers*

Singapore has three locally incorporated and headquartered insurers with a regional footprint. The largest among the three is Great Eastern, followed closely by Singlife and Income. Great Eastern has operating businesses and licences in Singapore, Malaysia and Indonesia. Singlife was born from mergers between erstwhile Singlife, the first insurance licence awarded after 1970, Aviva Singapore and Zurich Singapore. It currently has operating licences and businesses in Singapore and the Philippines. Finally, Income, initially a cooperative, has become a corporate with a licence in Singapore and leverages the insurance-as-a-service solution HIVE in Vietnam, Malaysia, Indonesia, Thailand and Japan.

▸ *Regional Neo-banks*

Singapore also has a few regional leaders in the neo-banking space with credible pan-ASEAN market leadership, primarily in SME financing and lending. For example, Validus and Funding Societies have licences and operations in most ASEAN markets with a combined annual volume of over SGD3B annually as of 2023. Aspire, which is on the other end of the spectrum of operating SME neo-banking services leveraging partner licences, is already one of the most significant players in ASEAN in the domain of SME neo-banking services.

Innovation Quiver

Globally, travel for business, work and leisure reached a standstill in 2020. The local market has been cultivated well, with dedication from the government materialising in the form of grants and innovation labs, resulting in a flourishing ecosystem. There has been a culture of openness and sharing, as seen in the innovation lab crawls. The main issue is the limitation in terms of volume and market size. For FinTech to mushroom, volume is necessary. To overcome this, the next generation of FinTech in Singapore needs to embrace remote work and digital servicing strengthened by the pandemic to serve the needs of their regional customers.

The challenge is that much talent can work remotely, thus challenging the ability to host talent in a central location. Therefore, in the post-pandemic world, Singapore needs to develop policies to facilitate swift talent movement, newer tax policies to embrace remote working and enable companies to adjust to the realities of a borderless world impacting their business.

The number of FinTech companies in Singapore has grown significantly from a few hundred to over 1,200. In the first phase of Singapore as The FinTech Nation, much impetus was placed on promoting new startups and ensuring accelerator and incubation units to develop the first generation of companies. As a result, new venture capitals formed in Singapore got through the cycle of their first few funds, and the ecosystem got ready to compete globally.

In something we describe as the **innovation quiver**, the two main sources of startups in the Singapore ecosystem are homegrown in Singapore or overseas companies which set up bases in Singapore either to service clients in Singapore or as the regional and international headquarters.

There have been several programmes from different agencies to support different sizes, scales and origins of startups since 2016. However, Singapore must also evolve its investments and resource allocation strategy as the world embraces remote working.

For homegrown start-ups, a key point to understand is that many smaller startups have been focused on pointed, one-off solutions. While most of them are unique in their regard, in the context of being adopted by a big corporation, they must be stitched together to form one cohesive, end-to-end solution.

One example of this has been Project Ubin, wherein many solution and service providers came together, each forming one part of the story. Singapore needs to bring more of these end-to-end solutions together to become trusted partners and to strengthen recognition for such alliances.

Another example is a Singapore startup, Canopy, stitching together API from different wealth management providers, including traditional brokers and new-age wealth robo-advisors. For Singapore to succeed in the next growth stage, it must have more such stories and alliances to enable corporates to undertake digital transformation successfully.

Singapore will continue to be an attractive place for international startups due to its tax, legal structures and ease of doing business so that part will continue to grow. However, at the same time, Singapore needs to build more solutions to enable digital business operations, reduce the leftover paper process and make it the best place in the world to set up their international entities.

Growth @ ASEAN

The concept of growth hacking was first invented in Silicon Valley. But how does the theory of growth apply to FinTechs in ASEAN, and what are the key strategies and local tactics that need to be considered?

Unlike Silicon Valley, ASEAN startups prefer evolutionary change, and even disruptors focus on creating value. The focus on avoiding a radical free-market approach and varying degrees of centralised planning makes the ASEAN growth model unique. ASEAN cherishes order amongst the chaos, alignment amongst debate and construction of the future before the disruption.

In this paradigm, ASEAN FinTechs apply an array of approaches to growth:

Humble Passion — In countries that grew out of centuries of colonial suppression, the attitude of founders and leaders is based on their commitment to demonstrate support for the local communities over affluent groups. Successful entrepreneurs amalgamate a mix of deep passion for building the future rooted in the humble origins of their own families and teams. The deep thread of humility to avoid upfront confrontation while aspiring to win the world is an ASEAN-specific oxymoron that powers the undying resilience of the ecosystem.

Transient Networks — As companies and investors are growing and evolving at an unprecedented pace while the overall size of networks is still tiny, the joke in ASEAN is that everyone in the startup ecosystem is only at two degrees of separation. ASEAN's unique phenomenon is networks that evolve faster than seasons. People share resources, investors, and vendors with each other, leaving one word obsolete in the lexicon, EXCLUSIVE. There is nothing exclusive about anything in ASEAN.

Fluid Identities — ASEAN FinTechs keep reinventing themselves, evolving their brands and positioning, adding complimentary services, exploring hybrid models, deepening their relations with existing users and catering to new segments, and ultimately pivoting into new territories and categories.

Conclusion

In conclusion, it is culture that drives success! The **Singanomics**, the *kiasu* syndrome and the opportunities revealed in this book have led to Singapore's success today. It takes a village to raise a child! Indeed, the success of setting Singapore as The FinTech Nation involves many players.

The ecosystem provides an open ground for experimentation and a route to facilitate innovation. In contrast, the accessibility of the ASEAN market provides the ideal hunting ground for new innovative startups.

Singapore stands as the epitome of excellence in the world of FinTech, where Singanomics, *kiasu* syndrome and the opportunities revealed the underlying factors that have propelled Singapore to success. Just as it takes a village to raise a child, the establishment of Singapore as The FinTech Nation involves the collective efforts of numerous stakeholders. Moreover, the accessibility of the ASEAN market serves as the ideal playground for budding startups seeking new opportunities. By addressing the industry's points and actively supporting our innovators, Singapore's regulators have created a nurturing environment that ensures the preservation of our coveted title, "The FinTech Nation, Excellence Unlocked!" Ultimately, it is the individuals with unwavering tenacity who will continue to push boundaries and chart new frontiers in the pursuit of excellence, with the thriving ecosystem that paves the way for innovation to flourish.

GLOSSARY OF TERMS

Accelerator — An accelerator, or seed accelerator or incubator, are fixed term cohort-based programmes that provide mentorship, education and guidance to develop an idea into a viable startup. Such programmes typically culminate in a public pitch or demo day to potentially attract further investment. Accelerators can be government funded or private funded with a focus on a full gamut of startup industries, though more recently they are associated with technology-based products and services.

AFIN – ASEAN Financial Innovation Network — AFIN is a non-profit organisation established in 2018 by the ASEAN Bankers Association (ABA), International Finance Corporation (IFC), a member of the World Bank Group, and the Monetary Authority of Singapore (MAS). AMTD Foundation and Mastercard are AFIN's Corporate Founding Members.

Agile methodology — Agile methodology is a project management tactic that involves breaking the project into phases and emphasises continuous group effort and improvement.

AML – Anti-money laundering — AML is a term used in the financial and legal industries to describe the legal controls that require financial institutions and other regulated industries to prevent, detect and report money laundering activities. AML guidelines differ across countries, but there are many efforts to align international standards to further clamp down on cross border money laundering.

API – Application Programming Interface — An API is a computing interface that defines interactions between multiple software intermediaries. APIs can be entirely custom, specific to a component or it can be designed based on an industry-standard.

ASEAN – Association of Southeast Asian Nations — ASEAN is a regional organisation of 10 Southeast Asian countries. While formalised into an organisation meant to collaborate on and promote the advancement of the region, it does not have legal frameworks like the European Union (EU).

AUM – Assets under management — AUM measures the total market value of all financial assets being managed by a financial institution or fund manager on behalf of clients or themselves.

Bancassurance — Bancassurance is an arrangement between a bank and an insurance company, through which the insurer can sell its products to the bank's customers.

Big data — Big data refers to the large, diverse sets of information that grow at exponential rates. These data sets tend to be too large or complex to be dealt with by traditional methods or software. While big data offers greater statistical power, the interpretation and predictive analytics for data story telling are aspects that make such data useful.

Blockchain — A blockchain is a decentralised distributed ledger that cryptographically secure peer-to-peer (P2P) transactions. It is a chain of digital "blocks". Each block stores information about transactions, cryptocurrencies, contracts, records or other information. The block is time-stamped and contains its own hash (a unique identifier) and the hash of the previous block. Hence, each block is connected to all the blocks before and after it.

Bootstrapping — Bootstrapping is the process of initiating and growing a business without external help or capital by using personal savings or existing resources rather than depending on on investors or loans.

Brokerage — A brokerage is a company or a middleman who links buyers and sellers to complete a business for stock shares and bonds.

Capital markets — Capital markets are the basis of a flourishing financial services hub.

CBDC – Central Bank Digital Currencies — A CBDC is the digital form of a fiat currency of a particular nation. The concept of a CBDC is directly inspired by the proliferation of crypto currencies such as Bitcoin but is significantly different as it would be regulated by the monetary authority of the country issuing it.

CPF – Central Provident Fund — The CPF is a compulsory comprehensive savings and pension plan for Singaporeans and Singapore Permanent Residents. The fund was created primarily to fund the retirement, healthcare and housing needs of those residing in Singapore. It is an employment-based scheme and the contribution comes from both the employers and the employees.

Crowdfunding — Crowdfunding is a form of crowdsourcing and alternative finance that refers to the practice of raising small amounts of capital from a large pool of individuals to finance a new business venture. This is typically done through the use of online sites and social media that help facilitate the matching of potential investors to entrepreneurs, while lowering the barriers to venture stage investment by spreading the capital requirement across a pool of investors.

Cryptocurrencies — A cryptocurrency is a digital asset designed to act as a medium of exchange and when stretched to its full potential, it is meant to replace traditional (fiat) currency. The advantages posed by proponents of cryptocurrencies is the secure nature of the underlying decentralised transactional database and the democratised control of the creation of additional coins.

Custodian — This refers to a custodian bank like a specialized financial institution or a department of a larger bank, that is responsible for the safeguarding of a client's financial assets. They may not necessarily be the originator or the broker of a transaction, but simply a trusted intermediary to hold the asset.

DAG – Digital Acceleration Grant — A DAG is a system that supports smaller financial institutions and FinTech firms in adopting digital solutions to improve productivity, strengthen operational resilience, manage risks, and serve customers better. It provides these smaller FIs and FinTech firms based in Singapore with 80% co-funding of qualifying expenses, including hardware, software, and professional services.

Democratisation — The action of improving access to a specific good or service to the larger population.

Digital Payment Token — Digital tokens are either intrinsic or created via software and assigned a specific function. Examples of intrinsic digital tokens are Bitcoin and Ether. Other types of tokens include asset backed coins which is issued to represent a claim on a redeemable asset such as precious metals or even real estate.

DLT – Distributed Ledger Technology — A DLT is a consensus of replicated, shared and synchronised digital data that is not limited by geographies. Unlike a traditional distributed database, the key difference is that there is no central administrator, and thus is colloquially known as a decentralised network.

Elevandi — It is a non-profit organisation that aims to advance FinTech in the digital economy by fostering an open dialogue between the public and private sectors.

ESG Registry – Environmental, social and governance registry — It is a blockchain-powered data platform supporting a tamperproof record of sustainability certifications and verified sustainability data across various sectors.

ETF – Exchange Traded Funds — An ETF is a type of investment fund traded on a stock exchange. An ETF holds assets such as stocks, bonds, currencies or other commodities to provide investment exposure.

FIs – Financial Institutions — FIs comprise corporations or public entities that provide services as intermediaries in the financial markets. Activities range from deposits, loans to investments, securities and currency brokerage. Examples of businesses classified as FIs include banks, trust companies, insurance companies and securities dealers.

FNF – Fintech Nation Fund — FNF is a venture capital fund that strongly emphasises community connectivity and deep-rooted ties to entrepreneurship in Singapore.

Fractional shares — Fractional shares is ownership of less than one full share of equity or other assets. Such shares may be the result of stock splits, dividend reinvestments or other corporate actions. It may also be intentional in cases where investors are trying to democratise an asset, such as bonds, which have a high investment cost.

Fractionalisation — Fractionalisation is a concept extensively practised in traditional financial markets, often enabled through asset-backed securities or mutual funds.

FX – Foreign Exchange — The FX market is a global, decentralised and over the counter (OTC) market for the trading of global currencies. This market determines the value of free-floating currencies against other currencies, such as the SGD against the USD. It should be noted that the FX market does not have as much sway on the value of nonfree floating currencies, such as those tightly controlled by central banks or countries that use the exchange rate as a form of monetary policy. In terms of trading volume, it is by far the largest market in the world with recent estimates reaching 6.6 trillion per day.

FX Spread — Within the foreign exchange markets, the spread refers to the difference between the buying price and selling price for a specific currency. In interbank FX markets, this spread can be razor thin as significant liquidity exists and there is little to no information asymmetry. However, further down the value chain the spread may expand significantly.

GDP – Gross Domestic Product — GDP is the monetary measure of the market value of all the final goods and services produced within a geographical boundary in a specified period. This is the most used gauge for the health of an economy. Nominal GDP however does not account for differences in cost of living and inflation rates between countries, which must be remembered when comparing across economies.

GFIN – Global Financial Innovation Network — The GFIN is the international network of financial regulators and related organisations committed to supporting financial innovation in the best interests of consumers. Formally launched in 2019 by an international group of financial regulators and related organizations.

GWP – Gross Written Premiums — GWP is the amount of an insurance company's premiums that are used to determine the amount of premiums owed to a reinsurer.

Hyperinflation — Hyperinflation in economics refers to a period of very high and typically accelerating rates of inflation. During these periods, the real value of local currency plummets and the price of all goods increase, causing people to minimise the holdings in the local currency. This tends to be a spiral situation, where if not dealt with correctly and early on, it will result in the collapse of the local currency. Generally accepted level of inflation that is hyperinflation is above 50% per month.

IoT – Internet of Things — It is a network of interrelated devices that connect and exchange communication between devices and the cloud.

IPO – Initial Public Offering — An initial public offering (IPO) refers to the process of offering shares of a private corporation to the public in a new stock issuance for the first time.

Kiasu — Kiasu is a Hokkien / Teochew word in Chinese dialect often used in Singapore that relates to the fear of missing out.

Kopi — Kopi is a type of traditional coffee local to Singapore and Malaysia. It is a black coffee typically served with milk and sugar. Also known as Nanyang coffee.

KYC – Know Your Customer — KYC refers to a standard or guideline in financial services that requires professionals and institutions to make an effort to verify the identity, suitability and risks involved with a client. This procedure also falls under the broader scope of the institution's AML requirements.

Kudo — Kudo is a leading online-to-off line (O2O) e-commerce platform in Indonesia that enables Indonesia's unbanked consumers to shop online by connecting them with online merchants and service providers through its vast existing network of agents and merchants across Indonesia.

Loan shark — A loan shark is a colloquial term that refers to individuals or organisations that offer loans at predatory or extremely high interest rates. A common feature of loan sharks are strict terms of collection and operation outside of regulated markets. Many times, these are associated with criminal organisations and in some cases, violence is used to collect outstanding loans.

Leverage — It is the use of debt or borrowed capital in order to undertake an investment or project that is commonly used as a way to boost an entity's equity base.

MAS – Monetary Authority of Singapore — The MAS is Singapore's central bank and financial regulatory authority, the combination of which is unique on the world stage. It administers various regulations pertaining to the financial sector in general in addition to currency issuance. It was originally established in 1971.

MoU – Memorandum of Understanding — It is an agreement between two or more parties that is outlined in a formal document. While not legally binding, it does signal a significant step towards moving forward with a formalised legal contract.

Network effect — A network effect is an economics and business concept that entails a scenario where an additional user of a good or service adds value to the use of the product to others. If a network effect persists, then the value of a product or service in question increases according to the number of users it has.

Neo-bank — It is a FinTech firm which function like banks and operate digitally through an assemblage of financial apps and services.

OTC – Over the counter — OTC refers to off-exchange trading. This means that trades are done directly between the two parties rather than through an intermediary such as an exchange. The largest known OTC market is the foreign exchange market as large global banks create the liquidity for the market rather than a centralised exchange. Equity markets have OTC transactions as well, specifically for illiquid or unlisted stocks.

P2P Lending – Peer to peer lending — P2P lending is lending capital to individuals or businesses without the traditional intermediary of a financial institution. This is typically done through online services that match lenders with borrowers, with clientele ranging from individuals to businesses.

Partior — Partior is a blockchain platform for payments, trade and foreign exchange settlements. It is a digitised M1 commercial money that can offer a credible alternative to the traditional cross-border payments "hub and spoke" model, allowing for more efficient payment clearance and settlement.

Payment rails — Payment rails are payments platform or network that facilitates the movement of money from one payer to payee. Parties involved could be retail or businesses and both parties can move funds on the network. Credit card rails are the most common type of payment rails while Blockchain applications is considered a new type of payment rail.

PolicyPal — Policypal was the first startup to graduate from the MAS FinTech Regulatory Sandbox.

Polytechnics — A polytechnic refers to an institute of higher learning leading to a diploma qualification. In some countries, they are also referred to as universities of applied sciences.

Private markets — Private markets refer to securities not actively traded on a publicly accessible format. They fall under the "alternatives" umbrella in portfolio construction and until recently were considered inaccessible, illiquid, hard to value or niche for traditional investors. More recently they are considered to provide additional diversity to a portfolio to reduce overall risk and improve returns by having low correlation to traditional securities.

Proliferation financing — It refers to the act of providing funds or financial services which are used, in whole or in part, for the manufacture, acquisition, possession, development, export, trans-shipment, brokering, transport, transfer, stockpiling or use of nuclear, chemical or biological weapons and their means of delivery and related materials (including both technologies and dual-use goods used for non-legitimate purposes), in contravention of national laws or, where applicable, international obligations.

Proxtera — Proxtera is the commercialisation of the Business sans Borders initiative led by the MAS and the Infocomm Media Development Authority.

POC – Proof-of-Concept — It is a demonstration of a product, developing and testing of innovative solutions in a live financial sector environment before turning into a reality.

POV – Proof-of-Value — It is a combination of technical evaluation to validate the product idea and demonstrate a likely return on investment for stakeholders.

Project Guardian — Project Guardian is a collaborative initiative with the financial industry that seeks to test the feasibility of applications in asset tokenisation while managing financial stability and integrity risks.

Public markets — Public markets refer to securities sold to the public, who can then subsequently trade them on a stock exchange or other relatively accessible method. Stocks and bonds are the traditional securities associated with public markets.

Regulatory Sandbox — A regulatory sandbox is a testing environment created by a regulator that allows FinTech startups and establishment players to conduct live experiments under a controlled environment. Sandboxes can be applied to experimentation in many FinTech applications ranging from operational innovation to new product types.

RegTech – Regulatory Technology — It is the application of emerging technology to improve the way businesses manage regulatory compliance.

Robo advisory — Robo advisory refers to a subsection of financial advisory that provides financial advice or investment management services with minimal human interaction, normally via online channels. The concept of robo advisory leans on the idea of removing human error and bias from the investment process by guiding the investment process with mathematical rules or algorithms.

Sandbox Express — Sandbox express is an approach where applicants can begin market testing in the predefined environment within 21 days of applying to MAS.

Sandwich generation — Sandwich generation is a term that refers to groups of adults who care for both their parents and their own children. This does not point towards any specific generation but rather is a phenomenon that can affect any generation based on the support needs in their extended family.

SEA – Southeast Asia — Southeast Asia is the region of Asia, south of China and east of India. It includes the area ranging from Myanmar at the north to the southern tip of Indonesia. The farthest east includes the Philippines and Papua New Guinea. Today the population of SEA stands at 665 million accounting for the 3rd largest concentration of people in the world outside of China and India.

SGX – Singapore Exchange — SGX is a listed investment holding company that manages Singapore's leading stock exchange and offers additional securities and derivatives trading services. It is a Self-Regulatory Organisation with a dual nature of commercial and regulatory obligations.

Smart contracts — A smart contract is a computer program or selfexecuting contract that is intended to automatically control or document events and actions relevant to the terms of a specific contract or agreement. The objective of a smart contract is to reduce the need of trusted intermediaries, arbitration costs, enforcement costs and instances of fraud.

SME – Small and Medium Enterprise — SMEs are businesses whose employee count falls below a certain limit. This limit depends on the country in question. SMEs outnumber large companies globally by a significant margin and actually account for the largest percentage of employment in most countries.

Stablecoins — Stablecoins are a key piece of infrastructure that bridges traditional payment systems with the digital-asset economy, facilitating trading, transactions and conversion to crypto from government-issued (fiat) money.

Structured FX notes — A structured note is an over the counter (OTC) derivative instrument that combines payoffs from multiple ordinary securities. These derivatives are not traded over an exchange but are rather structured "in-house" through a bank and marketed as illiquid instruments. Depending on the underlying securities, the name changes, for example, if it is linked to the FX markets then it is a FX note.

Tenant Banking — It is a digital bank model wherein risk management and regulatory reporting are the responsibility of the incumbent bank.

Tokenisation — Tokenisation is the process of replacing sensitive data with unique identification symbols that retain all the essential information about the data without compromising its security.

Unicorn — A unicorn in the business setting is a colloquial term to indicate a highly valuable privately held startup company. Generally, any startup valued at over a billion dollars, with continued expectation of fast growth, is considered a unicorn.

Utopic ecosystem —An ecosystem where businesses work in tandem with the regulators, leading to maximum compliance and operates based on a network of individual users.

VC – Venture Capital — Venture Capital is a form of private equity financing that specifically funds startups, early stage or emerging companies. These companies are deemed to have a high growth potential and thus the funding is expected to yield returns in excess of public markets.

Vitana — Vitana was the first to enter Singapore's FinTech Regulatory Sandbox. It was the first blockchain application and corporation to embark on a long journey, a lending testament to the applicability and flexibility of Singapore's regulations.

Warung — A warung is an Indonesian word for a type of small, typically family-owned, business such as a restaurant or cafe. The word is used in Indonesia and other parts of SEA too.

INDEX

A

C

E

G

H

I

N

O

P

U

V

Printed in the USA
CPSIA information can be obtained
at www.ICGtesting.com
JSHW050353231023
50616JS00007B/15

9 789811 250286